C000075637

No monkey business

FINANCIAL TIMES
Prentice Hall

This series brings you a new generation of business books: books about the way things might be, books about competing in a fast and networked economy and books which extend the edge and the energy of our working world. Above all, these are forward-looking books for those, like you, who are looking to the future.

These books will help make sense of a business landscape transformed by new ideas, technologies and trends, in which the inescapable rules of competition meet a new range of opportunities. We have selected a new generation of business authors to challenge comfortable assumptions and explore uncertain futures; to ask the questions and find the answers that will help and inspire you to compete creatively and profitably in a connected world.

So, this is a collection of books for wherever changing technology and culture mean business people can do things differently.

To find out more about our business publications, or tell us about the books you'd like to find, you can visit us at www.business-minds.com

Pearson Education

No monkey business

what investors need to know and why

Stuart Fowler

FINANCIAL TIMES
Prentice Hall

An imprint of **Pearson Education**
London / New York / San Francisco / Toronto / Sydney / Tokyo / Singapore
Hong Kong / Cape Town / Madrid / Paris / Milan / Munich / Amsterdam

PEARSON EDUCATION LIMITED

Head Office
Edinburgh Gate
Harlow CM20 2JE
Tel: +44 (0)1279 623623
Fax: +44 (0)1279 431059

London Office:
128 Long Acre, London WC2E 9AN
Tel: +44 (0)20 7447 2000
Fax: +44 (0)20 7240 5771
Website:www.financialminds.com

First published in Great Britain in 2002

© Pearson Education Limited 2002

The right of Stuart Fowler to be identified as Author of this Work has been
asserted by him in accordance with the Copyright, Designs and Patents Act 1988.

ISBN 0 273 65658 9

British Library Cataloguing in Publication Data
A CIP catalogue record for this book can be obtained from the British Library.

All rights reserved; no part of this publication may be reproduced, stored in a retrieval system,
or transmitted in any form or by any means, electronic, mechanical, photocopying, recording,
or otherwise without either the prior written permission of the Publishers or a licence permitting
restricted copying in the United Kingdom issued by the Copyright Licensing Agency Ltd,
90 Tottenham Court Road, London W1P 0LP. This book may not be lent, resold, hired out or
otherwise disposed of by way of trade in any form of binding or cover other than that in which
it is published, without the prior consent of the Publishers.

This publication is designed to provide accurate and authoritative information in regard to the
subject matter covered. It is sold with the understanding that neither the author nor the publisher
is engaged in rendering legal, investing, or any other professional service. If legal advice or other
expert assistance is required, the service of a competent professional person should be sought.

The publisher and contributors make no representation, express or implied, with regard to the
accuracy of the information contained in this book and cannot accept any responsibility or liability
for any errors or omissions that it may contain.

10 9 8 7 6 5 4 3 2 1

Designed by Sue Lamble
Typeset by Northern Phototypesetting Co. Ltd, Bolton
Printed and bound in Great Britain by Bell & Bain Ltd, Glasgow

The Publishers' policy is to use paper manufactured from sustainable forests.

Contents

Abbreviations

AIFA	Association of Independent Financial Advisers
APCIMS	Association of Private Client Investment Managers and Stockbrokers
AVC	additional voluntary contributions
CAT	charges, access and terms
CGT	capital gains tax
EPP	executive pension plan
ETF	exchange-traded fund
FSA	Financial Services Authority
FSAVC	free-standing additional voluntary contributions
IFA	independent financial adviser
IMRO	Investment Management Regulatory Organisation
IPA	individual pension account
ISA	individual savings account
MVA	market value adjustment
OEIC	open-ended investment company
OFT	Office of Fair Trading
PEP	personal equity plan
PIA	Personal Investment Authority
SERPS	state earnings-related pension scheme
SIB	Securities and Investment Board
SIPP	self-invested personal pension
SOFA	Society of Financial Advisers
SRO	self-regulating organization
SSAS	small self-administered scheme
VCT	venture capital trust

List of tables and figures

Introduction

Financial markets should have made it easy going for UK individual investors in the last two decades and information and ideas about investment were never so freely available. Yet we have all these walking wounded from bruising encounters with risk they did not anticipate, agents whose motives they did not appreciate and products they never understood properly.

Investors are waking up to their vulnerability to mistakes about products and agents for any number of reasons: mis-sold pensions, endowments that won't pay off the mortgage, having to pay for other people's guaranteed annuities, rip-off terms for getting into products, even bigger rip-offs when they try to get out, with-profits policies that look more like with-losses.

Misunderstandings about market behaviour also colour these mistaken choices. Vulnerability has been exposed by expectations that were only reasonable if inflation continued to be high and by classical investment bubbles, bursting first in emerging markets and then in technology stocks. With hindsight, the peak levels of major equity markets will be seen to have been another bubble waiting to burst and it will not be instructive merely to blame terror striking out of a clear blue sky.

The popularization of investment encouraged by newspapers, magazines, TV and the internet has failed to build strong educational foundations. Hype about 'consumer power' played up the frivolous benefits of information access, immediacy and new transaction platforms instead of the worthwhile goals of principles, planning and personal responsibility. Power does not lie in having a large-scale map unless you also know your destination, your starting point and the route that best connects them.

This book springs (would that it were actually that easy!) from a conviction born of over 30 years of working in the industry that it is never too late or too difficult for individuals to master the essential principles of investing and to learn how to deal safely with an industry whose help they need but whom they can ill afford to trust or depend on. Principles and a code of safe practice will get you as close as you can to peace of mind.

I like to think of this as money needing a good owner. For most of my career I have worked with what are known as 'institutional' funds, such as company pension schemes and endowment funds. Both involve trustees, and these are the people that we professionals have to treat as our client. What is special about trustees is that they have a legal code that requires them to act as if they were owners. This is perfectly reasonable since they act on behalf of the ultimate owners and must do so in the owners' best interests. But what it also presumes is that owners themselves act in a particular way: with responsibility, with reason, delegating only with well-informed control, not blindly, and not totally trusting. Good thinking – but it is not in fact how owners do usually act. To measure up to this model takes some effort on their part and some help from professionals who really want them to be good owners. Reading this account of what motivates the retail investment industry, you will see that there are a surprising number of reasons why firms are not genuinely committed to you being an educated and participating – let alone controlling – customer.

What makes good owners? They do not need to be clever but they do care more and have some general understanding, as a context for all the detail they will necessarily encounter. They do not need to be experts themselves but they need to be streetwise when dealing with experts. They know to respect the uncertainties inherent in investing and to mistrust false prophets. They know what kinds of decision matter and what are trivial. They choose their relationships with the industry, whose help even DIY investors need, cautiously and know how to control them, even when delegating. Good owners do not trust their money blindly to third parties or hope that whatever goes wrong there will be a scheme to bale them out. They know where their money is at work and they under- stand why. They have route maps.

This cannot promise a future without disappointment but it can minimize the chances of regret. So much of what has blighted individuals' recent experience of investing is coloured by regret. Our loud and angry voice cannot quite drown out a quieter and more reasonable one: 'I could – and should – have known better'.

What kind of knowledge does this call for? Many investors with bad experiences or anxieties about the future will probably assume that they need more of the 'know what' kind of knowledge. This book is mainly about the 'know why' kinds. Not only does it make it more interesting but it is also all that is needed to use knowledge of the essentials as an informing context and simplifying device to deal better with the confusing and often boring detail. 'Knowing what' treats the problem as one of inadequate grasp of the complexities of the industry, with its jumbled landscape of different types of firm and different investment products, and desperately complicated tax regime. 'Knowing what' is dealt with by trying to cram more factual information into your head.

It is served by manuals but there are already several published guides to the UK financial jungle and plenty of online glossaries of the jungle jargon. Instead, I invite you to follow a particular trail which has a deliberate, narrative logic. It starts with some elementary questions about what we want to achieve with our money, shows how we can use markets to achieve those goals or perform those tasks and then shows how to decide how best to implement that, including how to select who we want to work with in the industry and on what terms. Though it has a narrative thread, readers who prefer not to stick to the trail can use the index or chapter and section headings to pick out particular areas.

As a narrative, it has three protagonists: your money, the markets and the people in between. Relating investment to tasks for your money or personal life goals makes it more relevant but also helps you to keep control of the agenda. The idea of the markets is important because it is where your money is put to work that determines outcomes, and markets have characteristics, or 'behaviour', that make them more or less suitable for achieving goals. They function as systems, or engines, whose power you can harness. Markets, not people, get the job done for you. The concept of the people in between is important because, whereas you need to pass through industry firms or individuals to put your money to work, they do not determine the investment outcome as much as you may suppose, and they insert agenda conflicts and a cost wedge that are much more significant than you suppose.

The thread comes partly from history. Knowing the story of the development of the industry that inserts itself between us and the markets and seeing how many of our relationships and the products we buy are the accidents of history can help us to reshape our relationships so that they are deliberate and contemporary.

History flows into philosophy. Understanding the history encourages a mindset about ourselves, our goals, the nature of the power of capital markets, the limits of human intelligence and skill and the ubiquity of randomness which is arguably worth more than a thousand pages of detailed information about ISAs, SIPPs, SSASs and the rest of the investment industry paraphernalia. It is a mindset that many investment professionals could themselves usefully adopt! Of course, there should be monetary benefits from sound, rational and cost-controlled investment plans for you and your family. Yet the book also points to non-monetary benefits in terms of quality of life and the peace of mind associated with the clarity of well-articulated plans, the reduction in the stress of living with the short-term consequences of decisions made for their expected long-term outcome and with having well-educated expectations both about outcomes and about what can happen along the way.

It is also partly about psychology. It is impossible to tune up our antennae to detect the 'enemy without' unless we understand the motivation of the people in between us and the markets. It is difficult to exercise control sensibly unless we can also tame the 'enemy within': our own behavioural traits that are likely to drive us away from our investment goals.

The book does not propound any single theory in order to help you think about investment. However, it does offer a set of simplifying structures that impose an essentially rational process on an otherwise intuitive and emotive helter-skelter, and these certainly owe their origin to well-developed investment theories. They help you understand why clever people so often get it wrong, why planning is more important than management and why *strategy* – what markets – is more important than *implementation* – what products or what stocks. The book also points accusingly at the gulf between the commitment to theory-based investment techniques in the institutional market (where they also shape how those trustees exercise their responsibilities) and the rootless diversity and ambiguity of investment practice in the private client area.

I have tried to avoid a sensationalist exposé of the blatant abuses of customer trust that have seen so many great institutions, once pillars of the establishment, pilloried and humiliated in the press. Yet it is impossible to see this sad chapter in the story of the industry laid out again without being as astounded by the sheer cheek of these people as when the stories first broke, or to feel any less angry with ourselves at our capacity for gullibility. Nor should we be ice cold about the exposé of the much more subtle forms of corruption that have insinuated themselves into the very heart of the industry, in its conflicts of interest, flawed product design, unrealistic claims and excessive costs. Though we may feel less angry at ourselves for failing to spot the more subtle forms of system-wide corruption, why should we not be angry at the industry that works so efficiently and spends so extravagantly to institutionalize the myths that perpetuate these self-serving practices?

Though I assume most investors are not particularly numerate, the code of practice that is essential to the transfer of control from industry to consumer does rely heavily on the use of numbers instead of woolly flannel. Do not for one minute think that using numbers puts the professional at an advantage. Flannel suits their agenda far better. It is cheap, flexible and makes an excellent smokescreen. Control the language and you control the relationship.

Numbers allow you to describe your needs in an unambiguously explicit way, leaving the people in between no room to twist your description of your needs to fit what they want you to buy. Numbers, in the form of probabilities, are also the language that best conveys risks and how to make choices that involve uncertain outcomes. Why is it so few investment firms, even independent financial advisers (IFAs), can quantify the odds of achieving the targets you define with the resources at your disposal? Why can't an adviser recommending actively managed funds tell you what the odds are of making up the additional costs relative to an index-tracking fund? You wouldn't let a bookmaker get away with quoting flannel instead of odds. You wouldn't play roulette without being sure the house would pay out in proportion to the mathematical chances – pace the zero.

Some mathematical concepts and terms will be encountered on this trail but only when they serve to help communicate an essential principle or help you to translate the language that the industry may wish to confuse you with. Where possible I use a table or a picture to tell a story that relies on numbers.

More important than maths is an awareness of technology: investment engineering and the way you access it. This is an essential catalyst in the transfer of control from professional to customer. You should be able to see 'levers' of control and those levers should connect to 'engines' in the form of computer-based toolkits. You do not have to assess the performance of the engine or its design, which would be brilliant but unrealistic, only that it performs the functions you know you will require of it. This particularly includes the ability to deal with the uncertainties inherent in planning any investment task. It is the complexity of the uncertainties, of their relationship to each other, and of the trade-off decisions that typify the way the information is processed that makes computers, not clever people, the essential resource of investment firms. The use of engines is part of the story about how unaccountably differently the institutional and retail worlds have grown up. The engines and levers could be part of the technology of an adviser, such as an IFA or private client stockbroker; they could be sitting on the front end of the website of a unit trust group or insurance company that sells its own products, or on the website of a fund supermarket.

It is a book and it is a website: *www.nomonkey.biz*. The website adds detail and links to other sources but its main purpose is to take the book on from where the narrative ends, with the emphasis on practical implementation of the ideas in the book. It will keep up pressure on the industry, its regulators and law makers for consumer-friendly change. It covers new topics that are or should be compelling investors' attention. It takes sides. A conversation is always more interesting than a monologue and the website also allows people to respond and contribute – both customers and professionals. It can help investors find new industry relationships likely to be consistent with the No Monkey Business approach, whether DIY platforms, once-off advice, investment planning, ongoing advice or discretionary management. It may also be able to offer online planning and selection tools, connected to engines designed to be consistent with the book's approach. Some of these practical aims will require help from enlightened firms in the industry but even then it is possible that having useful interactive functions will mean that subscriptions need to be charged. What comes free is not necessarily a bargain but, as the book says, the internet can drastically cut the cost and ease of access to customised personal services based on state of the art investment engineering, and that will be a bargain.

In writing this book I had a simple purpose: to encourage you to trust yourselves more and the industry less. Use the industry to get the information you need and in the form you need it. Select people to work with whom you find personable and who inspire confidence but make sure they also meet your criteria, have the right mindset, will work on your terms and to your rules, whether you intend to delegate a lot or a little.

Take your time. Getting the relationships right is more important than anything else. Follow the code and only out of idle curiosity, in jest or as a trivial pursuit will you ever again ask an investment professional the question, 'What do you think the market's going to do?' Why on earth should they know? You will already know what the markets can do for you and your personal life goals. You are on journey, not in a race. Bon voyage – and travel safely.

Past preface

'Do you think we can afford it, Sal?' asked John. He and Sally had been sitting in their garden in the watery autumn sunlight poring over the particulars of a little house in the Tuscan hill-top village of Castellina, one of many they had explored that summer.

'The fact is, we really don't have much idea what we can afford,' was Sally's answer, to the point as ever.

She had been saying for some time that they needed proper financial plans. With two boys in school and grandparents' fee contributions starting to run out, and retirement (if they were lucky) in little more than a decade, there were certainly some question marks over the future. With two good incomes, they felt well enough off and they had money in the bank. But Sally was right: they had no real idea of what their money would buy them or what their future needs would add up to.

John's friend Chris had introduced them to his friend Colin who was a salesman at Rothbar Life. Colin was a very persuasive man who lived up to Chris's little joke about 'Crowbar' Life but John and Sally saw the good side of that. At least they could be sure they had covered every insurable adversity! They also had an endowment mortgage, several single-premium investment bonds, all from different companies, as well as a Rothbar personal pension plan apiece. John would also be getting some pension income from company schemes from earlier jobs.

They had more money going out the door to insurance companies every month than almost any other budget item. This gave them pause for thought every time they picked up the money section of the Sunday paper and read yet another story about rip-off insurance companies. They were not entirely comfortable being so reliant on a salesman from one of the companies, mate of a mate or not. On the other hand, they dreaded the prospect of going through yet another 'fact find'. At least Colin managed to liven them up – even the way he handled his Mont Blanc pen was full of theatrical flourish.

'Maybe it's time we talked to someone else. Ask around your friends, Sal. I bet some of them use an IFA for their financial planning.'

That was how they came to be sitting at the kitchen table with Neil from Independent Money Associates, drinking endless cups of coffee and struggling with yet another 'fact find'. Gone was the Mont Blanc but the tools of the IFA's trade were otherwise evidently the same: forms to fill and a calculator.

Almost every inch of the table top was covered by policy documents and product particulars that only ever saw the light of day when a Colin or a Neil came to visit. These represented the sum total of John and Sally's haphazard past attempts at managing both household risks and their investment needs. Even if they could remember why each had been bought at the time, they certainly would struggle to explain now why this collection of paper represented an efficient and effective way of managing the family finances.

Neil had a formula which he religiously followed, noting down John and Sally's responses to his list of questions or ticking boxes in yet another form as he went along. You did not have to be a genius to work out what the formula was, as the logic was so clear. Less clear to John and Sally was how their halting and far from logical responses seemed nonetheless to move the whole process on to the next stage. The alternative, though, was that Neil would be staying for lunch and dinner and that was worse.

After establishing how much money should be set aside for contingencies, including any more education bills, the conversation was then dominated by pensions. Neil got John and Sally to say how much they wanted to retire on and when. Neil wrote it down and tapped the same numbers into his calculator. Out popped the contribution rate. Neil checked the amount the calculator wanted them to save with what the tax man allowed them to contribute. Between the two was some room for Neil to talk the contribution rate up but in the end it just boiled down to what John and Sally said they were prepared to save. Neil accepted that but did point out it still did not leave much scope for the house in Tuscany.

Neil set about explaining why they should move away from Rothbar and start a new pension plan. It was something about high charges on the 'capital units'. There were two types of unit as well as different unit trusts they each held. John hoped Sally was paying attention but Sally for once was relying on her husband. Neil said he would make some proposals and send them in a report.

He talked about their 'best advice' process. It seemed Independent Money Associates spent a lot of their time analyzing all the different managers in the market, any of which they could recommend. As well as buying in state-of-the-art fund research they got to know the best managers personally, following their portfolios really closely. He mentioned a few and they recognized all of the company names and John thought he recognized some of the managers' names. It was evidently all about picking the investment group that had good performance in a spread of different investment funds, such as an income fund, a UK growth fund, an international fund and so on. It seems that on this basis Rothbar did not have 'strength in depth'.

Then it was back to forms and the formula, for what Neil described as 'the interesting bit'. This turned out to be about their investment preferences. He had a coloured graph with the cumulative returns of equities and the Halifax Gold savings account. Sally remembered from Halifax Gold that this was the same exhibit that Colin had once used. Between the two was another line for gilts. Here is a race, she thought, where the tortoises never seem to beat the hares.

Neil had another illustration that showed the way risk fell the longer you were invested in equities. John particularly liked that one. But he had not noticed that the columns that shrank as you moved across the page, showing progressively longer holding periods, were actually bands of *annualized* rates of return. If you compounded those progressively falling rates over the rising number of years equities were held, the bands of outcomes were not shrinking at all.

Neil evidently had some more boxes on his form and needed to put a tick in either 'high', 'medium' or 'low' to be able to identify their risk tolerance, individually. It was not entirely clear that each box would lead directly to some combination of equities, gilts or cash but the implication was that this was how their answers would end up being interpreted. However, there was also some discussion about smaller companies funds and emerging markets that also had a bearing. Neither John nor Sally was really clear what this bearing was. Sally was a bit distracted by wondering whether, if Neil had been sitting at her table a year earlier, the discussion would have included a technology fund because this had been curiously absent from the conversation.

With more coffee and much more discussion, it was still not obvious where the ticks should go but it seemed that 'medium' best captured the way both of them thought about market fluctuations.

Next up was a question about their 'investment philosophy'. John looked a little embarrassed when Sally asked, too bluntly he thought, if Neil could perhaps explain how philosophy fitted in. Neil's answer did not in fact have much to do with the meaning of life. Actually, he had another set of boxes with terms along the lines of 'long-term capital growth', 'balanced income and growth' and 'capital preservation'. Eventually the ticks went down.

At last it was time to clear away the paper. Neil scooped quite a lot of John and Sally's own documents into his briefcase. He would check what he called 'the protection policies' (men in black in the High Street?) and also the investment bonds to see whether any changes needed to be made and would include that in his report. All the individual fund recommendations would be set out, with reasons why, so they would have plenty more opportunity to consider them. He left the papers to do with John's occupational schemes, though. He had explained why he could not comment on those – something to do with the regulations brought in after the pension mis-selling scandal.

As they were heading for the door, Sally returned to the question she had first put to Neil. 'Do you really mean we don't pay you anything?'

'Absolutely' said Neil. 'We are only paid by the product companies and then only if you decide to buy a product. You are under no pressure, believe me.'

After Neil had left John and Sally wearily discussed the process. They both agreed they were not much clearer and did not have much confidence that the report, when it came, would give them a real grasp of their planning needs. Sure enough, when it came two weeks later, it was far from illuminating. There was a long section setting out all the information about themselves they had given Neil. So they knew that anyway. There were detailed reviews of the individual products they each held. There were several recommendations for changes. In each case there were three new candidates, all household names that they remembered Neil mentioning, with summaries of the different fund choices that Neil's firm liked best.

Each proposal was accompanied by a set of particulars, not quite as visually appealing as those for the house in Castellina. These were the

Key Features documents that John and Sally had encountered before. For the pension proposals there was also a set of projections that looked very much like the ones they already had from Rothbar.

'This is not what we're looking for, Sal.'

'Your right. It's just the same old muddle only with new names. There has to be a better way.'

part

I

You and the markets:
the system that works

1

Investment is about you

We are wiser than we know

In 1997 the Office of Fair Trading (OFT) produced a damning report on second-hand car sales. It had been immediately preceded by a report on 'consumer detriment' in the personal pensions industry. The irony of the juxtaposition would not have been lost on anyone who had their own good reasons for spotting the parallel between the folk figure of the second-hand car salesman and the investment professionals they had been dealing with. This was a bad time for investment advisers and financial product salesmen, coming at the peak of media scrutiny of mis-selling. The money business was fast becoming synonymous with monkey business.

The irony certainly did not escape me since I had found it helpful in the past to use the analogy of both buying and driving cars to persuade investors struggling with the off-putting complexity of investment that they can in fact manage very well, and protect themselves, with little knowledge and minimal information.

The analogy I had intended was not in fact about *caveat emptor*, or 'buyer beware'. With hindsight, though, it would have been better if customers of the investment industry had approached their chosen agents with the same intuitive suspicion and caution as when approaching the used car forecourt.

The analogy with driving was a simple one. You do not need to understand the workings of the internal combustion engine to drive a car. You need a set of basic principles and rules to follow that are reliable and consistent. You need to understand and be familiar with the means of control: throttle, brakes, steering, gears. You have to be confident the response to the controls will be as you expect. You only need a limited amount of factual information fed back to you: speed, fuel. To plan your journeys sensibly and realistically you need some facts and figures but you certainly do not need to be a mathematical genius to process them.

We can take this analogy one stage further and imagine that we can afford the luxury of employing a chauffeur. We then safely delegate the controls and the information feedback, confident in the knowledge they will be used in the context of exactly the same principles, applying the same essential rules. Employing a chauffeur does not mean that we have to give up ownership of the car, or lose the power to determine the journey and the route map or to dictate the manner in which we are driven and the risks taken. Where it counts, we still have control.

The analogy with buying a car, new or old, is also useful for the individual investor. We take it for granted that the overriding criterion is *purpose*. We probably do not buy a BMW Roadster or a Morgan for the school run and the shopping. Implicit but absolute is the fact that the purpose is determined by us and is individual to us. The car salesman is not trying to sell us on the need to take the kids to school or to go shopping. If we tell him our purpose, he may of course try to persuade us that a sports car is ideal for that purpose. How he measures up to the challenge of that particular pitch may be amusing to discover but we are unlikely to be moved from our own good sense.

Our sensible intuition also works well when it comes to the *performance* of a car. The chances are that we will see safety as a more important principle than performance. That does not mean we all want something slow and ponderous but it does mean we expect a car to be engineered to match its safety to its performance, as well as to our purpose.

You are likely to be reading this because you want clearer and more realistic expectations about the future. You want to roll back the clouds of confusion that surround the individual components of an investment strategy and that conceal any purpose and logic for the overall strategy. You want to be less dependent on third parties, and you want to understand exactly why you are working with the ones you choose. You may well be less trusting of professionals but on the other hand you may also be mistrustful of your own ability to take control. You want, in a word, *coaching*.

Though it is not necessary for the usefulness of the book, I am going to make certain assumptions about your wish to be coached. I will assume that you do not want investment to become an all-consuming hobby and are fearful of the time and effort it may require. You view control as different from DIY. I will also assume you do not want a writer to tell you what to do, any more than you want the industry to tell you what to do, but that you are willing to be educated towards a general understanding that can help you choose your own path.

I will also assume you are bored by tax and insurance and are not particularly turned on by the daily hubbub of stock markets, because this actually describes most of us and is what is least well catered for by educational material. The good news is such fascination is not necessary to being a good owner of personal investments.

What I will not assume is that you belong to any single group of personal investors, by age, gender or measures of affluence. The wish to understand what degree of control is sensible and responsible, and how to achieve it, crosses all different thresholds of personal wealth. It is as pressing for families with modest needs as for those with substantial assets to organize. Wealth differences may show up in different needs for tax planning or for trust arrangements but the essential principles of investment planning know no social or economic boundaries.

I need make no assumption about your existing relationships with the industry, whether you delegate a lot or a little, whether you use an adviser or make your own decisions, or whether you use securities or funds. The essential principles of individual investment are not affected by the chosen methods of implementation.

In the first part of the book we encounter the simplifying structures: a few key principles you need to understand and the techniques for achieving genuine participation and high-level control of your investment arrangements. This focuses on you and the markets, in terms that are easy to relate to, instead of products and professional paraphernalia that are difficult to relate to.

Investment does not have to be complicated. It does not have to be outside your control, certainly not when you take professional advice and not even when you delegate the management to professionals. Complexity and control are two sides of the same coin. The more complex, the harder it is to control and the more tempting to give up and depend blindly on third parties – or even your own poorly informed attempts at DIY. In Part II we will see that the complexity and control coin is one minted by the industry with the express purpose of gathering and managing assets in ways that best suit their business model. This has been and continues to be the source of great harm to customers.

The *knowledge* that allows you to control your own investments and avoid industry abuse is not the same knowledge that professionals need to perform all the functions of investment stewardship. That functional knowledge is equivalent to the engineering under the bonnet. I plan to leave it there.

Happily, the knowledge you need focuses on aspects of investment that you are more likely to find genuinely engaging and interesting. Control comes, after all, from concentrating on a higher level, above the day-to-day trivia and noise of markets. On this higher level, investment understanding ties in with 'big picture' themes of general interest, such as history, progress, beliefs, personality and social behaviour.

As for the *information* you need, it is probably very different from what you imagine. Most of what you may think important is found down on those lower levels and is not necessary for either control or clarity. Indeed, an obsession with trivial detail is one of the barriers that it suits the industry to erect between your money and the markets.

Investment is not about 'products' and 'securities'

Some 4,500 firms of independent financial advisers (IFAs), and several hundred companies who have 'packaged' about 30,000 individual financial products for sale, want you to believe that investment is all about products. The industry spends three or four times as much money promoting the idea of products as it spends managing investments. Firms bombard the newspapers and your doormat with product advertise-ments and leaflets. They would like nothing more than to pump up the 'let's go shopping' culture to the point where you start to covet your neighbour's ISA.

Stockbrokers and private client portfolio managers, smaller in number but controlling a large proportion of individual wealth, want you to believe investment is all about individual securities or industries – picking winners. Most newspaper coverage of finance and the growing fascination of television with the stock market promote the same idea that stocks are what matter. Much of the early presence of investment on the web has served the same model of trying to draw private clients into trading stocks directly.

Both sets of people, whether selling securities or selling packaged securities as products, want you to believe it is clever investment professionals with an 'information edge' who will fulfil your goals. It is not enough that you have to pass through investment professionals to get your money to work in financial markets. They need to make you believe that you have to depend on them for the money to work.

This is self-serving nonsense that plays on the typical private investor's ignorance of basic investment principles. *Money works for you just by being in the markets*. It does not need clever investment professionals. Clever or not, they are merely the gatekeepers to the markets, 'the people in between'.

In the rest of Part I we will encounter the characteristics of markets and portfolios that ensure it is market exposure that explains virtually all of the results of any portfolio strategy, whether that exposure is acquired through packaged products or through direct securities. We will meet the 'decision hierarchy' that separates the vital from the trivial and is therefore an important device for securing active participation and effective control by the owner of the money. It is also an important device for limiting the time owners need to spend on their investments.

Money and personal goals

Investment is certainly about exposure to financial markets but there are many different markets and they can be used in different ways, so markets can no more be the end purpose of investment than can products and securities. They are no more the end itself than a £20 note in your pocket is.

It is only when you imagine yourself converting your investment back into money that you can really see that the end itself, what you spend it on, or choose to enable someone else to spend it on, is always entirely personal and individual. The industry cannot tell you what to spend your money on or how much you need or when you will need it. The industry cannot force upon you some preferred level of confidence about future spending capacity. It does not know how you would value the possibility of having a greater amount to spend relative to the possibility of having less, when with risk taking either might occur.

This idea that investment is no different from money except in the deferral of its likely exchange for goods and services is both sensible and helpful. It is sensible because it captures the essential purpose of investment without pretensions or embarrassment. It is helpful because it allows you to plan the investment process, which you may not be familiar with, by reference to spending intentions that you are familiar with or can at least easily relate to. It is also motivational. The process of deferring the gratification that money can bring often involves sacrifice and focusing on the eventual object of gratification can in turn make that sacrifice easier to make.

This does not mean you have to be able to anticipate exactly what you will be buying in, say, 20 years' time. It could be you only need to think about levels of spending power and about the consequences of higher or lower levels of spending power.

Some tasks are obvious, like pensions and school fees. It is less obvious what task we allocate to general funds that do not have a single goal in mind and may even end up benefiting our heirs. However, even these can be defined as a separate goal or series of individual goals. Separately defined, they may take on very different characteristics, such as reserves against unforeseen expenditures or part of your estate planning, which in turn obviously imply quite different time horizons and investment approaches.

The motivational benefits of goal-based planning also attach to these general tasks. By attributing some notional purpose, such as the purchase of a second home, planning can reveal that what might otherwise seem a pipe dream is actually realistically achievable at a cost you are willing to bear. It can also frame the risk you want to take if, for example, the disappointment of failing to achieve a goal seems to you unlikely to outweigh the benefit of pulling off the improbable. You would not make the same gamble with your pension, because of the consequences of a shortfall, but you might in order to achieve that house in Tuscany.

Filling in some notional detail in plans for inheritable wealth can also be motivational for both donor and beneficiary. If, for example, you are in the happy position of being able to fund more than just your first priority for your children, the best education for them, you can focus on their eventual benefit from having investments in their own name, such as the equity in their first house or flat.

Early inheritance planning is usually tax efficient but as important may be the benefit to your children of involving them in an early investment education. The idea that assets are 'earmarked' for particular purposes will help them to play the game of deferring gratification and ordering priorities. The matching of investment strategies to their own particular purposes is a key part of their introduction to practising safe investment.

'Oh dear', you may be thinking, 'this is beginning to sound a little folksy'. It is true that we British are not particularly good about thinking in terms of personal aspirations so the idea of setting personal goals for different stages of our lives may at first make us feel slightly uncomfortable.

It is difficult to imagine the idea of a 'British Dream' catching on like the 'American Dream'. This difference also shows in attitudes to financial planning. To American ears, the common enough claims of financial planners to help their clients 'fulfil personal dreams' do not sound either extravagant or foolish. Yet, even accepting this difference, I would strongly urge you to give the motivational benefits of goal-based planning a decent chance.

Early in 2000 I was engaged in a market research project for a new internet-based investment business. We decided to use a series of 'focus groups' drawn from different age groups and each covering a wide range of levels of spending and saving. What they all had in common was initial embarrassment about discussing personal life goals: things they would really like to do or achieve if they only had a bit more money. It was surprising to see how, in a group, individuals can quickly take encouragement from each other to share their secrets or even perhaps to articulate ideas that were only vague and dreamy in their own minds. Every one of them had some goal that was real, beyond their apparent reach but not so far beyond as to be in the realm of wild fantasy. The reticence was perhaps not so much about setting goals as about talking about them.

Even if you are sure that aspirational planning is too folksy for your own taste, there is a good practical reason for adopting personal goal setting. Even if you only think about it as giving tasks to your money, it can be a pragmatic device for seizing the agenda back from the industry.

By relating all of the planning of your available resources to tasks that you define and control, you can in turn control the investment process and your relationships with the industry. You define exactly what information you want about risk, which is not the information the industry would otherwise give you, and the form of the information, related to the probabilities of achieving your personal goals. This ensures that you alone are at the heart of the investment process, where you belong.

These benefits will apply whatever the agents you choose to use, whatever the degree of delegation or discretion you decide to give them and whatever the chosen means of gaining your market exposure, be it packaged products or individual securities.

If any of this sounds unfamiliar, be assured that it is in fact the essential model for the way institutional funds, with advice from investment professionals, plan their own chosen balance of resources, goals and risk.

Planning versus management

A practical implication of choosing to relate all of your investment needs to personal goals is that the planning process becomes much more important and personally relevant, both at the outset and continuously thereafter. In fact, I recommend that you make no distinction in your own mind between planning and management, so that you come to see management as a continuous and dynamic planning process in which you always participate and which, at a high level, you control.

At first sight, this might well strike you as odd, based on your experience of dealing with the industry, but it does make perfect sense. Consider how the two are normally separated and what results from that separation.

If, for instance, your experience is of dealing with a stockbroker or having assets managed on a 'discretionary' basis[1] by a private client portfolio manager, you may recall some planning issues being discussed at the outset. There are, I suggest, two features of these discussions that are likely to hold true in most cases. Firstly, they have rarely been revisited later and are not constantly referred to as the basis for monitoring the portfolio's progress. Secondly, they were framed in language that related to investment, not to you, and required and presumed knowledge of investment on your part.

We can start by assuming you were asked how long the money was likely to be invested for. However, it is most unlikely your agreement was sought for any specific time horizon, either for the eventual liquidation of the portfolio or as a decision time frame.

A typical question: *'Is the purpose of the portfolio to produce income or capital growth or a combination?'* Did you perhaps wonder how you were meant to know how to balance income and growth or what the implica-

---

[1] 'Discretionary' is an industry term that means the investor's agent does not have to refer back to the investor before making any transactions, although there may be standing instructions that also govern how the adviser should manage the portfolio. Arrangements that require the investor's agent to refer to the investor for agreement to each transaction are called 'advisory'. Some agents, such as private client stockbrokers, offer a choice of service.

tions were of taking income out instead of reinvesting it? How were you supposed to know how your stated income objective would affect the entire investment strategy and eventual range of portfolio outcomes?

Another typical question runs along the lines, *'Is your risk tolerance high, medium or low?'* Did you perhaps wonder whether you were alone in not possessing some psychic barometer that would allow you simply to read off your personal risk tolerance? Did you wonder what the average risk tolerance was, and how and why? Did you wonder how high is high and how low is low? Even if you assumed one or other fitted you best, how did you know that it would mean the same to an investment professional as to you? Did you know the implications of your answer?

Were the risks even defined for you? If there were several sources of risk, such as market uncertainty and inflation uncertainty, how were you to be expected to reduce these in your own mind to a single measure of risk tolerance?

You might have been asked if you were willing to invest in foreign markets, which in turn might lead to questions about limiting exposure to

IF YOUR EXPERIENCE HAS BEEN WITH AN IFA, THERE IS A BETTER CHANCE THAT YOUR PLANNING DISCUSSIONS WILL HAVE BEEN MORE FORMALLY LINKED TO SPECIFIC GOALS

particular markets or about including or excluding emerging markets. When offering answers that would determine the type of assets and individual markets that you would be exposed to or the ranges of exposure, did you appreciate that those answers would end up determining much of the portfolio outcome over time, as well as the likely path of the portfolio value through time? Were those implications ever explained to you? Were they quantified?

Perhaps you were also asked if you wanted to invest in securities directly or via funds, such as unit trusts and investment trusts. If you were not asked, maybe it was because the people you approached only offered one of these options anyway. In either case, did you already have some assumptions and, if so, what were they based on?

All of these questions that portfolio managers and brokers typically ask require investment knowledge that you should not be expected to have. They all touch on the mathematics of investment, a book that should remain firmly closed for most investors. They certainly go far beyond the essential principles that should be all you need to control the way in which the portfolio is best matched to your personal needs.

If your experience has been not with a stockbroker or portfolio manager but with an IFA, there is a better chance that your planning discussions will have been more formally linked to specific goals that were personal to you. There is also a good chance that your IFA genuinely tried to help you articulate these goals.

IFAs are more planning orientated because more of the investment tasks they are asked to advise on require the calculation of *resources*, be it existing capital or savings you are prepared to set aside regularly, in order to meet, with the help of investment growth, some task-specific target. The commonest task IFAs advise on is retirement income. This is a task that lends itself readily to definitions using criteria personal to you, such as age, retirement date, a preferred level of retirement income. So does the funding of school fees, for example, or the investment of a settlement that has to produce a stream of income for life.

If you were dealing with an IFA you may therefore remember more precise and more meaningful discussions about targets and time horizons. Yet I would wager that the rest of the questions, about risk tolerance and types of investment exposure, were essentially the same and framed in the same way as I have described above for the typical stockbroker or portfolio manager.

What did you do if you found it difficult to relate to many of the questions in your planning process? Did you keep your unease to yourself? Were you perhaps worried about looking silly? Did you keep quiet because you assumed there is no other way? There is a better way and it involves as a first step extending the idea of personal goals to all of your investments.

The Three Ts that define personal goals

What you need from the industry, at the outset and from time to time afterwards, is a particular set of information which is based on the mathematics going on 'under the bonnet', which you prefer not to open. You, not the industry, frame the questions that dictate the form and content of this information.

You do so by defining your personal goals in terms of several specific features that you are aiming to fix and agree with your adviser or manager as the basis of your control.[2] These are the instructions to your

[2] In mathematical terms, which may not put off all readers, a quantity that is constant or fixed in the case being considered but which can be varied in different cases is called a 'parameter'. It is the same meaning that I intend for these 'defining features'.

chauffeur, to stay with that analogy. They are expressed as numbers or facts, not as woolly aspirations.

These defining features can be easily remembered as the Three Ts: Targets, Time Horizon and Tolerance of Risk. Like the Three Tenors, the Three T's must be in tune and in harmony: they must 'balance' by being consistent with each other. The idea of *balance* comes from an underlying theory that recurs throughout the book. It is the one from which the saying *'There is no such thing as a free lunch'* stems. You will also see that the idea of balance flows naturally from the way markets and economies behave over time, which we observe in the next chapter.

The information you need from the industry is simply the probabilities that apply specifically to the Three Ts and to the markets. You are using exposure to markets to achieve your target outcome at a particular date (or series of dates) in the future, with some desired level of confidence. So, depending on how risky or uncertain the market returns associated with a particular strategy are, you have a particular chance of hitting, exceeding or falling short of your target with that strategy. Those chances need to be quantified. It is equivalent to calling the odds.

YOU ARE USING EXPOSURE TO MARKETS TO ACHIEVE YOUR TARGET OUTCOME AT A PARTICULAR DATE (OR SERIES OF DATES) IN THE FUTURE, WITH SOME DESIRED LEVEL OF CONFIDENCE

Because the odds apply to things you can easily relate to and have yourself defined, and because we all tend to have a fairly good grasp of how to interpret odds, they are enough information for you to be able to make the choices that govern how the portfolio is managed. You determine the range of acceptable outcomes.

The process of using specific information about outcome probabilities is actually interactive and iterative: in other words, you have several goes at it. This is inherent in the idea of finding the balance of resources, targets and risk that is appropriate for you and personal to you.

As an example, we can briefly anticipate here a widely shared investment task that features prominently in Part II, when we look at the mis-selling scandals. I argue in Chapter 7 that most of the 6 million households who have endowment mortgages would never have opted for them, in preference to a simple repayment mortgage, if they had been given realistic probabilities. I suggest that it was in the nature of the task that most would have set a very high level of required confidence, or virtual certainty, on having enough money at maturity to pay off the loan in full. This seems logical given the consequences of a shortfall and the fact that they did not need to link repayment and investment. You may include yourself in that category if you have one of these products.

What the industry should have done is quote a monthly premium, or contribution level, that reflected both the true uncertainty inherent in the investment returns and in the rate of inflation over that time frame and the customer's own required level of certainty. Had the industry done so, it would have made endowments so much more expensive than a straight repayment schedule as to make them impossible to sell! But anxiety and regret would have been avoided.

We will be looking at how to operate this goal-based probability approach later. At this stage, it is sufficient to note that it will not limit you to any one type of relationship. You might prefer to be interacting with a personal adviser who has access to the information you need, and doing so either in his or her office or even in your home. You might be happy to interact with investment websites to obtain the information feedback, using goal-based investment planning 'work surfaces' that they provide on screen. Or you may prefer to delegate all of the day-to-day management to a discretionary manager in which case the goal-based process ensures you control how the portfolio is managed by reference to outcomes acceptable to you.

The only common denominator is that they should each have access to and be able to communicate the information in the form that you want it. Though the appropriate investment technology is widely used in the institutional market, it is woefully under-used in the retail sector. This means that if you are putting this approach into practice in the next few years the determining factor in your choice of actual firm may well be who has the methodology and technology rather than whether it is an IFA, stockbroker or money manager.

Since the information you need from the industry is about the probabilities of achieving your personal investment goals, and since these are specific not just to the goals themselves but also to the markets you are invested in, market exposure is a key element in any controlled investment process.

This in turn makes markets a key element of the little knowledge that you need. It takes the form of the nature of markets as a 'system', an idea we explore in the next chapter. Systems are great: in a chaotic world, they are one of the few things that obey rules and display an underlying order. We can use that.

2

The markets as a system

Economies, markets and board games

Market exposure is the key to different outcomes for any diversified investment strategy. Markets are reasonably predictable. On both counts, it is well worth understanding how markets behave. Speculating as to why they behave as they do is less important except as a means of grasping the essential principles and absorbing their sound good sense.

First, we need to be sure of some definitions. 'Market' here means an entire population of publicly traded securities of the same type and listed in one place. A market therefore represents the 'opportunity set' for that type and location available to the investor. Any difference between the way an entire market behaves and the way any less representative collection of securities behaves is likely to be explained by the nature of whole markets as a 'system'.

In economic terms a market is a system for allocating a nation's capital. It acts as a bridge between those who have surplus capital and those who need capital, for instance, to develop a business. Equity and bond markets allocate capital that is likely to be tied up for long periods. Shorter-term capital tends to be allocated via banks – another system.

Within a capital markets system, stock exchange investments compete with each other and with other uses of capital, including consumption, government spending and business investment, for example. It is like a board game in which the balance of advantage may temporarily shift between players over time but which can have no overall winner or loser.

We know this to be the case, for example, because we have seen in the UK's own experience how labour and capital competed brutally in the 1970s. Organized labour managed to grab a larger share of the cake but only at the expense of profits, jobs and investment, eventually undermining their own self-interest. In the sea change that followed, trade union reform and the rebuilding of company profits almost destroyed both organized labour and the political party that had come to depend upon it. Much of the unusually long period of subsequent growth in the UK economy, and the emergence of New Labour also, stems from a more sensible and sustainable balance in these competing claims on resources.

The allocation function of capital markets also allows for risk sharing or pooling, by spreading investment among a large number of individual recipients. This is sometimes described as a form of insurance because it removes the most intuitive of all capital market risks: total loss. Investors with well-diversified exposure to a large number of firms ensure that the failure of any one or of a few will not result in the loss of a high proportion of their total capital.

The entire market, or the majority of a market system as represented by a broad index of securities within that market, is by definition a diversified portfolio. Thus the FTSE All Share Index, with some 800 constituents, is a diversified index and an index fund that tracks it passively is also a diversified portfolio. By mimicking the constituents of a market index, an index fund, or 'tracker', will also mimic the behavioural characteristics of the market system. Other portfolios, based on a selection of securities, may not do this.

'Behaviour' in this context refers to all aspects of the returns or performance of a market over some time frame, such as levels, the changes in levels, rates of change. Applying a human characteristic, behaviour, to an inanimate object, a stock market, is appropriate in this case. Markets are after all a reflection of the totality of the actions of millions of individuals. Those actions are in turn the object both of their rationality and of their emotions: their fear, their greed or their impatience. Behaviour is for very good reasons the most popular way to describe market performance characteristics.

Types of asset are *money* itself, usually held in the form of a deposit, *fixed income* securities, which pay a rate of interest determined when they are issued and normally have a set date for repayment of principal, and *equities*, or shares in companies. These types of asset are also known as 'asset classes'.

These different asset classes are also represented in other countries so exposure to the same class of asset, such as equities, can be obtained by investing in the equity markets of different countries.

Overseas markets for any asset class also expose investors to exchange rate changes. Because currency exposure can only be obtained in conjunction with a deposit or an investment, currency is not really an asset class itself. Thus, whereas foreign equity markets are of the same class as UK equities, their behaviour is different as a result of the combination of market and currency characteristics.

The way investment is presented in this book, by reference to tasks for your money, means that markets can be further defined in terms partly specific to each task rather than some universal standard. This further definition takes the form of a distinction between all *risky assets*, that is to say, assets with uncertain outcomes over the horizon of the task, and a single *risk-free asset* that best matches the defining features (or parameters) of the individual task. It is only risk free if there is effectively negligible uncertainty about the outcome. Whatever that asset is in each case, we shall refer to it generically as the '*safe-harbour*' asset.

▨ Harnessing the power of markets

Now that we are sure of the definitions, we can look at how markets behave. What we are about to observe has all the appearance of a natural power, or 'dynamic', that can be 'harnessed'. A portfolio of individual investments, once harnessed to capital markets simply by exposure or 'being there', is carried by and dependent on the dynamics of market behaviour.

For those dynamics to be useful as a means of achieving some target outcome for your money, they must have certain characteristics that are not just random. Few people (and certainly not, for example, prudent pension fund trustees) would want the money set aside to meet future needs (or promises) to be carried by a power whose dynamics are no different from the toss of a coin or the throw of a die. Randomness is not the behaviour we are looking for.

The essential feature of the behaviour of markets that encourages us to use them as a means to an end is a return over some long holding period that normally exceeds a risk-free or safe-harbour return. The effect of this '*premium*' is that we may need less money to fund a particular target outcome than if we rely on a safe-harbour asset. A smaller commitment now, accumulating at a faster rate, will reach the same target at the same time. Alternatively, the same commitment (such as if it was all that we could afford) will accumulate over a given period to a larger sum than if we stay in our safe harbour.

However, it is a fundamental principle that markets that show this feature of a long-term premium also show very large and long-lasting swings around the upward 'trend' that results from the amount of the premium. These swings, often also referred to as deviations or even aberrations, represent the majority of the 'market risk' or uncertainty inherent in harnessing the power of markets. The practical impact is that you may either exceed or fall short of your target. This has to balanced against the fact that you may need less capital than if you rely on the safe-harbour asset. Because of this association with uncertainty, the premium is normally referred to as a 'risk premium'.

Fixed income and equity investments show different orders of both trend and deviation in risk premium, and both in turn depend on the asset they are compared with. As we will revisit this later in Part I, all we need to note here is a few summary observations.

For investment planning purposes, the fixed income return is a forward-looking yield to redemption, rather than a backward-looking achieved return. For an individual bond, it is a function of the known fixed rate of return given by the annual rate of interest (or 'coupon'), the current price of the security and the period to redemption. For a bond market as a whole, it corresponds to the average of all issues' redemption yields. (Representative yields are also often selected for groups of maturity, such as short-, medium- and long-dated bonds.)

The deviations stem from changes in the price and yield during the course of the life of a bond (or bond market). These are in turn largely a function of changes in the prevailing rate of interest. For private, non-government bond issues, how investors view credit risk, or default risk, is also dynamic. It reflects both the changing state of the economy as a whole and conditions specific to each borrower.

At any time you can check the forward-looking structure of risk premia by comparing published cash interest rates and bond redemption yields. Observations of the structure at various redemption dates, for example, from one-month deposits all the way out to a 30-year bond, often refer to the structure as a 'yield curve'.

For equities, the trend return is not fixed but can be estimated based on long histories, as can the deviations. When we look at some examples, we will be able to speculate about the underlying factors that explain the trend, such as by referring to the economy as a whole, since the market is part of the economy board game. We will also be able to extend the influence of these factors from a national perspective to a global perspective, as the economy is also part of a global system. Capital competition, allocation and risk spreading occur across as well as within national boundaries.

The uncertainty about the true extent of any underlying rising equity trend, which is directly related to the extent of the typical deviations for risky assets, introduces an additional source of planning uncertainty when funding future needs by exposure to equity markets. If the extent of the underlying trend is uncertain, there must also be uncertainty about where we are at any point in relation to that trend.

MEASURING A RISK PREMIUM IN TERMS OF THE WRONG SAFE HARBOUR IS A DANGEROUS ERROR AND CAN ALSO BE ONE OF THE INDUSTRY'S DELIBERATE MONKEY TRICKS

This higher order of uncertainty shows up in a higher typical risk premium for equities relative to fixed income. As we will see shortly, these different expected orders of uncertainty are significantly dependent on whether the behaviour that counts for an individual goal is 'nominal', including inflation, or 'real', measured after inflation and in terms therefore of purchasing power.

This distinction can be illustrated clearly by returning briefly to the example of the endowment mortgage. The repayment of an amount of debt that is fixed in money terms, like a mortgage, makes nominal returns the key. That in turn suggests that fixed-income investments are the natural safe harbour. However, a pension task is more likely to have a purchasing power target. Obviously, there is no point retiring with a target income fixed in money terms if at some stage it will no longer purchase enough of the goods and services we need to live without hardship. Fixed income is not the natural safe harbour for a pension task because it is only the nominal return that is fixed: the real return is highly uncertain because inflation is so poorly predictable.

Measuring a risk premium in terms of the wrong safe harbour is a dangerous error and can also be one of the industry's deliberate monkey tricks. It is implicit in most comparisons that professionals make between risky-asset returns and cash, as cash is rarely the natural safe-harbour asset.

My use of language in this chapter hints at another analogy related to the idea of investment as a journey. The power of risky markets can be compared with how early mariners viewed the power of wind and tide – although the consequences of the risks involved are quite different when a single crew cannot diversify its risk of total loss!

Though vessels under sail could readily harness those natural powers to carry crew and cargo from one port to another, their masters knew enough about the uncertainty of those elements to respect their power and remember their own limitations. Assuming mastery of the elements or of navigation was a dangerous delusion usually punished by disaster.

Respect for the power of the sea is still vital to the modern mariner but today's navigators do at least have better technical equipment and the uncertainty about exact position that characterizes equity markets is more akin to an earlier age of ocean sailing. Yet even with doubt about their exact position and about future conditions of wind and tide, it was still worthwhile for those early mariners to seek to use approximately predictable or dependable elements to achieve the aim of their enterprise.

A further analogy that is useful for private investors is to think of themselves as 'harvesting' risk premia: deliberately exposing their capital in a diversified way to capture the risk-premia incentives inherent in a competitive system.

What history can teach us

The behavioural characteristics of systems are not necessarily apparent in the pictures of historical series that you are most likely to see, such as a newspaper graph of an equity market index or a chart of the past returns of a diversified fund or portfolio. For a start the history may be too short to reveal what is really going on. More likely, though, the data itself has not first been transformed, as is usually necessary.

The most important transformation is from nominal to real terms. A country's measured rate of inflation or deflation is like a rising or falling tide that raises or lowers all boats but does not tell us anything about the boats themselves. Thus higher inflation will tend to raise the deposit rate of interest on cash, raise the yield on fixed-income bonds and increase both the trend return of equities and the size of the deviations from the trend. None of these necessarily make either old or new investors better off.

The failure to make actual, statistical adjustments for inflation, or indeed to make mental adjustments to thinking about risk and return in market systems, is often given the name of 'money illusion'. The UK's economic history in the twentieth century was marked not just by large changes in the rate of inflation but particularly by the widespread extent and damage of money illusion. Ignorance of history and poor education in long-term probabilities have not been confined to ordinary investors. They have been displayed with embarrassing obstinacy by professional investors, business managers and governments, all of whom should know better.

When my grandmother died in the 1970s she left just one investment that she had held for several decades: War Loan. She could not have known better. With the full security of the British government behind it, she had been educated that this was a safe and sound investment for the long term, yielding more than cash on deposit but with lower return potential (and also lower risk) than equities. She had implicitly decided that harvesting the equity risk premium was not her game but harvesting the smaller fixed-income premium was. At the time there was nothing unusual about her preference.

During the course of the approximate period that she held her War Loan, inflation in Britain rose from the typical pre-war average of about 2 per cent or 3 per cent per annum to around 5 per cent per annum immediately after the war. It fell back briefly and deceptively to the earlier level but by the late 1960s it was back on the rise again. The worst experience was in the 1970s, extending briefly into the 1980s. In the ten years from 1972, eight of the annual increases were at a double digit rate. The lowest annual rate was 7.7 per cent and the highest 24.9 per cent.

To provide any protection against the continuation of inflation at such alarming rates, fixed income bond yields needed to rise from the typical 3.5 per cent level before the war to around 11 per cent. Shortly before the peak of the inflation rate in 1975, gilt yields reached their own peak of nearly 18 per cent. This experience reduced the price of my grandmother's War Loan from its par value of 100 in the mid-1950s to just 30 in 1974. With both income and capital fixed only in money terms, the purchasing power of her investment fell by 90 per cent in just two decades. So much for 'safe and sound'!

Though War Loan, as an irredeemable gilt stock with no redemption date, was the worst victim of the adjustment of fixed-income assets to inflation, my grandmother's experience was not a lot worse than that of anyone living on, or partially dependent on, a fixed income. It was an expensive lesson in the importance of planning and forming expectations about the role and performance of investments *in real terms*.

With less excuse than my grandmother, life assurance actuaries and directors must now be mulling over how they could have been stupid enough to have offered guaranteed annuity rates that depended on a bet on a particular outcome for long-run inflation. The widely publicized problems of the Equitable Life that led to the humiliating closure of its life fund and forced sale to Halifax stemmed from this error of judgement.

Equitable started offering guaranteed annuities, also a fixed income for life, in the 1950s and continued to do so throughout the subsequent inflation. While inflation and yields were rising, the guarantee had little or no value but once inflation started to fall in the 1980s it acquired real value to the policyholder. This value could not be insured, or offset by any balancing investment, by the Equitable or by the other life assurance firms that had offered guaranteed annuity rates. Honouring the promise would inflict actual loss on the life companies. Where Equitable was different from the others was in not having the accumulated reserves to act as a cushion against such losses – a factor we return to in a later chapter on with-profits policies.

Figure 2.1 shows a long history of UK gilt yields and the percentage change in consumer prices, at annual intervals.[i] In the past, when changes in the price level had no trend, gilts tended to yield around 3 per cent. Note the extreme changes that have occurred in the rate of inflation and its direction and its momentum, all of which make it very difficult to anticipate. In investment planning terms, inflation uncertainty is a high risk.

Figure 2.1 ▦ **Annual percentage change in UK consumer prices and year-end gilt yield, 1756 to 2000**

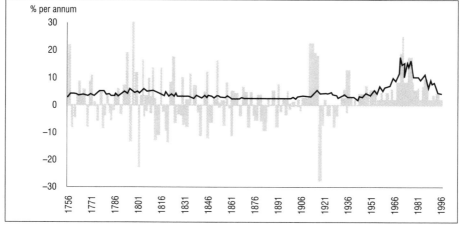

Nominal yields of around 3 per cent that were assumed to be equivalent on average to a real yield are close to the level of government bond yields on issues that guarantee inflation protection and so assure their holders of a real yield. These bonds, known as index-linked gilts, were first launched in the UK in 1984.

Their novel feature was the indexation, or automatic adjustment in line with the retail price index, of both income and capital. Full inflation protection is actually achieved by indexing the principal amount and applying the original coupon to that uplifted amount to calculate the interest payment. The coupon itself does not change. Note that if retail prices fall, the interest and principal will also be adjusted *downwards*. Because the real return at purchase is therefore fixed, whatever happens to retail prices, they are the natural safe-harbour asset for any investment task with a real return target.

When first issued, index-linked gilts had a scarcity value that was reflected in coupons of 2.5 per cent. Though the Treasury seemed to prefer to hold the coupon at the same level, issue prices had to fall to reflect a rise in investors' required real yield once the novelty wore off. After peaking at around 5 per cent, this subsequently dropped back to around 2 per cent for the longer dated issues.[3]

The period since 1984 is too short for the observed average real yield, or real expected return, on index linked to be a valid average in the future, for planning purposes. However, I believe we can also take advantage of our knowledge of the earlier history, when conventional fixed-income yields were assumed to be real, to suggest that the normal real yield for index-linked gilts will be about 3 per cent per annum.

As Figure 2.1 suggests, there is no such thing as a normal level of inflation. An average change on prices of zero, though consistent with past expectations, has not proved after the event to be a safe assumption. On the other hand, there is no natural tendency for prices to rise by a particular amount. Instability in the price level is a function of a large number of changing influences and circumstances that are not themselves predictable.

---

[3] This is a lower real yield than on inflation-proofed securities issued by other governments. It is probably due to strong demand for index-linked gilts by pension funds to match a segment of their liabilities – a market distortion that may be eased by recent changes to their solvency tests.

Since markets (and governments) must nonetheless estimate inflation in setting nominal short-term interest rates, it follows from inflation uncertainty that there is no 'normal' interest rate, before the event. After the event, however, we can see that historical interest rates adjusted by the inflation that did actually occur have averaged around 1 per cent per annum. If we make the same observations for other countries, and limit ourselves to countries that avoided hyperinflation, we find that 1 per cent per annum is a fairly typical rate for most of the last century.

It could be argued that if a system really could depend on stable prices, and if the supply and demand for short-term capital were normally in balance, there would be no real interest rate on cash, on average. If so, all of the 3 per cent real return on index linked is a risk premium. If we accept that 1 per cent is a valid estimate of future real interest rates, the index-linked risk premium is 2 per cent per annum.

Why would a system provide a risk premium incentive, whether 2 per cent or 3 per cent, for an asset with no uncertainty of outcome in real terms? The reason is that the carrying value of index linked, the market value 'along the way', is subject to volatility. It fluctuates under the influence of factors such as other risky asset prices (including conventional fixed-income stocks) and supply and demand imbalances (such as the pension fund matching referred to above). The problem of choosing between uncertainty along the way and uncertainty of outcome is one that features in all investment programmes and we will be returning to it.

These systematic return characteristics for the money and bond markets can now be compared with the systematic behaviour of equity markets.

History and equity market systems

To interpret the history of an equity market in the context of a system also calls for manipulation of the data. This takes several forms. First, we need to add together the two sources of equity return, income and change in capital value, in a measure known as *total return*. Second, we need to adjust this series for inflation. Finally, it is helpful if we present any graphs of real total return in logarithmic scale, or use 'natural logs', so as to maintain the proportionality of changes over time.

You may wonder why so many graphs for equity type investments (such as a market index, a fund or a share price) show exponential growth, with the series soaring to the top right corner with accelerating velocity. These are all distorted by the failure to use logs or a log scale which would probably show that there was no such change in velocity. Figure 2.2 shows an example of this illusion.

Figure 2.2 ▨ **Growth index over 64 time intervals of initial investment of £1 increasing by 5% in each interval together with natural logarithms of exactly the same price series**

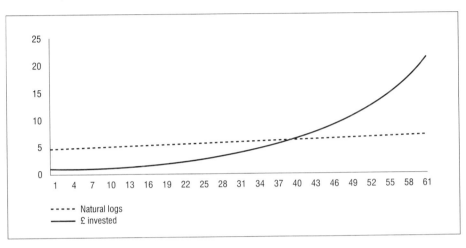

- - - - - Natural logs
———— £ invested

Viewed as the product of a system, real total return is the 'bottom line' of investing. It is unaffected by what happens just to dividend payments or just to share prices. It discounts the influence of investors within the system who, by reason of tax planning or personal need, choose to focus on one or the other. It is not distorted by changes in the tax or accounting treatment of income or capital gains from time to time. It is not distorted by cyclical trends, possibly long lived, in the proportion of company profits that are distributed as dividends. It is unaffected by companies buying back their shares in the market instead of paying dividends.

It is also the bottom line in terms of the way individual and institutional investors, at the margin, respond to past achieved returns in their own actions in the market. They do not necessarily do so because they are all using exactly the same measure but because the measure captures well enough the way investors view their changing wealth, as a part of the board game phenomenon.

Let us look at some manipulated data and see what it suggests. Figure 2.3 shows the real total returns for the UK investor with gross dividends reinvested (as if in a pension plan, for instance) expressed as an index starting at 100 in 1918. No charges have been deducted as this is based on the index itself, not a product. Tax and charges are adjustments that can be made once assumptions about the future behaviour of the market have been made. The source of this data is CSFB (formerly Barclays Capital).

Figure 2.3 ▓ **Real total return index, UK equities 1918 to 2000**

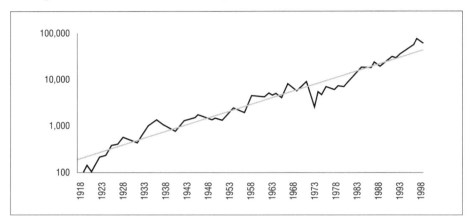

What is immediately apparent is that the market has a trend return, defined by an upward slope.[4] Because this is a logarithmic scale, the trend shows as a straight line. The annual deviations from the trend are large but the pattern of them is not necessarily regular. The deviations appear to be correlated with each other, which is natural as share prices themselves are 'serially correlated': that is, tomorrow's price is largely explained by yesterday's price. The two do not behave as if unrelated.

Though the deviations appear irregular, as distinct say from the swing of a pendulum, the extent of them nonetheless appears to be bounded, in the same way that a pendulum swings so far before losing momentum and reversing.

Systems that reveal these characteristics can be said to be *mean reverting*, or show reversion to the mean.[5] In a totally random system, like throwing dice or tossing a coin, mean reversion reveals itself after a large number of

---

[4] It is a 'regression' line that best fits all the data points rather than a line connecting the first and last data points. A regression is the best way to calculate a long-term trend that is least likely to be period-specific.
[5] The appearance of mean reversion from a graphical representation of a series, particularly one that we have already noted is 'serially correlated', can be a trap but on the website are documented some statistical tests of UK real total returns to demonstrate that the phenomenon is real.

throws as an equal number of instances of each number on the face of the die or the same number of heads and tails. It is sometimes called 'the law of large numbers' and is not at all an unfamiliar concept in every day life.

For this UK series the mean is a number equivalent to a real growth rate of about 4 per cent per annum. The ABN-Amro/LBS index which has been recalculated from 1900 to 2000 in *The Millennium Book: A Century of Investing*, shows an annualized percentage return of 5.9 per cent.

Figure 2.4 ⬛ **Real total return index US equities 1820 to 1999**

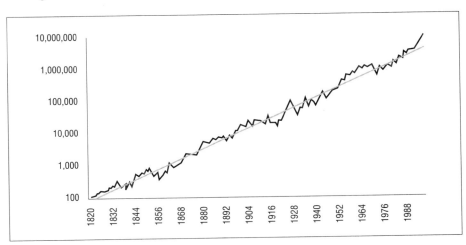

In Figure 2.4 we show an even longer data series for the US equity market, also real total returns, indexed from 1820. This data from leading American pension consultants Wilshire Associates shows the same pattern and the growth rate is also fractionally over 6 per cent per annum.

There are a number of aspects of these observations that are really quite extraordinary and which I found hard to accept when I first encountered them:

1 The trend is remarkably consistent whatever is happening to consumer prices, be they rising or even falling. Though the data has been deflated, we would still expect to see actual inflation causing a much larger hiatus in markets. With the exception of hyperinflation and currency collapse, which has proved a massive wealth destroyer and can even end the board game, price changes make little lasting impact.

2 The behaviour is affected remarkably little by wars.

3 It holds good whatever the stage of economic development. For the US series, for instance, much of the early data relates to an emerging economy.

4 It does not appear to be affected by the changing industry make-up of the market, such as the shift in the UK from a heavy weighting in railway stocks at the start of the century to a heavy weighting in telecommunications, media and technology stocks by the end.

The fact that the behaviour persists in spite of such contextual differences is itself evidence that the UK and US markets function as a system. Extraordinary though these observations are, they do at least make it less of a shock to find that the behaviour holds up in so many different equity markets, and not just in the Anglo-Saxon culture. Common behaviour overwhelms the expected differences due, for instance, to our perception of their economic development, economic performance and in the prevailing culture of investors.

The 6 per cent growth rate emerges as a remarkably common approximate trend in international equity markets. Using the Global Financial Data return database (there is an explanation and link on our website), it is possible to extract periods of history for other markets not affected by phases of hyperinflation that introduce discontinuities in the data series.

For Germany, real total returns from 1926 to 1999, after the distortion of the hyperinflation between the wars, show a growth trend of 5.9 per cent per annum. For Japan, the growth trend from 1960 to 1999, after the post-war hyperinflation and major industrial rebuilding, is 6.4 per cent per annum. The shorter data series for Europe as a whole, from 1969, shows a growth rate of 6.9 per cent but this is beginning to be too short to be representative of a true systematic return. It compares, for instance, with the UK rate over the same period of 8.3 per cent, faster than the longer period rate.

Analyzing the standard deviations[6] for these different series and the strength of the reversion to the mean in each case shows the same

---

[6] Standard deviation is a statistical term so widely used in all fields involving probability as to call for familiarity from all streetwise consumers. It measures the dispersion of a series of values, acting like an average of the amount by which all the values deviate from the mean of the distribution. The more widely distributed the values, the higher the standard deviation. Arbitrarily, it measures approximately the middle two-thirds of the distribution. A standard deviation of annual returns for, say, an equity market index of 25 per cent means that there are two chances in three that the market will return the average plus or minus 25 per cent. It is more informative than the average alone since two assets could have the same average yet very different distributions and hence uncertainty or risk.

remarkable similarity. It supports the idea of a global equity system, with domestic influences overlapping with international influences to affect capital allocation and risk spreading.

Whatever the precise number for different countries' trend growth or return from equity investing, the 6 per cent level is a good enough approximation of the size of the dynamic that investors can harness to try to achieve personal goals. Bear in mind, though, that it is before tax and before any charges have eaten into the market return. In Part II we will be seeing how vulnerable this small number is to the ravenous appetite of the financial services industry.

What about the equity risk premium? If the appropriate safe-harbour yield is 3 per cent per annum for the duration of an individual task, then a normal gross equity return of 6 per cent provides an equity risk premium of just 3 per cent per annum.

This might strike you as surprisingly low. We are all too easily tricked into thinking that equity returns are normally much higher than this, both because of money illusion and because we are not sufficiently familiar with long histories of market returns. The big number in investment planning is not normally the expected return or the expected risk premium, but *time*. Time and the power of compounding is the key to using the capital market system for personal goal planning.

THE 6 PER CENT LEVEL IS A GOOD ENOUGH APPROXIMATION OF THE SIZE OF THE DYNAMIC THAT INVESTORS CAN HARNESS TO TRY TO ACHIEVE PERSONAL GOALS

This view of markets focuses on normal returns and normal risk premia. However, it is clear from the size, duration and frequency of the deviations from normal market conditions in the graphs above that plotting a course based on a presumption of normal conditions is highly likely to lead to disappointment, even if it does not quite dash you on the rocks. We need outcome probabilities that are specific both to our own task and to actual market conditions at the time.

Modelling equity market returns

How can the professionals be expected to calculate, or form a reasonable estimate of, probable outcomes for individual equity markets? It is possible to do so by approximation or by eye and indeed any such attempt would probably be better than blindly assuming normal conditions and no uncertainty, which sadly typifies much investment planning advice.

However, the information for each market should then be further processed by the professionals using some mathematical and logical procedure in order to move from expected returns to an actual investment policy. This definitely should allow for the uncertainty associated with each individual estimate and the uncertainty associated with the combination of asset classes, markets and currencies. This is too complex to perform by eye. If complex processing power is needed for the next stage anyway, it might as well be used for the first stage of forming individual market estimates.

The normal form this processing power takes is known as a *'model'*. It makes the process a function of mathematical equations that replicate the observed behaviour of markets.

There are a number of different ways to skin this particular cat. I have chosen to demonstrate the essential features of equity market behaviour using past real total returns as the bottom line of investing, whether we are individuals or institutions, British or Japanese. However, most formal modelling of equity returns starts above the bottom line, filling formulae with values for possibly a large number of factors held to be causal influences on the 'after the event' bottom line returns. These factors tend to be economic and refer to what are usually known as 'fundamentals'. Examples of such fundamental factors are money supply, GDP growth, company profits, dividends and balance sheet net worth.

Most fundamental models either accept the empirical evidence of mean reversion or view markets as part of a board game 'equilibrium theory'. Either way, they tend to end up with a structure of expected returns that looks like the histories shown above for the bottom line returns. That is to say they show a small upward trend and bounded deviations.

For modellers and financial planners using models, mean reversion makes a big difference to their task. It means that returns are more predictable. The mean expected return is influenced by the current deviation from trend and the standard deviation or risk is dependent on the time horizon. The effect of the second is that the band of uncertainty shrinks faster with time than if the model assumes that returns are time independent, which in turn means that less money is required to fund a goal that is conditional on a given level of confidence. Assuming mean reversion makes funding with equities more attractive relative to a known safe harbour.

In fundamental models, what typically limits the deviations is the assumption that the factors that are assumed to drive them each have a mean to which they revert. Examples are a *normal* required risk premium, an *equilibrium* rate of return on capital employed in the economy as a whole, a *sustainable* dividend payout ratio, an *average* price earnings ratio and an *average* price to book value ratio. It is common sense, for example, that, if profitability becomes very high, competition will be attracted and returns will then be driven down again – hence mean reversion. It is also obvious that the proportion of profits paid out as dividends cannot keep falling or keep rising indefinitely.

Such assumptions are likely to produce fairly realistic models of future uncertainty. Different fundamental models will nonetheless produce different versions of where we are today, equivalent to the approximation that early navigators had to rely on. These show up as differences of opinion about market value, even when investors are working with the same fundamental measures. Thus whenever many are claiming markets are 'expensive', there are always some who argue that they are really 'fair value', even if there are few who actually claim them to be 'cheap'.

Most of these differences of opinion are explained by the requirement to forecast the future values for the model parameters, such as what is going to happen to corporate earnings. Economists, wherever they work, are not good at forecasting.

To get round this problem I believe it is better (and certainly requires much less time and effort) to model future real returns, which are what count for most investment tasks, directly from the bottom line past returns.

Chris Drew (my partner in a consulting business called Fifth Freedom that develops technology solutions) and I have modelled what we believe to be the consistent behaviour of international equities. We assumed a common long-term growth trend of a little over 6 per cent per annum, with a common structure of deviations reflecting the same strength of reversion to the mean. We also assumed that the correlation or degree of common movement between them was the same, even though over any particular time period they will turn out different.

Chris and I like this sort of approach because it is quite agnostic. It has the feel of respect for the inherent uncertainties that we expect of seafarers. We do not feel competent to forecast what is going to happen to any one economy and equity market but believe that history tells us that whatever can happen in one market can as easily happen in another. Each of the major markets has experienced exceptional overvaluation, or what after the event comes to be called a speculative bubble. Each has also at some point plumbed deep despair. These peaks and troughs do not necessarily occur together, as global phenomena. They may be specific to one economy and market.

We cannot avoid the problem mariners had of approximating their current position. This required us to work out how to fit the actual past real return data series to an assumed common trend of 6 per cent, and how to estimate the confidence in that calibration. We did this (at the end of 1998) with a combination of judgement and statistical tests related to the length of the data histories.

Where each market lies currently in relation to its long-term trend, in other words the latest level divided by the mean level, gives us a ratio that performs the same function as a fundamental measure of value. It should even suggest roughly the same conclusions about market value as fundamental models, provided the latest fundamental factors have been sensibly 'normalized' by their modellers.

Fifth Freedom's term for its measure is a Market Value Ratio. Figure 2.5 shows the historical ratios of the four major markets: the UK, Europe (excluding the UK), the USA and Japan.[7] As a ratio, it should be read as 'low is good, high is bad' on the basis that low past returns translate into a low ratio and imply high future returns, and vice versa. That is the practical implication of mean reversion.

There are several striking messages you should pick up from these measures. You can see that the US market reached a peak level in 2000 every bit as extreme as Japan reached in 1989. Some fundamental models, though, seem not to have delivered this important message, possibly because they were insufficiently agnostic, overestimated the extent and sustainability of the boost to profitability associated with the 'new economy' technology boom and failed therefore to adjust for a return to more 'normal' levels of profitability. In terms of model inputs, they failed to 'normalize' the factor values as successfully as did our agnostic, history-bound simplicity. Also striking is that the slump in Japan in the 1990s shows up as extreme in terms of duration but no deeper than occurred in several other countries in the bear market of 1974.

---

[7] Updated graphs of Market Value Ratios and of various other measures based on Fifth Freedom's investment modelling are maintained on the website with their permission and subject to their copyright.

Figure 2.5 ▣ **Market Value Ratios for the UK, Europe, the USA and Japan (in local currency)**

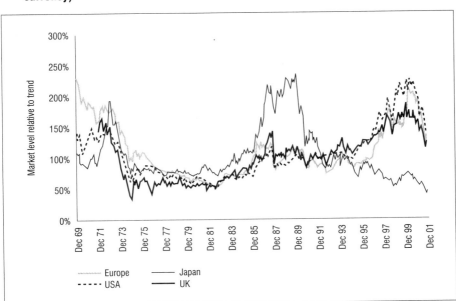

The graph captures both the essential similarities implied by a global system and the differences. 'Similarities' mean the same thing happening at the same time in different markets but also mean that what occurred once in one can also occur later in another. 'Differences' mean that though two markets might reach the same extreme, the speed and extent of the subsequent reversal is not precisely predictable. Such differences clearly limit the information equity models can be expected to provide for short-term performance or the benefits that a general understanding of market behaviour can provide for short-term decisions.

Most professional investors fret too much about the short term, and hence try to guess the specific profile of the next expected market move or cycle. Planners looking at an investor's horizon-specific outcome probabilities do not need to speculate in this way.

Whatever the precise way they model future returns, if they start with initial conditions at the same moment similar to those revealed by Fifth Freedom's ratios in Figure 2.5, they are likely to project a much higher mean expected return for Japan over the long term than for the USA, UK or Europe. That is actually more important information than what will happen over the next few years, which is essentially unpredictable. The mean reversion magnet is too weak to work its magic over such short periods.

Modelling currencies

The UK investor cannot achieve the same real return as the Japanese investor because of the additional exposure to currency movements. These can be 'hedged', such as by owning Japanese shares and selling the Yen forward for Sterling, but not that many funds or managers do this. Moreover, the nominal return deflated by Japanese retail prices may be the bottom line return for a Japanese investor but for a UK investor it is UK inflation that counts.

If the returns we are interested in for planning our investment tasks are real returns in Sterling, we need to take into account the possible differences in inflation between Japan and the UK. However, this is much less of a problem than it might appear because such differences will in theory be offset by an equal and opposite change in the exchange rate. They cancel each other out. The theory this is based on is called purchasing power theory.

In a nutshell (more detail on the website) the theory states that exchange rates adjust to differences in inflation so as to keep trade in balance. It is another version of a competitive system at work. Over long periods, it does indeed work quite well. When inflation differences are very large it even works over the short term. It would certainly be accepted by people living in Latin American countries with historically very high inflation who knew that doubling your salary in a month did not make it easier to buy an imported Mercedes because the exchange rate against the Deutschemark was likely to have halved.

Though the theory explains long-run exchange-rate movements excellently, it is subject (like an equity market's fundamental value) to large deviations. These can last for a number of years without any sign of correction. If returns are being modelled in real terms for a Sterling investor, as seems most appropriate, it is only these deviations that represent an additional return and risk component. It is not necessary to forecast each exchange rate and inflation rate. This might appear deceptively simplistic but it does stand to reason!

The deviations from the real exchange rate can fortunately be modelled without difficulty from past histories. Figure 2.6 shows Fifth Freedom's estimates of the historical deviations from the real exchange rate or the purchasing power parity. They are expressed in the same terms, as a ratio, which also therefore performs the function of a measure of relative currency value between two currencies. Low is good for future currency returns, high is bad.

Figure 2.6 ▓ Currency Value Ratios for Deutschemark (then Euro), Japanese Yen and US Dollar against Sterling

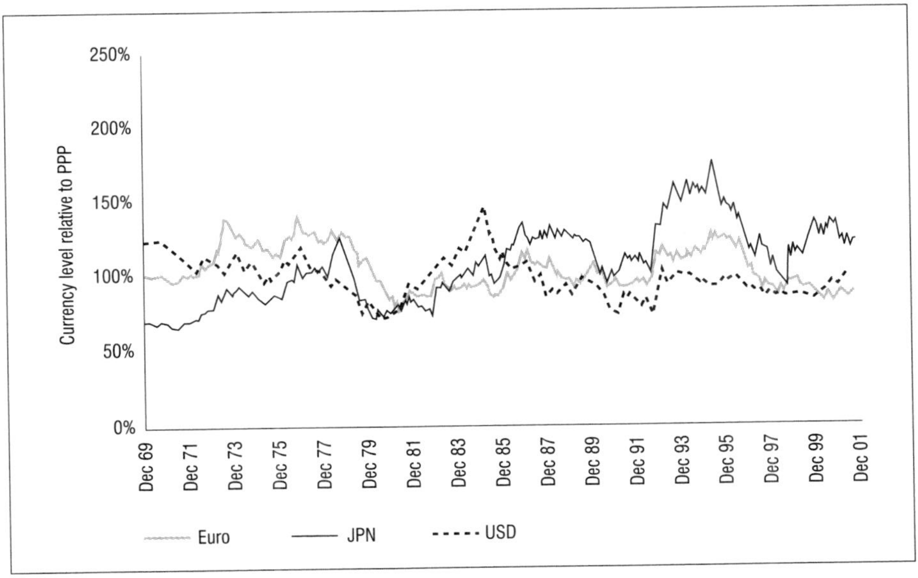

Note that there are some obvious similarities with equity valuations. Extremes have arisen in each case but not necessarily at the same time. The same extreme levels do not necessarily correct in the same way. There is a systematic dynamic that is dependable but any forecasts or estimates based on it will need to allow for uncertainty and estimation error – just like equity returns.

▓ Pulling it all together

This examination of the behaviour of equity markets and currencies would not be complete without seeing the effect of the two combined. It is shown in Figure 2.7 as Fifth Freedom's 'Combined Value Ratio'.

Figure 2.7 ▪ **Combined Value Ratios for the UK, Europe, the USA and Japan**

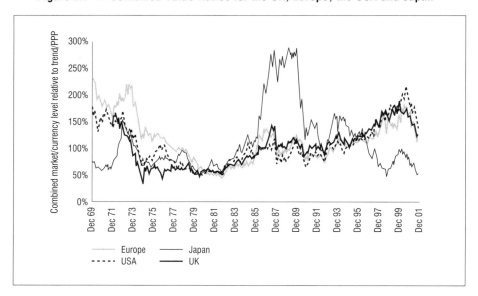

Note that unusual conditions can either coincide in each of markets and currency or they can occur separately. There appears to be no natural pattern for them to coincide. Likewise, when they do by chance coincide, they may as easily be high at the same time as low at the same time.

The essential messages of this chapter are as follows:

1 Equity markets, both UK and foreign, are poorly predictable over the short term, possibly even no better than random.

2 They offer a normal long-term real return that is higher than alternatives.

3 If starting conditions are not normal, future returns will either be higher than normal (if starting from below trend) or lower than normal (if starting from above trend).

4 Current conditions are not necessarily similar for different markets at the same time.

5 Future outcomes are uncertain but bounded.

6 The boundaries depend on the length of the time horizon.

7 Uncertain outcomes can be avoided by locking in a horizon-specific safe-harbour return but only at the expense of the equity risk premium.

To any investor used to the false certainties peddled by many investment professionals, this may sound like a pretty weak basis for planning an investment strategy. Given the true nature of the uncertainty, which can even appear chaotic, these behavioural characteristics are actually a firm foundation for investment planning. They provide the basis for modelling future real return probabilities.

Provided modelling techniques are sensible, healthily agnostic and long term in their focus, the resulting real return probabilities can in turn be used to inform the individual investor's own choice of balance of targets, resources and risk for each task they give their money. As we shall see in Chapter 13, this is exactly how institutions deal with investment planning problems.

You need only consider the practical benefits had such an approach been available to individual investors when endowment mortgages were being overpromoted in the 1970s and 1980s to realize how much can be done with very little. In the future, it is likely to be personal pension funding which turns out to be the next major source of disappointment and regret. Once again we will be able to point to the failure to apply basic investment principles and to use robust market modelling techniques. No doubt many investors caught by the boom in US stocks, and its attendant fashion for global technology, have already been ruing the absence of both principles and process that left them so vulnerable to regret.

3

The decision hierarchy

Asset allocation – or 'being there'

In the first two chapters we encountered two of three key principles that form the minimal knowledge that individual investors should have:

1 Investment should be based on defined personal investment goals.

2 It is the characteristics of market behaviour that allow goals to be planned for, resourced and managed with reasonable predictability.

The link between these two is the third and last key principle. It is that *market exposure, also known as asset allocation, explains most of the return behaviour of a diversified portfolio.* This principle applies whether what happens to the portfolio is measured in terms of the outcome at the time horizon of a personal goal or of the path of the portfolio along the way.

Other decisions, which to a private investor can appear important, are in fact relatively trivial compared with asset allocation. Their importance is often deliberately exaggerated by the industry, as the perceived value of the service they provide is likely to be diminished if the customer knows and shows the knowledge professed in Chapter 1: 'Money works for you just by being in the markets. It does not need clever investment professionals.'

The vast differences in importance of distinct types of investment decision, which may also be reflected in differences in professional functions or providers, are captured by the notion of a decision 'hierarchy'. This notion can prove very useful to understanding how results are achieved, how agents are selected for the different functions you need, how costs and benefits are best compared and how your relationships with the industry can be controlled instead of blindly dependent. This makes it a pretty handy principle.

The importance of the asset-allocation decision is empirical, that is to say, it is based on the observation of actual portfolios or simulations of test portfolios, rather than a theory. Like many aspects of investment, the facts and figures are nonetheless capable of being interpreted differently, either for a good reason or, more often, for making mischief. This chapter is all about the proof of both fact and significance.

The significance lies in the practical observation that asset allocation provides you with the levers that control, as far as is humanly possible, what happens to a portfolio. This applies whether you make all your own individual investment decisions, by providing a structure for them, or whether you prefer to hire and control professional investment agents.

If the contents of a portfolio are accumulated piecemeal over time, with no controlling structure, the resulting market exposure that determines what happens will be just an accident. This higgledy-piggledy, hit-or-miss approach is typical of most of the portfolios built up of investment products or funds that I have seen. A customer of financial planners who has been making contributions to his or her investments over many years could easily have between ten and 20 funds or 'policies' with a wide range of providers.

> IT MAKES SENSE OF YOUR INSISTENCE THAT THE PEOPLE IN THE INDUSTRY THAT YOU WORK WITH ARE ABLE TO QUANTIFY THE PROBABILITIES OF ACHIEVING YOUR GOALS

They may have been built up over the years by several different advisers or a combination of advice and DIY. The goal-based logic and the underlying asset allocation are usually lost in the confusion of portfolio contents.

In my experience, many customers of the industry in this position realize this is daft and are looking for a better way. Even if they do not yet realize the dominance of asset allocation, they know only too well that the contents of their portfolios were typically added as new resources became available and usually reflected the flavour of the month rather than a long-term strategic plan. That just does not feel right.

The dominance of the asset-allocation decision is a vital principle because it makes sense of your insistence that the people in the industry that you work with are able to quantify the probabilities of achieving your goals. This would only work if they could do so on the basis of the underlying portfolio market exposure, since they could never make so many assumptions for the millions of possible combinations of portfolio contents.

After reading this book, you are unlikely to view your options about individual securities, products or portfolio managers in the same light as before. This has huge practical significance. In the hierarchy, these are trivialized as merely implementation choices. In Part II, we will see that while their power to explain portfolio outcomes may be trivial relative to asset allocation, the harm they can do through excessive costs or by weakening your control is far from trivial.

One practical change in your approach to investing is likely to be a clearer distinction in your own mind between a portfolio intended to 'play the system', picking up the systematic features we encountered in the previous chapter, and a portfolio consisting of a small number of specific company bets. I suggest the use of the term 'entrepreneurial' for the latter will help keep the distinction clear, even if you do not quite see yourself as the new Warren Buffet or George Soros. We look at this alternative approach in the next chapter.

The hierarchy and the industry

Though most investment professionals in the institutional market now accept the evidence of the hierarchy and have built some version of it into their investment process, not all have. In the area of private client portfolio management and advice and investment planning, awareness of the hierarchy and its formal adoption in investment processes is very patchy.

Yet most financial planners and most portfolio managers, whatever school of investment they feel they belong to, do have an intuitive sense of the importance of a level of decision making loosely defined as asset allocation. This is reflected in widespread inclusion of references to asset allocation in material that you are likely to see, such as brochures, customer agreements, 'reasons why' letters, regular investment reports and newsletters. If you could go behind the scenes of a portfolio management firm you would see it in their committees and procedures.

Unfortunately, you cannot assume from any of this that they understand the same thing by asset allocation, that they have any formal process for dealing with it, that they even know the overall underlying asset allocation of a portfolio or accept the implications of the hierarchy. Confusion and obfuscation arise for several reasons:

1 The same asset allocation terminology is widely used with different intended meaning, to suit the objectives of the user.

2 Precision that would actually help the private investor is lost in the attempt to dumb down descriptions of an investment process.

3 Many professionals are themselves a little dumb about the precise use of the terminology in the financial literature.

4 The way professionals typically claim responsibility for performance results exaggerates their true contribution.

To avoid being pushed about or confused, it is helpful for you to adopt some precise definitions of the terminology that suit your agenda and make sure that the professionals you work with know exactly what you understand by each. I suggest a three-tier approach to the hierarchy, using the expressions *'policy'*, *'strategy'* and *'implementation'*.

Top level: 'policy'

The Three Ts, or any equivalent defining features of your individual personal goals, belong on the top level under the title 'policy'. Each task-based portfolio should have a clearly articulated and agreed policy.

Resist any attempt to deal with policy as a single wishy-washy framework that covers a range of different tasks or goals and all of your individual investments. This makes the false assumption that your time horizons and risk tolerance are general rather than specific and that one portfolio can be best for any goal. The effect is to allow your agents to control the agenda and select whatever portfolio structure and contents suits them best. In Part II we shall see the problems this wishy-washy approach causes when things go wrong.

Policy should also include any client-driven decisions about which asset classes or individual markets are eligible for exposure, what exposure limits should apply and which asset is the right safe harbour for each task.

In Chapter 2 we saw that portfolio management should be a continuous planning process, always focused on the goal-specific time horizon and target and always matched to the goal's risk tolerance via calculation of the latest probabilities based on prevailing market conditions. This means that the top level, policy, must always dominate and be tied into the next level, 'strategy', which deals with the way the asset class and market exposure of the portfolio might change over time.

Next level: 'strategy'

Strategy is a term that some in the industry use instead of policy, in which case the term they use for the next level may be 'tactics'. Indeed, there is a particular approach to dynamic asset allocation that is actually known as Tactical Asset Allocation or TAA. This is usually very active, makes big changes and is focused on short decision horizons rather than longer planning horizons. Because of the level of activity and transaction costs, TAA mostly uses derivatives (such as index futures) rather than actively managed portfolios or products. For all of these reasons it is less common in the retail market. Because TAA bets and payoffs are usually independent of customer goals or individual risk tolerance, it has no place in a customized investment approach that matches assets to personal goal outcomes. I prefer to think of it as another version of an entrepreneurial activity.

If you adopt the approach of matching assets to your personal goals, then, for as long as you do not alter the policy description, any transactions made to alter the portfolio's market exposure should be made only because of changing market conditions. These transactions do not need to be frequent and, as we shall see, must always take trading costs into account. Where contributions are being made to an existing portfolio, such as a pension plan, those contributions can also be used to effect a change in market exposure.

Why bother with a dynamic strategy? In Chapter 2 we saw that changing market conditions significantly affect expected returns. Deviations from a normal 6 per cent return could translate into mean expected returns as low as 3 per cent and as high as 9 per cent. To invest as if all positions will always earn the normal return entails two serious flaws and one lost opportunity:

1 The actual portfolio outcomes are unlikely to match the policy parameters or the assumptions on which the resources required for the task (initial capital or subsequent contributions) were calculated.

2 The ability to control risk, in the form of the acceptable range of outcomes, by dynamically combining risky assets and the safe-harbour asset will be lost.

3 The opportunity to lock in 'planning gains' by switching from overvalued to undervalued assets from time to time will be given up.

Based on simulations of the model referred to in the previous chapter, by way of example, planning gains could lift outcome ranges by up to 1 per cent per annum relative to a passive asset allocation strategy. It may sound small beer but over a long period 1 per cent compounds to a large difference in outcome. Even this small margin assumes relatively infrequent but large changes in the asset mix and that advantage is taken of opportunities in overseas equity markets. The more constrained the policy, the less the potential for planning gains.

The bottom level: 'implementation'

With policy and strategy dealt with, the third level naturally becomes 'implementation', in other words the selection of the portfolio contents that give the same market exposure as called for by the dynamic strategy, with as close a match as you and your agent have agreed.

Implementation is a word worth bringing regularly into your vocabulary with your chosen investment agents. It is a suitably diminishing sort of word. It acts as a constant reminder of the hierarchy as a controlling framework and of your own relative indifference to the precise contents of the portfolio, provided they are to give effect to a strategy that matches the policy.

The implementing contents are several, as follows:

- diversified combinations of securities that represent each asset class and market (as distinct from an entrepreneurial portfolio)

- products, such as country-specific equity funds (either unit trusts or investment trusts)

- a combination of securities and products (such as individual UK equities and gilts plus funds for international equity exposure)

- funds, either actively or passively managed (trackers that replicate or mimic a market index offer the tightest method of implementing a strategy because they are bound to pick up the behavioural characteristics on which the plan is based).

Your agency relationships for implementing the strategy are also several:

- advisory, such as with an IFA or stockbroker
- discretionary, such as with a stockbroker or portfolio management firm
- using industry firms to plan your policy and strategy and then making your own selection of implementing contents
- relying entirely on DIY, on- or offline.

After reading Part II, you will have a much better idea about preferences for implementation options, both contents and agents. You are likely to be influenced by three factors you will learn about:

1 agency conflicts of interest
2 the level and impact of typical industry costs
3 the long odds, between 4–1 and 10–1, against making up the additional cost of actively managed portfolios compared with using trackers.

▨ The evidence of a hierarchy: the '90 per cent rule'

What is often referred to for convenience as 'the 90 per cent rule' refers to the proportion of the overall return path of a diversified portfolio that is 'explained' by the underlying asset allocation. It is worth being absolutely clear what this means but that does call for some more maths. You can skip to the end of the section if you feel you can live without the explanation.

The calculation to which this refers requires the contents of a portfolio to be classified by the underlying exposure to different asset classes and markets. For instance, there may be 25 individual UK stocks held as part of a portfolio that in total account for 30 per cent of the entire portfolio value. Alternatively, there may be several UK funds and some managed or balanced funds within which UK equity exposure collectively accounts for the same 30 per cent of the total portfolio value. The overall asset mix might then be: 30 per cent in UK equities, 20 per cent in UK gilts, 10 per cent in US equities and so on.

This classification allows the return actually earned (by adding up the performance of all the actual contents) to be compared with the notional underlying asset allocation return. This is the return calculated by attributing to the proportion of the portfolio exposed to a separate market the appropriate market return (as if invested without costs in a representative index) and then summing all those return contributions. In the example above, the notional asset allocation return is the FTSE All Share Index return weighted by 30 per cent, plus an appropriate gilt index return weighted by 20 per cent, and so on.

Each set of returns in individual periods (such as monthly or quarterly) can then be strung together to create a long series of changes such as +0.6 per cent, −1.6 per cent, −0,4 per cent, +0.7 per cent and so on. The actual portfolio return series can then be mathematically 'regressed' on the notional asset allocation return series to calculate the proportion of explained variance, also known as R squared. (The regression technique is the same one we encountered in Chapter 2 where it was preferred to 'point-to-point' or start-to-end growth rates as a means of estimating a true underlying trend that best fits all of the data points instead of just the first and last.)

A 90 per cent proportion means that the two fit very closely. The pattern of changes in the actual portfolio value each month (or quarter) is very close to the path of monthly changes that would have arisen from holding exactly the same market exposure but earning the market return.

This approach to explaining where returns come from is identical to one widely used to explain the risk of an equity portfolio invested in a single market, where the actual security returns are regressed on the host market return. An R squared of 90 per cent to 95 per cent is fairly typical for an actively managed fund in the UK equity market measured against the FTSE All Share Index. The lower the R squared, the less like the index the fund can be expected to behave. The less like the index, the higher the relative return variance: that is to say, the higher the standard deviation of the return of the portfolio when divided by the return of the index. R squared is therefore a measure of relative, not absolute risk, which is appropriate when assessing the suitability of a fund to match an asset allocation strategy.

The 90 per cent figure, or thereabouts, that is most often quoted refers to two particular research studies. However, precision about the proportion is really spurious because it depends on the sample of portfolios: how diversified they are and how similar are the members of the sample to each other. No two studies should be expected to confirm an exact number.

The original analysis was carried out by Gary Brinson (of Chicago-based money managers Brinson Partners that was later bought by Swiss bankers UBS), Randolph Hood and Gilbert Beebower, who worked for pension consultants (and performance measurers) SEI and who therefore had access to the real portfolio return data the analysis required. Their study, titled 'Determinants of Portfolio Performance', was published in the USA in the *Financial Analysts Journal* in 1986. Remarkably, prior to that time there had been no published analyses of where performance came from!

Brinson *et al* analyzed the returns of 91 large US pension funds between 1974 and 1983. Using a standard regression approach they found that on average 93.6 per cent of the total variance in actual performance was explained by what they defined as the asset allocation decision. A further paper followed in 1991[ii] covering 82 large pension plans over the 1977–87 period. It found that, on average, asset allocation explained 91.5 per cent of the variation in quarterly returns.

How they defined asset allocation and how their findings are interpreted by the industry (and are typically quoted) are not necessarily the same. Briefly, the authors inferred from the changing actual mix a normal mix that they referred to as the 'policy mix' and then regressed the actual returns on the returns of this notional policy mix. Because returns in the period for the different markets were not widely distributed and because US pension managers kept to a similar mix, both over time and between them (to reduce their own business risk), the regression may misrepresent the typical strength of the hierarchy.

What the authors could have done is simply regress the actual returns in each period on the notional return in the same period had they held the same mix but earned the index return. This, though, would have failed to distinguish (usefully) between the normal exposure ('being there') and the managers' actual choice.

Had they done so, however, I do not believe the result would have been very different. A 90 per cent fit emerged from analysis of the returns of simulated portfolios carried out in 1993 by the company I was then associated with, Valu-Trac Investment Management. Using data for the average allocations for an actual sample of UK pension funds (The WM Company UK pension fund universe), we simulated dynamic ranges of allocations around that average, based on historical limits for the relative bets. The idea of simulations was to reflect the managers' typical behaviour, based on history, but to avoid the conclusions being too specific to the actual return differences in that particular period of history.

These conclusions do not depend on mixing different asset classes, such as equities and gilts. They also apply to portfolios diversified between different equity markets. In the early 1990s Valu-Trac pioneered in the USA and Canada a new approach to managing international equity portfolios, based on the hierarchy, which became known as Active/Passive management. It is now an accepted investment approach adopted by many US institutional investors and by a few in the UK, as well as by a few UK private client managers and advisers. To support its approach, Valu-Trac also analyzed the importance of the country decision in a globally diversified equity portfolio, again using simulations rather than actual portfolios.

Some of the initial conclusions, along with further research, were later published in an article I wrote for the *Professional Investor* journal in February 1997, titled 'Asset Allocation: Too Important to be Left to Money Managers', from which the following is extracted.

Regressions based on multiple randomly selected portfolios of 50 stocks in any of 18 MSCI World Index constituent markets over a 12-year period from 1980 show that 85 per cent of the US dollar returns and 86 per cent of the local currency returns are explained by the country decision and the high proportion of explained variance holds in most years.

OK, it was not quite 90 per cent – but that illustrates the point about approximating the scale of relative importance.

Why definitions matter

Beware that anything as precise in its calculation as is the 90 per cent rule will tend to be misrepresented by the industry. On our website we pick up a trail of exchanges, sometimes quite heated, between both academics and practitioners about the various claims that are based on the research. It includes a report by John Nuttall on his own website devoted to this subject. He refers to 'literally thousands of claims' made for one or other investment service or approach that seek to attach to themselves the credibility of the Brinson articles.

These claims appear in printed promotional material, magazine and newspaper articles, books, and increasingly on the Internet. In a report written with my daughter in 1998 are listed over 50 examples of such claims. The astonishing fact is that all but one of these claims misquoted the results stated in the

Brinson articles. That one correct quotation has now disappeared from its site, and has been replaced by an incorrect version. The claims often differ in only a few words from the Brinson articles, but these differences completely change the meaning of the statements.

The typical mistakes have been to assume that the proportion of explained variance is interchangeable with the difference between the paths of returns of any two portfolios and the difference between the outcome of two portfolios at the end of some long period. They are not the same.

Two authors associated with the American investment research firm Ibbotson Associates, who had been criticized by Nuttall for this same error, picked up on this distinction and later published a paper called 'Does Asset Allocation Explain 40 per cent, 90 per cent or 100 per cent of Performance?' in the *Financial Analysts Journal* of January / February 2000. An abstract, which is available on their website,[iii] is shown in full below:

Disagreement about the importance of asset allocation policy stems from differences in what is considered important. Using data on balanced mutual funds and pension funds, we explore the ability of asset allocation policy to explain variability of returns across time, variation in return across funds, and the average level of return. We find that about 90 per cent of the variability of returns of a typical fund across time is explained by policy; about 40 per cent of the variation of returns across funds is explained by policy; and that on average, about 100 per cent of the return level is explained by policy return.

Like the Brinson authors, they regress actual results on a 'normal' policy mix, so the results are biased by this assumption of a common benchmark both between funds and over time.

For the investment approach recommended in this book, outcomes are every bit as important as the observations of the hierarchy based on what happens to portfolios along the way. Some customers may feel outcomes are all that counts. The conclusion in Ibbotson's research that on average all of the return level, hence all of the long-term outcome, is explained by asset allocation follows naturally from the assumption that for any representative sample of managers the average *relative* return from stock selection must be about zero.

In Part II we will see how sensible this assumption is, because of the random nature of active management results. The contribution of stock selection to portfolio outcomes diminishes over time for the same reason that tossing a coin many times produces results bunched closely around 50:50. Any one manager's results over a long period may still be explained partially by stock selection but the asset allocation R squared is unlikely to be much less than 100 per cent.

Stealing the credit

In its most widespread and pernicious form, abuse of the hierarchy evidence consists of managers taking for themselves the credit for the asset allocation return contribution that rightly belongs to the client, because of the client's own policy choices and willingness to 'be there'. If 90 per cent or more of the return, however defined, is explained by the asset mix, most of that in turn reflects the express willingness of the client systematically to bear market risk as part of the process of harvesting risk premia.

As the Ibbotson report points out with reference to the typical high values for R squared, they are 'high simply because funds participate in the capital markets in general and not because they follow a specific asset allocation policy'.

In the research we have encountered here, the policy mix is inferred from the history of actual past allocations, perhaps as an average. This is only an approximation after the event of what should properly have been articulated before the event as an agreed policy benchmark. In spite of its shortcomings, it still helps underline how little of the asset allocation performance credit actually belongs to the typical fund manager. Needless to say, this does not deter managers from staking their claim to the 90 per cent proportion.

On our website are extracts from and links to further analysis that separates the contribution of the policy mix and the 'added value' of managers' strategy changes, or 'bets off the policy mix'. It includes a report by US pension consultants the Russell Company[iv] which puts fund managers' contribution at about one-tenth of the customer's contribution!

Where critics of the hierarchy are right is in arguing that, within the one-tenth that managers typically contribute, the small bets off the client's own policy exposure could easily be no greater than the performance contribution of their security selection. Stock pickers are right to complain that other firms who want to play up their strategic skills pinch all of the policy return and attribute it to strategy, whereas if they wanted to play up their stock picking skills by adding the policy return to their stock selection return, it would never wash. It is a reasonable grouse but the fact is neither should be claiming it.

Under the hierarchy, the fact that the policy contribution is seen to belong to the customer, as a systematic reward for taking exposure risk, prevents active managers from overstating their own importance. It is hardly surprising that this is a form of customer intelligence that they do not welcome.

If you really want to share the credit, share it with those in the industry who can help you plan the resources, targets and risk tolerance that will become the defining features of your top-level policy, goal by goal.

4

The entrepreneurial alternative

System player or entrepreneur?

'Playing the system' is a simple concept even if it as an unfamiliar one and with the help of the decision hierarchy it is easy for any equity investor to implement. Yet not all exposure to an equity market will necessarily provide the system risks and payoffs. An equity portfolio that is not diversified may not behave like a system.

In terms of money invested, most UK equity holdings are well diversified, but in terms of numbers of investors, a significant proportion is not. In America, for instance, where individual equity ownership is more common, non-diversified portfolios are estimated to outnumber diversified ones. Owners of non-diversified equity holdings almost certainly do not realise that they have a set of risks and payoffs that are 'outlaws', that is, not subject to the few laws that systems appear to observe and on which sound planning and customer control can be based.

In the previous chapter, I suggested that the use of the term 'entrepreneurial' is a handy way to keep a distinction clear in your own mind between playing the system and a non-diversified equity portfolio. This is a useful description even if you do not see yourself as a business investor.

There are other types of investment that are similarly poorly predictable and therefore 'unmanageable'. These also belong in the category of entrepreneurial investing. The distinction between playing the system and venture capital and hedge funds, for instance, is not one that will be obvious to most investors from the way they are marketed, though they may at least have an intuitive sense of the greater uncertainty of outcome.

They will probably not appreciate that they are literally 'on their own', totally dependent on a small number of bets made by professionals that they cannot control, instead of dependent on the systematic effects of being part of a vast national class of equity market owners. Risk premia are earned by crowds, exacted by their collective power and weight of numbers in a capital market system that has to balance. There is no guarantee of a risk premium to the lonely entrepreneur.

The distinction between system risks and payoffs and entrepreneurial performance is worth understanding so that what eventually results from the latter is unlikely to be a cause of regret. Non-diversified equity portfolios, hedge funds and venture capital may still have a role to play in the context of a goal-based approach to planning and organizing personal investment, but it is more likely to be for the house in Tuscany than retirement income or school fees. They may also have a role outside any goal-based approach, as a free-standing activity separate from all other portfolio investment that is planned.

The equity entrepreneur

The term 'entrepreneurial' suits the owner of a non-diversified equity portfolio because entrepreneurs, when they invest in companies, embrace the risk and return characteristics of individual investments rather than seek to diversify them away in favour of the system characteristics. This is true even if they seek some degree of risk spreading across different firms or even different industries.

They are not denying the existence of the decision hierarchy, merely saying that they deliberately want to turn it up the other way. They believe the individual contents of their portfolio have intrinsic merit and they want that to dominate their risks and payoffs. In the language of the previous chapter, their return path and their outcome will be explained to a greater extent by factors other than the host market behaviour, even though they may not be able to escape some influence from the market as a whole.

Though you may not see yourself as an entrepreneurial investor, your risks and payoffs may effectively be the same as if you were. How do you come to fall into this category as an equity investor? There are a few classical 'types' that are easy to recognize.

If you own a collection of say six or even ten stocks that have been privatized or demutualized, you will not be well diversified and will not pick up all of the systematic behaviour of markets. This is likely even if the individual stocks are large companies, each with a significant weight in the FTSE All Share Index and FTSE 100 Index. Many people became this type of entrepreneurial investor without realizing it, although with time and the purchase of more stocks their risks may well have declined sharply from how they started out on this unmapped journey.

If you particularly like or know about one type of industry, such as media or IT, and focus your portfolio on that, your portfolio will not behave like a system. If the industry you focus on also happens to be the same one that pays you a living, for instance, as an IT consultant, your overall risk exposure may be even greater than for an entrepreneur doing the same thing!

If you use the newspapers, website news pages and chat rooms or talk to your stockbroker to trawl for particular firms to invest in, your portfolio may not behave like the market even if you spread the money across several sectors or industries.

If your equity portfolio is dominated by a single share, perhaps through inheritance or your employment, it is unlikely to behave like the market even if the rest of your positions are well diversified. If the structure of your portfolio is dictated by large capital gains liabilities that cause similar concentration, it may not behave like the system even though market indices may themselves be quite concentrated in a small number of giant corporations.

In all of these cases, the link between planning and controlling how you meet your financial goals is broken because the assumptions about behaviour, and hence about probabilities, may no longer be matched by your implementation choices. The contents cannot be relied upon to do the job, at the strategy and policy levels, that you want them to do. The leakage, or mismatch, is far greater for an entrepreneurial portfolio than it is for a well- diversified yet actively managed equity portfolio, such as a general equity unit trust or investment trust.

If we try to quantify the expected outcomes of an entrepreneurial portfolio, we are highly likely to make very large estimation errors in the upside potential and downside risk. This is because we are inclined to attribute to individual securities the same kind of behaviour that we recognize in the market as a system. That means we are too confident about the risk of a single stock losing a large amount of money. If and when it does, we are likely to overestimate the likelihood that it will then bounce back.

This reflects a behavioural bias that is not present in the system: we run our losses and cut our profits. This typical individual tendency, which we will return to in Part III when we look at the psychology of individual investing, is the opposite of the dynamics of the market as a whole. This is odd. If the market is the sum of all individual actions, how can it demonstrate different behaviour collectively from that of most investors individually? Part of the answer is the fact that the market as represented by an index is an artificial construct.

Though we think of market indices as 'passive', like the name more often used by institutional investors for index tracking, the fact is that index constituents are altered by the index 'owners' from time to time. I like to think of this as 'refreshing' them, because it reflects a Darwinian process of the survival of the fittest that accurately captures the dynamism of the company sector of an economy. This is the process that, at the margin, forces losers out and keeps winners in. Everything else, not at the margin, can be viewed as neutral or mediocre in terms of Darwinian dynamics.

Entrepreneurial investors, in common with many professional equity managers, do not normally embrace this kind of discipline. They may either trade actively instead of refreshing occasionally or else they fail to refresh at all. They tend to place a higher value on a future price rise for a stock that has done badly than they do for a stock that has done well, hoping for the same kind of mean reversion for their own holdings as the market as a whole displays. Hence they run their losses (or poor performers) and cut their profits (or better performers).

Unfortunately, individual company returns do not enjoy mean reversion. Though a part of the same board game they can actually lose and drop out of the game completely. Their risks are not bounded and nobody owes them a risk premium. Their management and their shareholders are also 'on their own'.

Using business knowledge

The private client portfolio most closely matches the entrepreneur when business knowledge is being applied to equity selection. This is not necessarily the same thing as the knowledge sought by the professional portfolio manager, as it is likely to be much more narrowly focused on a small number of firms and sectors, or even a single sector.

Putting business knowledge to work in the stock market has always been better on paper than in real life, and disappointment is common-

PUTTING BUSINESS KNOWLEDGE TO WORK IN THE STOCK MARKET HAS ALWAYS BEEN BETTER ON PAPER THAN IN REAL LIFE

place. The simplest manifestation of it is that the knowledge turns out to be wrong. It does happen! A more subtle form is that though the knowledge is right the stock fails to do what you expected. This can be frustrating and perplexing but in fact it also happens in the market as a system. The market at any one point reflects the expectations of all participants. So if reality merely confirms the expectations, nothing new has occurred and at the margin there is no new buying and selling because of it. In stock market speak, if the 'world and his wife' have already 'bought the story', there is nobody left to buy it even when it turns out to be true.

Should you want your investment results to be specific to a particular area because of a knowledge advantage, it is surprisingly difficult to achieve. If you invest, for instance, in technology stocks where your experience of, say, broadband communications gives you a possible edge, your stocks will be moved by much else other than the changing expectations for and realities of broadband. There will be an association with other telecoms stocks and technology stocks in general, however different their trading prospects or long-term industry dynamics. There will also be some association with the market as a whole.

■ Diversification or dilution?

Those individual investors who deliberately hold focused equity portfolios rather than drift into it by accident may well believe they have some specific knowledge that gives them an edge or that they can accumulate enough information about their securities to watch them closely and keep out of trouble. Both are effectively following the economist Lord Keynes's advice about diversification, which was *to not put too many eggs in one basket and to watch the basket*.

Keynes is rather passé as a role model for private investors but his spectacular success between the wars in charge, as Bursar, of the endowment fund of Kings College, Cambridge, makes him one of the legendary figures in the story of investment. Nowadays, we are more likely to follow US individual investors as they try to follow in the tracks of a living icon: Warren Buffet, the so-called Sage of Omaha. Through his holding company Berkshire Hathaway he is one of the world's largest private investors. Books have been dedicated to his investment approach and 'Buffetology' has entered into the ordinary American investor's lexicon.

Buffetology is very much about a small number of eggs in the basket. The trick is to limit the contents to those whose business any non-professional can understand and which have natural advantages, such as an unimpeachable consumer franchise, that we can easily identify. He holds, for instance, more Coca-Cola stock than all the American mutual funds put together. Such a concentrated portfolio of excellent companies needs little or no activity, Buffet maintains. Indeed, his maxim is 'only buy the stock if you would like to buy the whole company'.

For Buffet, avoiding diversification has paid off handsomely, hence his legendary status. Yet he really is a business investor. He holds his investments within a tax-favoured insurance business, he deals directly with investment bankers and he can negotiate terms for acquiring large stakes in businesses that the rest of us cannot emulate, including special classes of preferred securities and options with different risk and rewards to shares bought in the market. Whatever his advantages as an entrepreneurial investor, underlying his track record must lie some genuine skill. If so, it is one that with characteristic modesty he has deliberately played down. Yet it is really a rather dangerous assumed modesty that suggests any of the rest of us can mimic his homespun selection criteria and simple management disciplines and achieve the same success.

It is in Part II that we will investigate the triumph of hope over experience that leads investors (individual or professional) to exaggerate perceived advantages, whether homespun or sophisticated, as selectors of individual securities. We will show that stock selection results or, in other words, performance relative to the market is essentially random and that there is no proof that individual advantages exist, notwithstanding a few legends like Buffet and Keynes.

The perennial excuse that professional managers playing this lottery have been able to make is that they are forced by the need for diversification to swamp their good ideas with so much dross. If you think about it, though, this excuse simply does not wash. They have always had the option of splitting their hand and playing each one differently.

They could hold enough of their portfolio 'in the index' to obtain the diversification required by their marketing or regulatory mandate and then focus all of their so-called skill on their best ideas, at the margin. Only their best ideas, an entrepreneurial sub-portfolio, would then contribute all of their relative performance against the index. It may be a different product from a concentrated equity portfolio but at least it would demonstrate, and offer exposure to, any selection skill they had.

In spite of the evidence that the 'skill' is actually a misnomer, the institutionalization of entrepreneurial portfolios is now coming in the shape of products that have come to be known as 'aggressive' funds. These invest in 20 to 50 securities instead of the 100 or more that most general, single country, equity unit trusts and investment trusts hold. They are the 20 to 50 best ideas of the manager (who in all cases already manages diversified products). But do not buy one without first reading Chapter 10, The Performance Lie!

Diversification and the system

How does diversification work in an equity portfolio and why does it make such as difference? When you play the system, the risks that have been diversified are those *specific* to a single company rather than those that attach to all equities, leaving you only the non-diversifiable *systematic* risk. If you removed all of the systematic market risk, you could no longer expect to harvest the system risk premium.[8]

A PORTFOLIO OF 30 STOCKS WILL STILL BEHAVE DIFFERENTLY FROM A DIVERSIFIED UNIT TRUST OR INVESTMENT TRUST

Diversification is a matter of degree. An entrepreneurial portfolio will behave very differently if it is spread between six stocks instead of focused on one only, just as you would expect a business investor's risk to be lower if capital is spread between six firms. However, a portfolio of 30 stocks, more typical of the accidental entrepreneurial investor, will still behave differently from a diversified unit trust or investment trust.

It is mainly a numbers game and it is one to which the law of diminishing returns applies. Risk, measured by the fluctuations in the path of

---

[8] If you are put off by the terminology and feel a daunting realization that you may not recognize a specific risk even if you tried, the entrepreneurial approach to equity investing may not, after all, be for you!

returns along the way, approximately halves by holding two stocks instead of one and further significant reductions in risk (outcome or along the way) can be achieved by adding 15 to 20 stocks. The academic literature[9] suggests that between 25 and 50 stocks are enough to get close to the index characteristics but to be sure of replicating the systematic features it requires a quantum leap in the number of holdings. That is why most diversified institutional portfolios hold well over 100 shares.

Quantifying diversification effects is a dangerous enough game for statisticians, let alone the rest of us. The literature may suggest that the standard deviation of a 30–50 stock portfolio is no more than 25 per cent higher than the market, but it does not necessarily point out that this is very sample-specific and that the standard deviation is itself difficult to estimate. Neither do most entrepreneurial portfolios with a relatively large number of holdings look like the samples in the literature. For a start, they do not usually have the equal weightings that statisticians normally but arbitrarily assume (a beneficial but naïve influence on the risk of a portfolio that we will encounter in Part II).

If, as an entrepreneurial investor, you are concerned about the impact of an extreme event, such as the bankruptcy of one or more of the companies you own, or a major collapse of an entire sector, your risk may not be well captured by the statistics quoted. To reduce this risk to the level of an index tracking portfolio or of a typical actively managed unit trust requires both many more holdings and specific features for the construction of the portfolio. There is no simple halfway house between the typical packaged product and the typical entrepreneurial portfolio.

This is highly relevant for owners of UK equity portfolios managed by stockbrokers. These often contain fewer than 30 stocks, are rarely constructed with a view to minimizing the leakage from the systematic characteristics and are usually distorted by capital gains liabilities. Where the relationship is advisory they typically reflect a haphazard cocktail of the broker's own attempts at integrity of portfolio construction, the unstructured biases of the client's responses to suggestions, a few individual stocks chosen by the client and a few privatization stocks and demutualization entitlements. The chances of such a portfolio behaving like the system are pretty small and, indeed, a matter of luck.

Mainly a numbers game, diversification is also a more subtle function of exposure to sectors and common influences (also known as 'factors'),

---

[9] This is summarized on the website – see Diversification.

such as interest rates, exchange rates or energy prices. The system also reflects a particular combination of sectors and influences but they are not the same for any one entrepreneurial portfolio. This leads naturally to a practical problem for the entrepreneurial private investor. Their specific risks are well nigh impossible to measure unless they have access to vast amounts of statistical information. Even most private client advisers and managers, including stockbrokers, are poorly equipped with quantitative portfolio construction technology.

The basis of the measurement of specific risk is our old friend from earlier chapters, regression analysis. This allows you, after the event, to measure the association between, or explanatory power of, one data series and another. In this case, you need the data for the market and for all the individual securities you might own. Ideally, you also need data for associations with all the separate influences on returns that differentiate the risk profile of a security and its host market. The cost of the database and processing techniques needed to monitor risk exposure would be irrational at the typical size of most such portfolios. Even then, these associations are shifting over the time so assumptions made before the event may not hold after the event. Even with all the numbers, you may be no more in control than if you were flying blind.

The fact is that, if you want to be an entrepreneurial investor, you should embrace specific risk. If you want to get rid of it, you are no entrepreneur and you should buy a diversified product. You should make a conscious choice, even if it is, quite logically, a different choice for different tasks.

Other entrepreneurial investments

Non-diversified equity portfolios are not the only assets that may not behave like a system. No such convenient natural powers attach to two other types of risky asset – hedge funds and venture capital investing. These also belong in the entrepreneurial category and carry specific risks and payoffs that are far harder to estimate.

In Chapter 2 we saw that the essence of systematic market behaviour is that we can quantify future outcomes with some confidence. When we play the system we attempt nothing cleverer than to ally ourselves with the great majority of investors, the dull, faceless but powerful majority. We rely on the weight and safety of numbers to ensure that there will be a reward for risk taking, that extreme market conditions will correct themselves, that history will repeat itself in a general if not precise way. When we detach ourselves from the safety of numbers, no one owes us, as an individual, a risk premium, let alone one that compensates adequately for the risks taken. Outside the crowd, these are lonely investments, dependent on our own skill or good fortune in selecting where we place our money, if we are to do it ourselves, or where we place our trust, if we are to hire professionals as advisers or managers.

The precise features of assets with systematic return behaviour were identified as:

1 a trend real rate of return that can be readily estimated with enough data

2 stable long-run deviations from trend

3 reasonable certainty about the current position.

These features do not apply to hedge funds, for instance. Because hedge funds typically represent a string of independent bets, there is no underlying current or market power to which they have hitched their wagon. Success depends not on being there and on time but on enough of the string of bets being winners. In Part II we will be looking at evidence for a range of different types of hedge fund strategies, or bets, that winning streaks have only a random chance of occurring.

Equity hedge funds that actually 'hedge' the market risk, or systematic risk, by selling securities they do not own (known as 'shorting') or by selling the index through a futures contract, are effectively detaching the system harness and leaving only the relative return bets. These so-called 'market neutral' funds may do better over time than cash but there is no reason to assume, for planning purposes, that a string of relative return bets will earn as much as cash, let alone the equity market return, even when market returns are below the 'normal' level of 6 per cent.

Hedge funds are often promoted on the basis of the risks and payoffs measured in absolute and nominal terms. With no benefit of systematic mean reversion, it is sensible to assume that returns are independent from one period to the next and benefit less from longer holding periods. With no underlying equilibrium theory at work on real, inflation-adjusted returns earned, there is no reason to assume that hedge funds match a purchasing power target. With no system behind them, there is no reason to assume that risk can be estimated properly and will be consistent over time, even when the fund has a track record.

To the extent that some equilibrium theory might be applicable to a hedge fund strategy, it is more likely to be the victim than the beneficiary. The typical strategy involves exploiting anomalies but with substantial and hyperactive hedge fund capital roaming around these should be quickly arbitraged out of existence. Here is an industry whose very commercial success is likely to defeat its own plans for investment success.

Venture capital investment by individuals is usually packaged and most often in tax-favoured investments such as venture capital trusts (VCTs). These serve to spread the specific risk between a number of ventures and thereby lower the impact of failures and reduce the risk. Since the funds are effectively tied up for some time, we are at least encouraged to see risk in terms of longer-term outcomes rather than short term ones.

The range of probable outcomes is very difficult if not impossible to estimate, lying anywhere between losing most of the investment and winning several times the investment. Uncertainty arises less from the lack of historical data, which might anyway be misleading, as the dispersion of results for the entire population of potential investments. Within any single portfolio, the outcome is highly dependent on the balance of total losses and big wins (unlike diversified equity portfolios) as a few successes have to carry a much larger number of disappointments.

Investment theory would have a risk premium attach itself to the overall long-period return for the sector. The evidence that it can normally be achieved over long periods is in fact far from convincing, even if allowance is made for tax subsidies (some of which are anyway only deferrals). Even if across the venture capital sector as a whole, in all its vehicles and forms, the mean return provides a risk premium, the tiny sample of the potential population of venture opportunities that any one portfolio represents means there is no assurance that your portfolio will receive it. These characteristics place venture capital firmly in the category of entrepreneurial investing, if not on some further boundary with speculation.

Playing the system via a hierarchical asset allocation strategy using major markets and diversified portfolios within each is likely to be the most suitable approach for most individual investment tasks where the target and time horizon can be readily quantified and the consequences of different outcomes can be easily conceived. Pensions and school fees are good examples.

There may still be a role for entrepreneurial portfolios for other investment goals where the time horizon and purpose are more fuzzy than fixed, the consequences of adverse outcomes are not so grave as to cause regret and the rewards of a favourable outcome, even if remote, are appealing – hence the house in Tuscany.

5

Making sense of risk

A better way

In the first four chapters we have seen that there are only a few essential principles you need to grasp in order to be a successful private investor, delegating to the industry if you want to but without losing control:

- Control and clarity come from relating investment to individual goals, defined and quantified in terms of the Three Ts.

- The only firm foundation for any investment programme is to have a rational, internally consistent balance between your targets, the money available and your risk tolerance – there are no free lunches.

- All an investment strategy has to do is match your Three Ts – preferably dynamically and certainly always focused on your planning time horizons.

- Matching is at the level of asset allocation and requires nothing more complex than exposure to market systems, their risks and pay-offs.

- This is guaranteed by index-tracking funds but active funds or stock portfolios can be chosen, less rationally, for their suitability to implement the asset-allocation strategy.

- 'Entrepreneurial investing', though not to be dismissed, does not offer the same scope for planning your resources, controlling managers, matching assets to your goals or managing the risks.

Drawing these core principles together, the overwhelming advantage they assure is a better way of dealing with risk. Why is this so important? Because the industry has failed to come up with a way of measuring, communicating and agreeing the risks that clients sign up to that is meaningful and relevant to them. This is not just a matter of inconvenience. Most of the problems the customer has had with the industry involve this failure. There is no point in investors trying to understand investment better and take more responsibility for their investment planning unless it is to control the risks and pay-offs they agree to expose their money to.

From my own experience of working with customers, the most important thing the industry can do for them is help them to understand the risk issues and to involve themselves directly in their own decisions about risk.

It has to be done at the point of every sale of products, whenever advice is sought from independent practitioners and when funds are handed over to professionals to manage as a personal portfolio. It has to use every available media of dialogue with customers. It has to be so integrated into a firm's processes and technology that it is not at all dependent on the intelligence or honesty of each individual practitioner, whether salesman, adviser or manager.

Quoting the odds

Can it be done? Half the battle is having customers better educated as to basic principles. That's not so difficult! The other half is reduction to the most essential information: the probabilities of achieving your goals. Feedback to the customer about the odds can dramatically alter the way advice is given, suitability assessed and responsibility taken for risk choices. It so changes the culture and language of investment relationships as to eliminate most of the 'agency problems' we will encounter in Part II.

The most powerful and revolutionary use of feedback is at the stage when you are defining and prioritizing your goals. It transforms a major part of the boring process of the 'fact find', the gathering of customer information, into a dynamic conversation that is totally relevant and individual. This stage is no longer an administrative formality but is instead all about setting your Three Ts and ensuring, with the aid of the feedback about probabilities, that the defining features of your goal do actually balance, make sense to you, are realistic and give a feeling of 'ownership'.

The variables that are common to any particular application of this general approach consist of one set within your own control and another set dependent on the financial markets, with risk tolerance as the balancing device:

- *You define* the money available, as a capital sum today, the contributions you are prepared to make in the future, the target outcomes you choose at the time horizon you set.

- *Financial markets define* the systematic return ranges, in terms of normal or average behaviour but better still in terms of market conditions today (which will affect the return applicable to capital currently available and to a lesser extent to the contributions you make in the future).

- *Altering the risk tolerance* will change the asset allocation that achieves the required balance or match between the variables you control and what the markets can do for you.

Underneath the bonnet the industry has some proven engineering, based on a theory called 'utility', for capturing risk tolerance. In essence, it measures how you value incremental upside relative to downside potential, on the realistic basis that this trade-off is conditional (such as on how sure you want to be about the worst outcome or how close you are to your target outcome, both of which vary with time and wealth levels).[10]

Because risk tolerance under utility theory is conceptual, when translated into a set of numbers or settings these mean no more to the customer than abstracts like 'low', 'medium' or 'high'. That is why they belong under the bonnet. However, by altering the setting the resulting answers, as fed back to the customer, are explicit and relevant and so make it easy for the customer to make a choice.

We have already referred to a typical situation, endowment mortgages, where investors are likely to place a greater importance on a shortfall of, say, £15,000 from the capital sum required at maturity to pay

---

[10] Risk tolerance in the context of utility theory is explored in more detail on the website.

off the mortgage than they would attach to a 'nice little nest egg' in the shape of a surplus of £15,000. The difference in importance emerges from thinking about the *consequences*. Though this 'utility' may be typical in such a case, a different investor who can meet a shortfall from other means may attach more importance to a higher outcome. This investor may not need the reassurance that at the quoted rate of premium they have a very high probability (98 per cent is probably as near certain as you can be) of avoiding a shortfall. He or she may be happy to accept no better than a 70 per cent probability so as to leave open the possibility of a surplus.

With an endowment mortgage, the person selling (or recommending) the policy has a vested interest in keeping the premium, which is equivalent to the resources available, as low as possible so as to ensure it looks tempting relative to a straight repayment. The last thing they want you to know is that the odds are only 50:50. Pension planning, however, should be less prone to bias. Here, probability feedback can make a big difference to how you decide what resources you need to commit in order to achieve your target retirement income. Feedback can also help you to make trade-offs between the level of contributions and the risk setting.

> WITH AN ENDOWMENT MORTGAGE, THE PERSON SELLING (OR RECOMMENDING) THE POLICY HAS A VESTED INTEREST IN KEEPING THE PREMIUM AS LOW AS POSSIBLE

For instance, let us assume you feel your planned pension contributions are really at the maximum you will be able to afford and that you instinctively want to try a low-risk setting. If the likely result is that you have no better than a 50 per cent chance of achieving your target, you will be prompted either to take more risk or lower your target. If you increase your risk, you also have to accept that the amount by which you could fall short of your target is also then increased, which you may see as not very different from accepting a lower target. If you do not want to budge on the target or take more risk, the only choice is to throw more money at the task.

Most of us find it easier to make this kind of decision if we define two targets: our desired target and our floor target. By implication, the floor target is always one we want to be near certain of achieving. For the endowment mortgage it is probably the nominal amount of the loan. For a pension task it is an after-tax monthly income, in real terms, pitched at a level that we think we could 'get by on'. It is very easy to see how changing the contributions and risk tolerance affects the chances of hitting our floor target. Clearly, taking more risk without dedicating more resources could jeopardize the target but taking less risk will also reduce the likely pension at every level of certainty below 98 per cent. That might be a sufficient incentive to increase the planned contributions.

Feedback about goal-specific probabilities can also be used to balance resources and risks across several tasks. There is no point, for instance, having a Rolls-Royce of a pension plan if it means you may run out of funds for school fees before your kids have completed their education.

Quoting odds can also be used to inform your choices where there is no specific target or time horizon. For instance, you might prefer to keep large cash balances in the bank even if the chances are most of them will not be needed for any eventuality. You just feel more comfortable. Imagine that you knew the odds of absolute loss and incremental return over different time frames as a result of committing some of that cash to risky assets. You might then feel tempted to risk some of the capital, perhaps with such tight risk tolerance as to make you only a fair-weather investor, on the basis that the scale of the possible loss does not damage the comfort role of the liquidity cushion.

If you are considering investing part of a cash 'float', a rolling five-year time horizon might be appropriate to control the risks. However, you may have pockets of 'longer-term' money with no particular time horizon or purpose, perhaps as part of your inheritable estate, where you are also intuitively scared of risk. Investing this money might be more appealing if you set a rolling target of ten years, say, and then in turn defined a limit on your chance of loss (or loss in purchasing power).

In every case, probability feedback is the essential language for ensuring that both parties have realistic and agreed expectations. That alone is worth changing your investment arrangements for, as unrealistic expectations are the commonest cause of regret!

The permutations are endless. That is the whole point: the trade-offs that achieve a realistic balance for the plan have to be personal. They cannot be standardized. You cannot delegate them. If you do, there will be no clear basis for managing the risks and payoffs. If things turn out differently from your expectations, however unreasonable, your agent is protected. They will only have to demonstrate that they went through the bare minimum of woolly procedures for discussing your objectives and attitude to risk to destroy any claim you may make against them. The only way for you to protect yourself is to control the risk agenda yourself, at the outset and going forward.

The permutations for the style and format of this sort of dialogue with the industry are also many, if not exactly endless. In the institutional market, investment consultants normally present a series of options, extracting a range of combinations of funding and risk tolerance and often using graphs as well as tables to assist choice. The normal format is a trustee meeting. Though consulting actuaries have impressive technology, the dialogue is rarely interactive or online, with trustees actually accessing the actuarial models to play around with the funding variables.

This direct interactivity with models is far more likely to be the way goal-based investment is presented in the retail market. Access could be via the internet from your home computer or you could be sitting at your IFA's laptop at home or in his or her office or indeed at your stockbroker or portfolio manager's PC.

Where a real person is involved as your agent, you of course need never have operated a computer or tapped at a keyboard. Nor does interacting with models to determine your goal parameters have to be instantaneous. There is no reason why customers and professionals should not work at the slower pace of conventional advisory channels, like the typical trustee format, with a range of proposals sent out in the mail to support individual choices, discussed in a subsequent meeting or on the telephone.

Are there no awkward issues raised by this approach to risk? Other than the fact that no investment approach can make all uncertainties go away, there are four worth touching on briefly in the rest of this chapter. If we do not, you are likely to encounter them or be aware of them already and wonder how they can be reconciled with the approach that the book recommends. They are:

1 the perceived conflict between two approaches to risk management: *matching* and *diversification*

2 the use of a unique, goal-specific safe-harbour asset

3 the need to choose between risk *along the way* and uncertainty of *outcome*

4 the effect of simplifying the range of suitable portfolio building blocks.

Diversification versus matching

In Chapter 4 we explored the difference that diversification makes as between being sure to pick up the systematic behaviour of markets and having a more entrepreneurial set of risks with greater (and less measurable) uncertainty of outcome. At the implementation level of the hierarchy, diversification is a very important principle. However, diversification at the asset allocation strategy level is a mixed blessing. Adding more asset classes, such as fixed interest, and adding more equity markets, such as emerging markets, may be intuitively risk-reducing but actually push you away from the bounded uncertainties of market systems and towards less predictable entrepreneurial investing.

Diversification to control risk is anyway less relevant, as well as less effective, when the principal means of managing outcomes is by combining risky assets with a unique safe-harbour asset, which is the next issue coming up.

The importance the industry attaches to diversification of the asset mix reflects a different agenda from matching. As we shall see in Part II, their approach is based not on customization but on standardization, for two reasons. First, the economics of managing money for a large number of different clients favour forcing them into common pools. Second, performance is the raw material of their marketing strategy and so they need to control their investment risks to ensure they suit their commercial risks. The economics of advising on investment are all too often about selling and switching products and so a wider range of portfolio contents also offers more scope for transactions.

Many investment professionals, whether technology-based or 'flying by the seat of their pants', also overestimate the genuine customer benefits of spreading money across a large number of asset classes or markets. Technology-based firms tend to use some form of 'portfolio optimization' software in their asset allocation process. Any firm capable of measuring portfolio probabilities specific to a particular asset strategy, as this book recommends, is also highly likely to be using portfolio optimization. This relies on a mathematical process for maximizing the 'efficiency' of the risk and return trade-off.[11]

Optimizing combinations of risky assets requires precise numbers for the return and risk of each asset in the opportunity set, which is

---

[11] Often referred to as 'mean variance optimization', the inputs are the mean expected return and the standard deviation (as a measure of risk). Connecting all the different possible portfolios that have the highest expected return (usually shown on the y or left axis) at each level of risk (on the x or bottom axis) describes a familiar curve from the bottom left quadrant to the top right quadrant, known as the 'efficient frontier'. The principles, different techniques of portfolio optimization and their strengths and weaknesses are described in more detail on the website.

challenging enough. It also requires a precise number for the co-movement, or covariance, of the assets, that is, how they behave when combined. Both measures of risky behaviour, singly and combined, are subject to change over time and so observations based on particular time frames tend to lead to spurious precision. Allowing for this estimation error significantly reduces the apparent gains in portfolio efficiency from throwing more assets into the pot.

The intuitive appeal of diversification for long-term planning is that it reduces the chance of your main market suffering a disappointing outcome. However, for that to be worth while requires a degree of risk spreading that is most unlikely amongst private investors, or even institutional investors. In practice, constraints placed by the client or professional on the exposure to international equities or other diversifying asset classes, often to trivial levels, make diversification of little actual benefit. The advantage of probability feedback is that you can at least see what difference, say, 10 per cent foreign exposure makes compared with none at all. If it makes insignificant difference, do not worry about ignoring it altogether. If it makes a real difference, try 50 per cent or more and see whether the feedback makes better sense than 10 per cent!

We saw in Chapter 2 that value ratios for the major equity markets tend to move together most of the time but that occasionally one may move apart from the others for reasons specific to its own economy. At the time of writing, this is what has happened to Japan, with unusually high value and expected real returns at a time when most markets are only offering lower than normal returns. In practice, this means that to benefit from higher exposure to international markets requires heavy concentration within the foreign component. Whether you can stomach heavy exposure to Japan will also be helped by probability feedback. At least it will be your choice. The practitioner's job is to quote the odds.

The unique safe harbour

Any theory-based investment firm that can measure and quote probabilities is likely to follow one of two approaches to varying the risk and return trade-offs for a portfolio, based on different interpretations of portfolio theory:

■ One involves narrowing or expanding the band of expected returns by altering the mix of risky assets, that is, *taking bigger or smaller bets*.

■ The other takes a portfolio of risky assets that offers an efficient mix of risk and return and varies the band of future returns by *mixing more or less of the safe-harbour or risk-free asset.*

Should you care which? I am going to stick my neck out and suggest that you want an adviser or manager who will use your safe-harbour asset to control the range of outcomes. Managers or advisers who seek to make bigger or smaller bets waste the one certainty in investment planning: a known risk-free rate of return for each goal. Why manage your risks by playing around with assets whose own risk characteristics are subject to uncertainty and whose common movement is uncertain, with lots of room for estimation error, when you can use a certainty?

In the process I described at the beginning of this chapter of using risk tolerance as a variable to achieve a balance of resources and targets, it should be changes in the ratio of risky to safe harbour that alter your outcome probabilities, like adding more water to your Scotch. It is a simple and intuitive process.

In Part III, when we get practical about selecting agents and implementation options, we will deal with the issue of how to achieve your safe harbour exposure. This is ideally via a horizon-matched security but you may need to approximate the match if individual securities are not an option or if the rules relating to a particular tax 'wrapper' (in which you hold the portfolio) restrict your choice.

Outcomes and what happens along the way

Do not be fooled: there is no way to satisfy your appetite for fixing the uncertainty of outcome without accepting the consequences in terms of fluctuations in the portfolio value – and vice versa. Both are genuine measures of risk but you need to choose consistently between them.

To demonstrate this quandary, let us consider the features of a safe-harbour asset. If you wished to reduce short-term fluctuations in the value of your portfolio you would dilute it with cash. Because cash is subject to uncertainty about the nominal yield and about inflation, this will increase the range of potential outcomes in real terms, which makes it more risky in terms of outcomes. You have to choose which form of uncertainty is most relevant to your goal and should preoccupy you and which you can 'educate' yourself to tolerate.

If it is a pension task, for instance, you are likely to view spending power outcomes as the dominant risk. So that makes index-linked gilts the natural matching safe harbour. These have virtually no uncertainty of outcome in real terms. Whatever happens along the way, you will still know that the return to your planning horizon is fixed. What can happen along the way to a long-dated index-linked gilt is that its price can swing around quite sharply. Its volatility is somewhere between that of an equity and a conventional gilt (equivalent to a standard deviation of annual returns of about 15 per cent). Accepting this volatility along the way is the price for fixing the outcome certainty.

Most risk priorities are common sense, yet there is plenty of evidence that people value the 'wrong' measure. Consider the case of a young employee saving for a pension. At age 28, for instance, the proportion that the present value of the embryonic pension fund represents of the expected final value is trivial, yet he or she may still fret about a short-term decline in the value of the fund.

Worse yet, the same investor, out of concern for what happens along the way, may opt for a personal pension based on a with-profits policy or 'managed fund' which typically holds conventional fixed-income securities as part of a 'balanced' diversification strategy. The fixed-income proportion is, say, 15 per cent. The significance of any reduction in volatility will be totally overwhelmed by the compounding effect of replacing the systematic equity risk premium on 15 per cent of every contribution by a smaller (and uncertain) fixed-income return. The asset mix 'mis-match' acts like a ball and chain that could leave their pension up to 20 per cent below its potential level with very little chance of it being as high. Is anyone quoting those odds?

Such 'errors' are made when the need to choose between risk priorities has not been properly communicated and the different probabilities have not been articulated. In my experience, the key to making a more rational choice, that is, one based more objectively on the nature of the goal, is for the investor to feel confident about planning outcomes.

How many building blocks?

If risk is managed largely by diluting the risky portfolio with your safe-harbour asset, if diversification benefits within your risky-asset portfolio tend anyway to be wrongly specified and if most of the available asset-allocation building blocks show entrepreneurial risks and payoffs, the answer has to be: *very few* are needed. You really can keep it simple.

In Chapter 2 we identified three individual equity markets that show reliable systematic features: the UK, USA and Japan. Though the USA and Japan also introduce currency behaviour, there is no essential difference in their use to a UK individual investor as building blocks.

The analysis of long historical data series that this was based on also found that most European markets displayed mean reversion and bounded deviations. Though the histories vary in length, they seem to fit the idea of a common global trend of about 6 per cent per annum in real total returns. Their use to a UK investor is only different because there is more uncertainty about how to fit past histories to a common trend, because exposure to Europe is in practice about a new single market rather than to 12 or so separate markets. Combining past data into a single series, 'Europe, ex-UK', poses some statistical challenges for the engineers but the additional doubt can be allowed for somehow in the assumed risk structure for Europe that is used as the input to a model.

Adding Europe to the other three, the total of the world equity market capitalization that these four building blocks account for is about 90 per cent: not bad representation. They are also easily implemented through index-tracking funds, both onshore and (with less choice) offshore. The broad geographical sweep of this approach omits, illogically, Australia and Canada: two markets with long histories and system-like character-istics. There is no reason to object to their inclusion from time to time in a dynamic asset-allocation strategy but they are harder to track passively. It also omits a large category of emerging markets, which account for most of the balance of the world market by size. This omission is deliberate.

The sales pitch for investing in newly developing economies, like most sales pitches, is crude: '*growth will be higher so returns will be higher*'. There is in fact no reliable long-term evidence of a higher return from emerging markets as a systematic feature. This should not surprise us now that we know (from Chapter 2) that today's developed markets provided the same real return trend for investors at their early stages of development as they have more recently.

What there is evidence of is a one-off higher return as investors in developed countries moved into emerging markets for the first time. There is a certain neat irony in regarding this, not economic development, as the relevant process of 'emergence' for investors! This is apparent in Figure 5.1. It shows the cumulative returns in Sterling terms of two repre-sentative indices: the MSCI Emerging Markets Index and the FTSE World Index of developed markets.[v] Both are diversified indices of lots of different markets, weighted by their size. The emergence phase can be seen in the early 1990s. The graph also shows clearly that a portfolio of emerging markets is bound to have been much more volatile, at almost every stage, than a portfolio of developed markets.

Figure 5.1 ▨ **Indexed cumulative total returns in £ (base 100 in Feb 1987) for MSCI Emerging Markets Index and FTSE World Index**

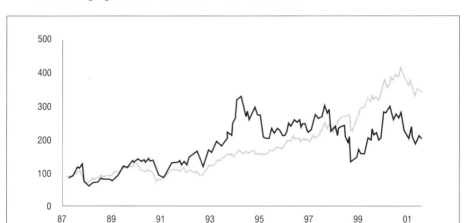

If there were a system at work, we would expect to see a higher return to reward this higher volatility. Why do we not? It is not like venture capital, where it is not possible to gain exposure to a full enough sample of opportunities to be sure of a risk premium. You can buy well-diversified emerging-market funds. It is not like hedge funds, where the risks and payoffs stem from a series of independent bets, unrelated to any convenient equilibrium system. I do not know the answer and propose to leave speculation to the website.

What we can safely assume is that one other element of the typical sales pitch is flawed: that emerging markets and developed markets are not closely correlated (in other words that they do not move together) and therefore are useful for creating more efficient portfolios. Of course they used to be weakly correlated; they were completely ignored by most investors in the developed markets. Once they emerged centre-stage and were widely held in global portfolios, it is hardly surprising that their movements then became more closely correlated.[12] Forget the diversification sales pitch and the high-growth sales pitch. If you are going to invest, treat it as strictly entrepreneurial and keep your wits about you.

You may find that some advisers and money managers break down the major markets to a further degree, as between larger and smaller companies or between value and growth stocks. This concept of 'sub-building blocks' is sufficiently well developed in the US to have led to indices for each, creating a matrix of large growth, large value, small growth and small value.

The assumption the concept depends on is that they all behave differently and that they are each reasonably predictable; in other words, they also have the attributes of systems. The logic is impeccable: if an equity market is a subsystem of an economic system, then why should not certain types of equity be subsystems of the equity system? Is this borne out and how useful to you is it?

This is also a large and complex area of developing debate amongst academics and practitioners.[13] Summarizing the mixed evidence about systematic features, we can note the following:

1 The 'small companies effect', in the shape of higher returns, that was observed in most host markets, and became the basis of debate about whether it was an anomaly or a systematic risk premium, has been plunged into doubt by a long period of poor relative returns.

2 If there is no long-term-risk premium for smaller companies, there may be no diversification attraction to investors with long-horizon goals.

3 'Fixing your position' in smaller companies is difficult so market conditions may need to be really unusual to allow for estimation error.

4 There is persuasive long-term evidence of outperformance by value-over growth stocks.

5 The indices this is based on require a high level of rebalancing of their constituents, suggesting that companies do not stay in one category for long, in turn casting doubt on any assumptions of systematic behaviour.

---

[12] The moral is that even the brightest minds can be incredibly silly when it comes to interpreting data histories. Numbers are only numbers; you have to think about what is going on.
[13] It is dealt with in detail on the website, under the heading of Styles.

6 Category inconsistency also suggests that the transaction costs of a style-specialized portfolio may erode any theoretical gain from passive exposure to value.

7 It is hard to find funds in all markets, particularly the UK, to implement any systematic play on value and growth.

8 The evidence nonetheless acts as a powerful warning to the individual investor to be careful about the industry's bias in favour of growth-stock investing, as displayed by many IFAs and portfolio managers.

Do not be easily persuaded that portfolio strategy needs to be complex or rich in diversity to be robust and sensible. These are widespread misconceptions amongst the people in between. Professionals are biased because of the seductively intuitive assumption that a complex world needs complex solutions. They are also biased as a result of the desire to play up their own importance and to increase your perceived dependence upon them. As we are about to see in Part II, this is a devilish agenda.

The people in between: a system corrupted

6

Products of history

System failure

In Part II we will see how an industry that based its customer relationships on a long tradition of trust and dependence, whether a patrician tradition at one end of the social scale or a working-class self-help tradition at the other, came to abuse that trust.

'My word is my bond' is the Stock Exchange motto and Lloyds' is 'Fidentia'. In both cases the notion of trust has often seemed to refer more to the way professionals deal with each other and honour each other's word (or a hand shake) than how they see their customer relationships. Indeed, it was the very exclusivity of the City 'insiders' that spurred the growth of financial institutions like life assurance companies, building societies and friendly societies.

THE NOTION OF TRUST HAS OFTEN SEEMED TO REFER MORE TO THE WAY PROFESSIONALS DEAL WITH EACH OTHER AND HONOUR EACH OTHER'S WORD THAN HOW THEY SEE THEIR CUSTOMER RELATIONSHIPS

Both of these rival traditions have managed to disarm consumers over the years. In other consumer markets the fundamental principle of *caveat emptor*, 'let the buyer beware', has tended to keep the customer alert and encouraged an effort to understand what was being bought, but when it comes to investment, caveat emptor is too easily suspended in favour of blind trust.

Apart from the traditions that companies have been able to exploit, there are a number of features specific to investment products that have helped the people in between to seize and control the agenda.

Investment products are 'credence goods': you do not find out when you get them home (or when the salesman leaves your home) whether they work or are suitable. You buy on trust and find out much later. They are also sufficiently complicated and removed from everyday experience to make their acceptability dependent on a high degree of trust. When we look briefly at the story of how the industry developed, we see that the underlying complexity of investment products has increased as their focus has moved from contracts based on fixed-income investments to contracts based on equities. We will also see that the experience of unusual inflation in the last 50 years has disorientated the conventional wisdom that investors had come to rely on.

Perhaps the most surprising feature of the customer's loss of the agenda has been the role of successive governments whose constant tinkering with the tax system and recourse to incentives to boost private investment and thrift have made the retail investment market ever more complex. All of these factors have made it too easy for companies to exploit consumer confusion.

In this story, acts of fraud or downright dishonesty are relatively rare, and certainly rarer than in many other activities that are less closely scrutinized by professional bodies and regulators. When they come to light, they make lurid copy for the media but their very sensationalism may draw attention away from the more subtle forms of institutionalized abuse of trust.

It is only in recent years that the media have been willing to dig deeper, down to the mundane detail, to expose whatever they judge is likely to be seen by ordinary people as crossing the boundaries of common decency, even if these are not boundaries in law or regulation. Even the widespread disgrace of pension mis-selling uncovered in the late 1990s might have been discounted as an exceptional blot on the industry's copybook rather than a symptom of serious industry-wide problems had it not been for the antennae of a number of journalists. The consumer watchdog style of financial journalism, more than a little challenging for a media that benefits from heavy advertising of financial products, has been in evidence in all of the widely read financial sections.

Credit must also go to a government that, even if only sensing the popular mood, was prepared to name and shame companies or practices that crossed those boundaries of common decency.

If journalists or law makers had any doubt that maybe this was just populist fodder rather than a big issue, or that they had got the wrong end of the stick in a complicated story, they only had to turn to authoritative, reasoned arguments from the Treasury, the Office of Fair Trading, the Consumers' Association and the Financial Services Authority (FSA) for support. Though most of the industry bodies just try to defend their interests whenever attacked, the Institute and Faculty of Actuaries, standing slightly removed from the special interests of the industries that employ its members, has also been an authoritative critic from within.

The system may not be corrupt but it is *fundamentally corrupted* in the sense that it has endemic structural flaws that act to the detriment of the customer and only benefit the industry. Because of those flaws, the system is failing the customer. It is particularly failing the customers with the least wealth and the most to gain from efficient investment programmes. In the next few chapters, as we look at what is wrong with the industry, four types of corruption of the system are recurrent themes.

The most obvious is *bad practice*. This ranges from professional incompetence, including ignorance of the body of science of markets, to sharp or shady practice. We examine the *conflicting agenda* that are inherent in all agency roles. They are particularly acute in financial services yet consumers are strangely insensitive to them. We see how *bad design* of investment products and services distorts market dynamics and, for no good reason, ends up complicating what could be a much simpler process and preys on investors' irrational instincts. We see the damage done to investors' chances of success in their investment goals as a direct result of *excessive costs*. When we look at why costs are so high, we see that it is mostly because of the industry's need to keep peddling a false prospectus about the importance of past performance. We are bribed with our own money to buy into this myth and the bribes are handled by both investment managers and advisers.

These are not isolated or marginal shortcomings and all too often they combine. It is normal that a customer of the industry will encounter a professional who has scant understanding of or respect for the inherent uncertainties of investment, will fail to spot the conflicts of interests that colour their advice, will buy products that are not suitable and will pay a price that makes it highly unlikely they will achieve their objectives.

When this awful combination later causes disappointment or alarm, the chances are that instead of finding someone who will put the situation right they will simply go through another version of the same flawed process with different agents and different products.

As we examine the evidence of system failure it will inevitably raise questions about our own culpability, as it is our capacity for irrationality, greed and cutting corners that the industry has managed so successfully to exploit. If we make monkeys of ourselves we are likely to encourage monkey business.

It is not just that we give the industry the opportunity. In my experience, it is even more significant that we also give it the excuse of some pretence of moral justification. All too often I have heard decent people working in all branches of the industry, who I know are aware of its shortcomings, blame the customer. They can argue that they are only giving them what they want. They can swear they know it from their personal interaction with customers, and, besides, they keep coming back for more. Convenient it may be but it is a doubtful justification if, as we shall see is probably the case, customers are not so much revealing their innate preferences as reflecting back to the professionals the beliefs and expectations that the industry has assiduously and expensively conditioned in them.

IF WE MAKE MONKEYS OF OURSELVES WE ARE LIKELY TO ENCOURAGE MONKEY BUSINESS

To understand what is wrong with the industry, and to reflect on our own role as less than streetwise consumers, it is helpful to see how we came to have the services, products, business structures and relationships that define it today.

The Victorian order

Private clients' investment arrangements are typically the accident of history, trapped in a structure stridently at odds with the fluidity of the 'new consumerism'. They reflect an essentially Victorian landscape, with strong definitions provided by specialist mutual societies and specialist shareholder-owned financial institutions and by rigid enclosures that separated the types of relationship according to wealth and social background. That this archaic landscape has survived at all testifies to the snobbery that attaches itself easily to money, particularly in Britain.

Behind its social enclosure, equity investing in the nineteenth century had been a preserve of those with considerable wealth and a far greater appetite for risk than we require today. I have heard it said (but do not know the source) that most of the world's stock of equity capital at the end of that century was owned by just 100 families, mainly of European origin.

Equity investment was essentially entrepreneurial. Investors were either the original family backers of a business, whose stakes collectively accounted for most of the market capitalization (precisely because equity investment had not yet been institutionalized), or they were speculators. Speculative activity was usually trading orientated. A main objective of the speculator's approach to risk management was to minimize the risk of loss by exploiting inside information! Integrity mattered when it came to the workings of the system, such as transactions and settlements, but integrity was willingly traded in order to get as close as possible to the tips that made money.

Occasionally more widely owned money was sucked into new equity issues, such as in the railway mania that in the early part of the century gripped the nation as effectively as any subsequent technology boom. Once these fevers had blown themselves out, as they always do, losers retreated leaving stock speculation once again to a braver and wealthier minority – at least until the next irresistible new issue fashion came round.

The gateway to the stock market was a stockbroker. There was no institutionalized packaging of equity investments until the following century, and as we shall see, financial institutions did not typically invest in equities themselves. A broker in the nineteenth century could expect to conduct the great majority of his (not her!) business in fixed income securities since this was the main form in which personal investments were held. Investment was predominantly undertaken for income and the main preoccupation was with loss of principal, even if the instrument was a bond. This was a real risk. Thus bonds or mortgages issued by private borrowers paid a higher coupon, or interest payment, than a government bond to compensate for the possible default of the issuer. The search for high yields, albeit at a greater risk, often lead British investors to foreign markets as the opportunities for investment in UK borrowers were limited. This would continue to characterize British investing until the early twentieth century when the world became a much more dangerous place.

The Victorian inheritance of snobbery and hope of being at the heart of a money-making clique has survived in the way old money still gravitates naturally to stockbrokers and is prejudiced against the institutions and brokers of packaged products. It even shows in the assumption among many who come into new money that at their new level of wealth it is natural to head off to the City, be it to a stockbroker or a 'private bank', rather than to an IFA or a DIY investment website. These prejudices are unfounded and, as we shall see in Part III, are likely to lead to irrational and inefficient choices.

The role of financial institutions in packaging investment solutions for individuals also began with contracts based on fixed income. These were life assurance and one of the world's oldest financial products – the annuity.[14] The need to convert a capital sum into a stream of income, such as on marriage, inheritance or the sale of property, has long been one of the commonest tasks of household finance. Once provided by wealthy (and sometimes unscrupulous) individuals, annuities were later provided by governments, to whom they represented another source of finance, before becoming the prerogative of insurance companies as they are today.

Life assurance and annuities are opposite bets on life expectancy, long and short, and so it was logical that companies should provide both. For the buyer of life cover or an annuity, risk was all about not getting paid and so the integrity of the provider as well as its financial strength were paramount concerns. Before the middle of the nineteenth century, confidence in financial institutions was actually far more fragile than today. It was only the introduction of accounting and reporting rules and of regulation by professional bodies and government agencies that established high levels of consumer trust.

The assets held by insurance companies to back their annuity contracts and their life (or general insurance) contracts were not equities but fixed-income investments, such as debt issued by governments or private companies and utilities and also mortgages. Managing the assets of an insurance company was about matching streams of income in and payments out. Income was subject to default risk and changes in market

---

[14] In *Against the Gods* Peter Bernstein writes: 'The first record we have of the concept of annuities goes back to 225 AD, when an authoritative set of tables of life expectanies was developed by a leading Roman jurist named Ulpian. Ulpian's tables were the last word for over 1400 years.'

yields. Payments were subject to claims uncertainty of which the prime source was the way the actual life span of the policyholders panned out by comparison with the estimates of the actuary based on mortality tables.

The origins of the life companies were very different from the patrician and exclusive life of the City. Shortly after Prudential was founded in 1848 it began to build its business on the collection of small weekly savings, door to door, from workers from the Potteries and the weaving districts of Cheshire and Lancashire.[vi] Some had no greater hope than to save for funeral expenses. Combining life cover and rainy day savings in a single simple payment of premium was the origin of the 'endowment' policy. Larger by far than any of the other Victorian 'industrial branch' life companies, 'the Pru' had a total of just £100 million of policies on its books at the start of the First World War[vii] which is tiny by comparison with private holdings of gilts, for instance.

There were other differences less obvious to customers. Because of the nature of their risks, insurance companies were staffed and often run by actuaries or mathematicians. When I started my working life in the City in 1969 as a stockbroker, there were just 28 actuaries employed in Stock Exchange firms and almost the entire professional body worked in insurance.[viii] Maths and the science of investment were alien to the amateur culture of the City which was more comfortable with instinct, gut feel and the practical experience that comes with trading stocks. Though much has changed, there is still a form of 'technical' snobbery that divides the City and the institutions.

Participation in bond markets was also institutionalized by the advent in the last 30 years of the nineteenth century of investment trust companies. Their purpose was to gather assets from the growing middle class of savers created by the post-Industrial Revolution boom in Victorian Britain. Like many of the older insurance companies, promoters were particularly drawn to the thrifty Scots who were more into financial planning than their brethren south of the border. Several founders of investment trust management companies later moved south, however, including Robert Fleming and George Touche (whose firm of investment trust secretaries was the origin of the accountants Touche Ross, out of which was later spun the investment trust managers, Touche Remnant).

Investment trusts originally invested in loans and mortgages and mainly in developing economies outside Britain: emerging markets and venture capital rolled into a single vehicle. In a brief history of investment trusts on the website of the Association of Investment Trust Companies John Newlands writes:

The investment trust industry could take pride in having helped to finance the railways, at home and abroad; the burgeoning economy of the United States, and Canada; the gauchos of South America, the farmers of Australia, and the worldwide development of telegraph and cable systems.

Newlands makes the point, not so widely appreciated, that it was only in the 1920s that trusts started to invest in equities.

During that decade the introduction of Corporation Profits Tax, and the onset of inflation began to erode the benefits of investing in fixed-interest securities. Many trusts, seeking income which had already borne tax – franked income – made their first moves into equity investment during this period. Liebig's Extract of Meat, Peninsular & Oriental, Swedish Match and Texas Gulf Sulphur were the first industrials bought by one of the largest trusts, in 1926.

It is a fair bet that trusts were also attracted by the boom in American stocks that occurred in the 1920s. The boom was tracked by markets from London to Tokyo. Though it eventually proved to be a bubble that burst spectacularly, it was accompanied by the first serious public debate about the role of equities as a means of capital accumulation. This focused for the first time on the concept of the market as a system that we introduced in Part I.

By linking a theory of markets to the underlying growth engines of the economy, an automatic link also began to be established in the minds of investors between equity investing and growth stock investing. Arguments about the relative importance of growth and value, which usually means income, went on to dominate debate about approaches to equities for most of the rest of the century.

Though the world after the Great War looked very different from the Victorian order, investment relationships did not alter greatly. The institutions and the City continued to appeal to two very different social constituencies. The stockbroker remained the gateway to exposure to equity markets. Even investment trusts, as securities traded on the London Stock Exchange, were bought and sold like equities through a broker. The greatest change was in the breadth of participation in the market, but this was mainly to occur after the Second World War, when equity capital became popular with individuals and institutions alike.

The rise of people's capitalism

I have taken the phrase for the title of this section from one of the giants of the American mutual fund industry, John Bogle, founder of Vanguard. He used it (probably not for the first time) in a lecture in Cleveland in October 2000 in which he looked back on the second half of the twentieth century since, as a student in Princeton in 1949, he happened to take as subject for a thesis the then tiny mutual fund industry.[ix] The American equivalent of a unit trust, mutual funds had been introduced as the first collective vehicle for equity exposure in time to take advantage of the 1920s boom. However, the 1930s bust, followed by the Second World War, did not exactly make for a brilliant sales pitch for the early promoters of these public funds.

In Britain, as in America, the institutionalization and democratization of the equity market took off in the 1950s. Though the young unit trust movement helped to broaden participation in the market it was not the vehicle that was the cause. For this we must look to what was beginning to be accepted as the first ever 'systematic' price inflation.

For several hundred years, price stability was the norm but it was punctuated by bouts of inflation and deflation caused principally by factors beyond the control of those with responsibility for the management of the economy: war and climate. Though historically episodes of currency collapse and hyperinflation were mercifully rare, they had occurred in France, Germany, Austria, Hungary, Poland and Russia between the wars, and in Japan, Italy and France in the immediate aftermath of the Second World War. If we look at the problem strictly in terms of numbers, it is likely that for most families hyperinflation was worse than war. Financial ruin was more likely to be caused by the mass repudiation of debts and worthlessness of pensions, annuities and all paper assets than by occupation or bombs.

Though Britain had escaped this fate, its leaders and its people were presumably sensitive to the dangers of tolerating rising prices of wages and goods. In spite of this, it became widely accepted in post-war Britain that 'a little inflation was a good thing', as though the drug could in fact be controlled. The prescient Lord Aldenham, however, as Chairman of the Westminster Bank, wrote in his Chairman's Report of 1955:[x]

The idea of a 'gently inflationary' economy for Britain was not without its supporters. There are some people who think we ought to reconcile ourselves to a permanent condition of gradually rising prices. What this seems to me to amount to is that wage earners and profit earners would constantly be increasing their slice of the cake at the expense of pensioners and of other persons with fixed incomes, and of future savers. And the size of that cake would most likely become smaller and smaller as high costs led to the loss of oversea markets and ultimately to the depreciation of the pound sterling.

I single out inflation because it is the change in thinking about the nature of the riskiness of equities that most accounted for the boom in stocks in the 1950s and which continued, with occasional setbacks, until the early 1970s, rather than exceptional performance of the economy.

In 1955 City stockbrokers de Zoete & Gorton (the 'Z' in Barclays' Big Bang amalgam, BZW Securities) published the first of their annual series called the 'Equity Gilt Study'. Gilt redemption yields were then 3.8 per cent and equities were yielding 4.4 per cent.[xi] Though this margin of additional yield for equities was lower than it had often been in Victorian times, it still implies concern then about loss of principal or risk of omitted dividends rather than positive focus on long-term growth in dividends and in the capital value of the enterprise.

By the end of 1972 (three years after I had become the first of de Zoete's new graduate recruitment programme), the yield on gilts had risen to 9.6 per cent and the equity yield had fallen to 3.2 per cent. In terms of relative returns, with income reinvested and adjusted for inflation, equities outperformed gilts by a factor of 5.6 times!

This change in the 'rating' of each of equities and gilts is exactly what was implied by Lord Aldenham, as steadily compounding inflation ate away at the real value of fixed incomes whilst equities benefited from the rising claim, in money terms, of profits. This was before double-digit inflation and in only five of those years did the annual rate exceed 5 per cent and it never reached 10 per cent. It was the fact that inflation had become systematic and apparently permanent that was the new and important information for markets. The 'cult of the equity' was born.

For the people's capitalism, however, it is helpful to look at it the other way round. The financial instruments that had been the people's choice for centuries, bonds, deposits and annuities, all of which were exposed to the corrosive damage of steady inflation, were suddenly vulnerable to a sales pitch that tried to push investors towards higher-margin equity-linked products.

The relative return path between equities and gilts, or equities and cash, became a standard part of the marketing of the people's capitalism.

It is still disingenuously wheeled out (even if for much shorter periods of history) in the form of a graph showing the cumulative return path of £100 invested in so-and-so's 'Super UK Growth Fund' soaring off like a rocket to the top right corner, compared with £100 in a building society savings account, barely managing to rise off the bottom of the graph.

How insurance companies were handed the show

At about the time in the 1950s that the Equitable Life (and others) first started offering guaranteed annuity rates on pension products, insurance companies also began to move from fixed income to equity investments. This was partly to match better the way their own liabilities were sensitive to inflation and also because they could ride on the coat tails of the equity marketing pitch to generate sales of 'riskier' products. Foremost amongst them was the with-profits policy which had been designed as a derivative of bond markets.

In Chapter 9 we will see how the inherent tension between equity volatility and the smoothing of returns in a with-profits policy ultimately came to be stretched to breaking point. There is no question that for much of the last 30 years the smoke and mirrors of a with-profits policy have allowed insurance company sales staff and advisers and brokers to sell equity investment exposure to investors who still hankered after the nominal safety of cash and bonds. In the light of the superior return, and the genuine protection against inflation, which they may only have enjoyed as a result of this deception, it is difficult not to see this as a blessing in disguise.

FOR POPULAR CAPITALISM, THE INSURANCE INDUSTRY WAS THE WORST POSSIBLE INSTITUTIONAL AGENT TO INSERT BETWEEN OUR MONEY AND THE MARKETS

The UK retail investment market is today dominated not by banks, as in most other countries, but by insurance companies. The popular appeal of with-profits policies and the social origins of the industry are not the only, or even main, reason for this. It is rather the peculiar feature of the British tax code that (for a long time) made life insurance premiums deductible from taxable income, even if the premium was largely an investment.

For popular capitalism, the insurance industry was the worst possible institutional agent to insert between our money and the markets. I believe they hijacked the product agenda, the language and the approach to marketing in a way that is principally now responsible for many of the industry's overall failings.

If you imagine yourself two decades or so ago passing on a single piece of advice about investment to, for instance, a young godchild, with the benefit of hindsight you might well choose the simple rule, 'Never mix investment and insurance.' That alone would have enabled the beneficiary of your wisdom to avoid the traps of endowment mortgages and pension mortgages and to avoid many of the worst excesses of hidden charges and penalties, all of which we explore in the next few chapters.

There are probably many reasons why Americans are so fascinated by investment markets and are turned on by personal goals and why, in Britain, markets excite little more than a yawn and goal setting is embarrassing. Maybe it is a genuine cultural difference but, if so, we got the culture we deserve in the shape of insurance companies. Finding themselves as the main distributors of investment products, they took their negative language from insuring against adverse events and applied exactly the same language to one of the really important positive ways we can think about money: our personal investment goals.

It is not just that the language of 'protection' is more negative than 'achievement'. It is also that the language is irrelevant to everyday life, irrelevant to the nature and basic principles of investing, even to the fun of investing, and is trapped in ancient history. Why is an investment product called a 'policy'? Why does it 'lapse'? Why are the amounts you invest called 'premiums'? Why is some part of your share of the return earned by a life fund on your money described as a 'bonus'? Why a 'reversionary bonus'? What on earth does that mean? Come to think of it, what does 'endowment' mean? Is this really people's capitalism or is it capitalists' capitalism, a form of producer power over the customer?

Insurance companies really stole the show when an outsider showed them how. In 1961 Mark Weinburg, a South African with a finance background, was the driving entrepreneurial force behind the formation of Abbey Life, which introduced 'unit-linked' life policies in the UK.

These retained the life insurance element necessary to obtain life assurance premium relief against tax but as soon as the money was received by Abbey Life it was separated into two streams, one, a trickle, going to pay for life cover, and the rest going into a unit trust that looked like and was indeed exactly like a normal unit trust. By contrast with a with-profits policy, you could now see exactly what was happening to the value of the assets. The concept did not really take off until the tax relief was extended to lump sum investments in 1968.

So transparent a method of obtaining a tax benefit from an investment you would otherwise have made anyway would appear to invalidate the advice not to mix insurance and investment. However, transparency came at the expense of complex and opaque methods for charging that were both onerous and heavily front-end loaded, to pay the large selling incentives to the direct sales force.

Rather than change the advice to your godchild, it should have been accompanied by a small gift of shares in Hambro Life, which Weinburg went on to found and which was the main engine of the popularization of unit-linked investing. Though the shares traded at a discount when first issued, they went on to be an outstanding investment, highly geared to the rise in market values after the 1974 bear market.

The real significance of the unit-linked concept to the story of the retail investment industry lies in its introduction of highly professional direct-selling techniques. Though they had been around for decades in the USA you would probably not have encountered them in the UK unless you found at your door a salesman for the *Encyclopaedia Britannica* or for the infamous Bernie Cornfeld's Dover Plan.

Though Mark Weinburg has the public profile, the man who really stole the show for the insurance industry was Hambro Life's Marketing Director, Mike Wilson. Running like a golden vein through the story of the industry over the last three decades, Wilson is the showman who taught the super salesmen who transformed the art of direct sales from its 'Man from the Pru' roots.

The training techniques and essential structures had all been installed first at Abbey Life and then at Hambro Life before Wilson arrived on the scene in 1975. They had been set up by Dan Dane who brought them with him from Sun Life of Canada who had in turn imported them from the USA. Direct selling the American way is clinically orchestrated, rooted in analysis of what makes people tick, whatever side of the coffee table they are sitting. Sales training did not only run to techniques for getting beyond the door to the coffee table. For selling on the telephone you would be trained to talk to your prospect looking into a mirror and smiling, on the basis that this lightened your tone and made you more likeable.

It took Mike Wilson to hone and perfect these structures and inject the personal magic and magnetism that can truly inspire successful selling. Part of the essential structure he perfected and attached his personality to was what amounts in effect to pyramid selling. At the lowest level, small units of sales staff were led, motivated and mothered by unit managers who were themselves successful sales people and good motivators. They were in turn managed and coached by a tier above them who themselves reported to the senior marketing team under Wilson. Each individual in a leadership role participated in the commissions brought in by every one below them in their own line of the 'family tree'. Effective mortar for the economics of direct selling, these mutual hierarchical dependencies also encouraged family bonds that could be powerfully motivating.

It was this pyramid structure of commission payments that contributed to some of the worst abuses of mis-selling and the successor firm of Hambro Life, Allied Dunbar, was itself among the offending life companies. Although the customer could not know of the performance outcomes until later, Allied Dunbar has also delivered mediocre performance. It shows that the quality of the offering counts for very little if the selling methods are good enough.

Until the 1990s there was so much ignorance of the schemes used by the industry to conceal the true cost of investing that it was possible to extract enough from the customer to pay the extravagant price of super direct sales, with its pyramid commissions structures, intensive training, sales conventions and exotic travel rewards for top performing sales agents. Allied Dunbar/Hambro Life has turned out to be one of the worst providers in terms of both hidden and disclosed charges, particularly for lapsed pension policies.

The Wilson showmanship has lived on in one more form. When Jacob Rothschild set up J. Rothschild Assurance (now St James's Capital) he attracted many of Allied Dunbar's staff and followed essentially the same model. Wilson is now its Chief Executive. In the more critical climate since the 1990s the worst charging excesses are no longer possible. To sustain the extravagant cost of highly trained and motivated agents, J.Rothschild Assurance needed to move up market, focusing on investors with bigger sums to commit. The product, after all, is still just a commodity.

The broker as adviser: enter the IFA

It was another Whitehall initiative that prompted the next important chapter in the story of the people in between. In 1986 the Conservative government passed the Financial Services Act which has shaped the regulatory controls over the investment industry ever since. It was a piece of 'consumer protection' legislation and the Thatcher government took the view that a basic protection the consumer needed was to know whether someone selling a long-term product was a representative of a company that manufactures products or an independent broker who advises on and transacts on other people's products.

The distinction is not unlike that between agent and principal in the stock market and the implication was that the advice of a salesman for a product manufacturer cannot be independent whereas the advice of a broker is untainted by ties to a manufacturer. The distinction is not necessarily between a salesman and an adviser since both can give generic advice that informs the decision to purchase.

The process by which selling agents had to choose which they wanted to be was called polarization. There is surely only one way to interpret that word: the difference is meant to be significant. We will see that in fact it never was.

Polarization gave birth to a new practitioner: the independent financial adviser. Many high street or City insurance brokers who already arranged life and pension contracts immediately registered under the Act as IFAs. Most of the rest came from the insurance companies themselves. It was a self-selecting process as only those confident of their ability to make a living out of selling products would choose it. The bias of the business towards selling, rather than advising or consulting, was predetermined in its formation. Indeed, in the early stages, the industry tried to 'look through' the new structure and set about wooing IFAs with the same kind of head office support they were used to, on the basis that this was more likely to secure them the agencies they sought than competing on the basis the Act intended, namely the curiously named 'best advice' process. 'Best advice' was supposed to ensure IFAs selected their recommendations on the strength of the intrinsic merit of the products and the providers rather than on the relationships between agency and producer. This intention was paramount, hence the implication of polarization and hence the 'independence' in the title.

IFAs have been highly successful in promoting the products of the institutions but they also helped City firms, such as investment trust companies and merchant banks, to compete on equal terms by emulating the commissions and support structures that the insurance industry had always understood. These same structures also allowed new specialist unit trust managers, such as Perpetual and Jupiter, to compete using the distribution channel of IFAs. I say 'equal terms' but in fact the City firms and the specialists have tended to be able to charge higher management fees than the insurance companies, replicating once again the hope of an 'inside edge'.

In the following chapters we will see how IFAs play a key role, both as victims and as perpetrators, in a number of the structural flaws of the industry as a whole. In particular I will highlight the persistence of accidental and archaic social divisions, the corruptive influence of commissions, the excessive focus on marketing skills, the paucity of investment skills, the vested interest in feeding a popular myth about performance and an obsession with implementation that turns the decision hierarchy on its head. In all of these respects the business of IFAs has been instrumental in allowing the product manufacturers to control the agenda of what gets sold, how and at what price.

The industry's accomplice: the Inland Revenue

One of the main reasons why advisers have been necessary, even for relatively low levels of wealth, is the complexity of the British tax system. However, the Inland Revenue's contribution to the transfer of power from customer to producer goes further than complexity. Successive governments have used tax breaks as an incentive to increase saving and though the aim may have been right it has had two pernicious effects. First, it contributed to the consumer's belief that investment is all about products, not personal goals and markets. Second, tax savings created a pot of investors' money that product provider's could raid to boost their own charges.

As we will see in the next few chapters, the industry has exploited complexity, the scope for high 'wrapper' charges and other terms for tax-favoured investments. In many cases the level of charges consumed all of any likely tax savings! Worse, because the tax code often trapped the investor's money in a scheme it gave the scheme provider licence to rip the customer off right up to maturity.

It has turned the end of the fiscal year into a marketing fest for first PEPs and then ISAs. This hype has reduced investment selection to the lowest common denominator, sucking in massive amounts into the best-performing funds and the best-performing sectors without regard to the evidence about the sustainability of high returns. Usually divorced from purposes for the money or personal goals, without the context of a long-term plan, they have become consumer goods in themselves, subject to the desire for instant gratification.

▨ Regulation no substitute for self-protection

The decade following the introduction of the Financial Services Act in 1986 witnessed the worst abuses of consumer trust in living memory, yet the Act was conceived almost entirely as consumer protection legislation. Was it just badly conceived or did consumer protection lull people into thinking that if protected by the law they did not need to protect themselves? Both are probably correct.

THE DECADE FOLLOWING THE INTRODUCTION OF THE FINANCIAL SERVICES ACT IN 1986 WITNESSED THE WORST ABUSES OF CONSUMER TRUST IN LIVING MEMORY, YET THE ACT WAS CONCEIVED ALMOST ENTIRELY AS CONSUMER PROTECTION LEGISLATION

The Act was badly conceived because it relied too much on structures and not enough on education. Strangely, for one of the most radical of governments, it was not accompanied by an attempt to win the hearts and minds of the consumer. There was no attempt to turn complacent attitudes into outright hostility against the industry (in the way that trade union reform did) though there were strong enough grounds, in conflicts of interest, pressurized selling, excessive charges and entrapment practices, to justify turning up the temperature.

As we have seen, the structure of polarization encouraged the false notion of a distinction between agent and principal and encouraged acceptance of implied, not true, independence. Instead of highlighting the problem of conflicts of interest, this sent the wrong signals: *no need to worry, we have dealt with the problem*.

The cooling off facility, which allowed customers to cancel contracts in packaged products as a protection against pressurized selling, was an important innovation but it could be turned by salesmen into a feature of the sales pitch itself: *no need to worry, you can change your mind*.

The main protection against rip-off terms for packaged products was the 'disclosure' regime, introduced reluctantly by the Securities and Investments Board (SIB) in 1995 after pressure from the Office of Fair Trading. The essential element of this structure was the 'key features document', the effect of which was to shift the information the regulator thought the customer should know into a separate document from both marketing material and written recommendations (or 'reasons why', to use the terminology required by the Act). It is typically dense, confusing and unfriendly. This is hardly surprising as it contains all the items likely to be contentious or inconvenient.

The Consumers' Association undertook some research with NOP in 1997 to examine whether the 'key features document' works. Their findings suggest a fundamental inconsistency: customers were mistrustful of the sales process and saw providers as a necessary evil yet they took more notice of verbal advice than written material and the majority had not even read the key features document. Put off by complexity and multiple choice, most only considered the products of a single provider.[xii] It is hardly surprising, therefore, if the introduction of disclosure failed to make an impact on rip-off terms.

A fundamental flaw of the legislation was the principle of self-policing. This meant that the relevant self-regulated organization (SRO) for the retail market, the Personal Investment Authority (PIA), was effectively heavily influenced by very senior professionals working in the industry, many of whose firms were amongst the offenders that the PIA later had to investigate and fine.

As the example of Investment Management Regulatory Organisation (IMRO), that is, the institutional fund managers' SRO, shows, it was possible to run a self-policing body without compromising the purpose of the legislation so it might be wrong to dismiss the legislators as hopelessly naïve. The failure of the PIA, under the influence of leading industry figures, to balance the interests of consumer and industry in the way self-regulation required is one of the most shaming aspects of the industry's recent record.

Learning from history: the FSA

The Financial Services and Markets Act 2000 is the regulation we should have had first time round and clearly lessons have been learned from the failures of the 1986 Act to control providers of retail investment services. Bringing the separate SROs together in a single regulator, the FSA, with a board constituted almost entirely of people with no conflict of interest with the enforcement of regulations and backed by stronger legal enforcement powers, is real progress. More important from the perspective of this book is the strong emphasis this time round on *caveat emptor*. Though not in so many words, it is written into the statutes that dictate the form and style of regulation.[15] Everything the FSA has

---

[15] When Sir Howard Davies, Executive Chairman of the FSA (who since leaving McKinsey has also run the Audit Commission and the CBI) translates caveat emptor as 'beware of the dog', as he is fond of doing, he is not referring to the regulator but reminding us of how we ought to respect the possible danger posed by the people in between.

published to date, as well as conversations I have had, persuades me it is deeply and genuinely ingrained in the culture of the new regulator.

Putting the onus back on the buyer is nonetheless an admission that in Britain's legal system it is not possible to legislate against the kind of bad practice that we investigate in the following chapters which in many cases breaches the boundaries of common decency but not necessarily of law. Regulators also have to tread a fine line between serving consumers' interests by outlawing certain practices and harming them by preventing healthy innovation and competition. They also have to avoid repeating the tendency of the first legislation to make people overreliant on someone other than themselves to protect them.

It seems as though the FSA will rely on three different means in order to change consumer behaviour:

■ general education

■ specific information

■ benchmarking.

As a long-term programme, *education* starts with schools and the FSA is working with the government to ensure basic principles of household finance are included in the national curriculum. This is good but it needs a broader context too. Understanding how to use the financial system needs an approach to the teaching of maths that equips kids with streetwise numeracy, so that they are able to think probabilistically and have an intuitive sense of mathematical relationships and orders of magnitude. Without these even a maths graduate can be easily caught out by the misrepresentation of financial products and expectations for their performance.

The FSA sees educating today's consumers as a long-term challenge. As Christine Farnish, the FSA's Director of Consumer Affairs has said, 'We cannot change a wide spread attitude that money matters are too complicated for most people to understand with a handful of leaflets and a poster campaign'.[xiii]

Specific information is a potentially powerful weapon because it can be timed and targeted. Early examples are the letters they required endowment policy providers to send to all policy holders using endowment policies to pay off a mortgage and the advice for Equitable Life policy holders that it has been running on the Consumer Help section of the FSA website.

Under the heading of *benchmarking* I include any of the subtler ways of changing behaviour of which the two to date suggest clever and powerful use of a new tool. These are the CAT marking of the stakeholder pension and the official information tables for products. The credit for stakeholder properly goes to the Treasury. Stakeholder is a specific type of product with a particular application and particular target consumers. It has been given special privileges that are conditional upon meeting benchmarks for each of three areas of risk of rip-off: *charges*, *access* and *terms*, hence 'CAT marking'.

The cleverness of stakeholder lies not just in its immediate objective, in that target market for those target customers, but in the way it gets round the problem that governments cannot easily legislate limits or prescribe levels across the industry. By releasing stakeholder into the marketplace it has successfully established the same CAT standards as a benchmark for other products that wish to be seen as 'consumer friendly'. It has already done more than anything else to improve product terms and to force the industry to address the kind of IT investment that will enable it to lower its costs. There is no way this kind of initiative could have been conceived inside the PIA, with its vested interests to preserve the status quo.

The official tables of information about products are also smart thinking. Growing familiarity with them will help to shape consumer attitudes to the information they need, and need to compare, to make sensible choices. As we will see in Chapter 10, the tables are intended to act as a wake-up call to consumers taken in by the industry's fixation with past performance.

These subtler means point to a possible switch in emphasis from trying to regulate firms and methods of selling to regulating the design of products. This is the only way the FSA can effectively stop consumer detriment before it has already happened. As FSA Chairman Davies has noted, 'Being cast permanently as the man who followed the Lord Mayor's show with a shovel and a bucket is not an attractive role.'

Though much remains to be proven, and while the consumer should not hang about waiting for a lead from the authorities, the radical reformist front formed by the Treasury, the FSA and the Office of Fair Trading does offer the first real hope of a break with our dismal history.

Top of the class

Though the political focus is on improving financial provision for those that can least afford it, the message is not confined to a single constituency. Smart money is classless and it is dumb to hang on the stereotypes of ancient history. There is no reason why the products and services designed for the less well off or less articulate should be second best. There is every reason to expect them to be the rational choice for anyone wanting to use exposure to markets to achieve personal life goals and to do so with the minimum interference from the people in between.

It is not the most affluent or best educated who are top of the class. From what we know about the way investment assets are held by different socio-economic groups, we can assume that most of the victims of the abuses we will look at in the next chapter are middle-class, middle-income, well-educated and articulate people. They have possibly been highly responsible about the need to plan their finances but they have been irresponsible in their blind trust and dependency. Victims of the industry, they have also contributed to their own disappointment, by cutting corners and lazily setting aside their intuition to beware of the dog.

7

A culture of mis-selling

Petty criminals and organized crime

The Chicago Pizza Pie Factory brought to the London restaurant scene deep-dish pizzas, slick American management and queues around the block, three novelties in the late 1970s. The company behind it, My Kinda Town, had been backed by a little-known venture capital fund which was managed by a small insurance broking firm which also had an investment management business. The firm was called Norton Warburg. When its founder, Andrew Warburg, suddenly caught a plane to Spain one day in 1980, his well-to-do clients were astounded to learn the reason for his flight. Many were also his friends, even members of his family, and never for a moment doubted either his good character or his business success. Yet Warburg had a weakness they had not suspected.

With the exception of the brilliantly successful My Kinda Town, everything else the little venture capital fund had invested in was proving to be a disaster. To try to shore up all the bad investments, Warburg first borrowed against the shares in My Kinda Town. Still the businesses bled. Next he pumped in new money from a loan secured without the board's knowledge against Norton Warburg's office. When even that was not enough, as a last resort he 'borrowed' from client moneys deposited with the firm as an integral part of its investment business, though nothing to do with the venture capital fund. When it finally dawned on him that it was all good money after bad and would never be recovered, he headed for the airport. He had slipped unwittingly into the role of one of the investment industry's very few post-war frauds, possibly without even lining his own pocket along the way.

Though the victims were small in number and for the most part well enough off not to be ruined, and though the total sum misappropriated was no more than £4 million, it happened to coincide closely with another more deliberate fraud by a firm of commodities brokers called Doxford. Together these two exceptional events had a highly significant consequence as they were influential in the setting up of the Gower Committee to investigate the need for 'investor protection'. Formed in January 1981, Professor Gower's committee eventually reported to the government in January 1984. Out of its report came the Financial Services Act of 1986 that put in place the first far-reaching and elaborate regulatory framework for investor protection.

It is difficult to know whether this new regime succeeded in stopping other weak and witless Warburgs or devious Doxfords. There have certainly been other frauds with the same sort of irregularity as before the regime. Yet this is a trivial debate besides the overwhelming scale of institutionalized fraud that the new regulatory bodies totally failed to prevent for the first decade of their existence.

This was systematic deception on a massive scale, tolerated by greedy and misguided industry bosses, ignored by government and going on under the nose of the regulators every day, across the industry as a whole.

These sharp practices were a predictable consequence of a number of government initiatives that were taken without appropriate safeguards. They were predicted by civil servants at the time and after evidence started to show up of sharp practice a number of senior professionals in the industry were vocal in their warnings to government and regulators.

Deception led to a bill to make good funds actually defrauded that run into several billion pounds. Yet it also ended up generating billions of additional income for the industry that would never be recoverable by its customers. Not least, it effectively exposed unwitting investors to huge additional risk. The few million pounds of frauds like Norton Warburg and Doxford pale almost into insignificance besides the 'organized crime' of the late 1980s and early 1990s.

Where were the regulators? What was all that money being spent on if it could not prevent system-wide fraud? It was at least for the most part industry money, as regulations were paid for by levies on registered firms rather than out of the public purse. Precisely because the purse strings were held by industry representatives, they proved remarkably slow to turn on their own. They were eventually forced to bow to pressure to act but their delay and prevarication contributed significantly to the scale of the final bill.

The so-called mis-selling scandals that we are now so wise about after the event are the sale of personal pensions to people better off staying in their company schemes, and deception or negligence in the sale of endowment policies in conjunction with a mortgage. There were a few other smaller scale abuses.

In this chapter we look at the facts and form a view on how widespread the practices were and how the customer might have been expected to be able to resist abuse. We will highlight the culture of the industry that contributed to institutionalized deception, and later on also look at the conflicts of interest, bad product design and people flaws that are part of the context in which mis-selling arose. Forearmed with this knowledge, we will be better equipped to develop the self-protection rules in Part III.

▨ Pension mis-selling

So appalling was the record of occupational pension funds in ripping off members who could not remain in a scheme for the whole of their working life that the Conservative government was determined to act. They clamped down on the abuse of early leavers and they also introduced fully portable personal pensions to suit people likely to move around from job to job.

The new portable pensions had to be 'managed' by banks or insurance companies. This meant that they could either sell 'wrappers' that in turn held individual unit trusts, or they could sell with-profits contracts that formed a part of an existing life fund. The banks who wanted to play had to set up new life and pension subsidiaries but the dominant insurers were able to get to work fast to exploit the new opportunity. So were insurance brokers, many of whom were already organized to sell investment products. Between them, they ensured that it was the life assurance industry that was best able to take advantage of the personal pensions marketing bonanza. The combination of expensive and inflexible products, politicians trying to promote the concept, insurance sales forces trying to push their new products and brokers trying to get into the fast growing market for pensions advice proved to be lethal.

These new pension contracts may have been portable but they were certainly not flexible. Policies were designed with high and hidden charges penalizing people who for whatever reason were unable to maintain regular contributions for the life of the contract, replicating the same feature in occupational schemes that the government had slammed. The fact that a high proportion never kept up their contributions beyond even a few years suggests that the selling processes for both insurance companies and brokers, knowing the structure and conditions of the policies, were careless of the suitability of the product for buyers. The PIA reported in 1997 that as many as one-third of polices sold by companies had lapsed after just three years, and it was nearly a quarter for policies brokered by IFAs. At five years, the lapse rate had extended to 44 per cent for companies and 32 per cent for IFAs.[xiv] Lapse rates were also excessively high for endowment policies so the suitability problem was not specific to pensions or the nature of the labour market.

Until 1995, when the PIA put in place the new disclosure requirements, companies were on average seizing half the plan value in charges on policies transferred to a different plan after five years. For shorter transfers it was possible to get nothing back of the premiums paid. Though the circumstances in which policyholders had second thoughts are bound to be varied, the pattern is too marked and the consequences too severe to absolve the industry of blame for over-selling these contracts to the wrong people.

Personal pensions were also sold to individuals who were in an occupational scheme and who stood to lose out on valuable benefits in those schemes that the new products could not match. There were also many instances of inappropriate advice to contract out of the state-run secondary pension provision, the state earnings-related pension scheme (SERPS).

A feature of pension mis-selling is that there was deliberate targeting of people vulnerable to difficulties in making the comparisons and without easy access to advice from their occupational scheme managers, such as nurses and teachers. Selling techniques that were focused on groups of workers often relied on the enlistment of victims as introducers to friends and colleagues in a similar position. Unscrupulous sales staff also targeted associations of workers, notably the miners' unions. Some £730 million of assets were transferred out of the Miners' Pension Fund to personal pension schemes on behalf of mine workers, the highest of any group of workers.[xv]

Based on the evidence in specific cases, it appears that there was widespread and deliberately lying by sales staff about the benefits their victims were leaving behind by transferring out of good occupational schemes.

It is likely that in cases where targeted customers of sales representatives and advisers had the good sense to approach someone in their own firm who dealt with the pension scheme to check out the merit of transferring, they were properly warned off. Without that, the number of people caught out might have been even higher. However, it also seems that far too many employers must have cynically connived at members exercising the choice of leaving their schemes simply because they stood to gain by paying less in contributions and insurance cover. Some even argued after the event that the regulations prevented them from giving any advice because they were not registered advisers![xvi]

When you hear about pension mis-selling, it refers normally only to the second category, people being talked out of an occupational scheme or wrongly advised to contract out of SERPS, rather than people for whom the contracts' disguised inflexibility meant they were unlikely to be suitable. It also normally refers to the policies sold in a particular period because these are the cases for which the regulator set up a review and redress process. Though the instances revealed by that review are shocking enough, bad advice motivated by a culture of selling was in fact broader in reach and went on longer than the regulatory process suggests.

The SIB, which the 1986 Act established as the agent of the Treasury to oversee the framework of the different self-regulatory bodies, did not start their review until 1994, that is, only after six years of continued mis-selling since the Act came into force. They decided they had no powers to do anything after the event for people who had been fleeced by heavy charges when they found they could not maintain pension contributions. All they could do after the event was ensure that anyone who suffered an actual loss by being advised to come out of an occupational scheme in favour of an inferior personal scheme was reimbursed for that loss. They also had powers to fine firms for administrative or procedural oversights and in many cases these were contributors to mis-selling.

Because of the emerging scale of the problem, they split the exercise into two phases, the first being people close to retirement and the second the rest. The SIB completed the first phase but the second is still going on under the supervision of the FSA and is not due to be completed before June 2002.

Both procedures only deal with the sale of products between 29 April 1988 and 30 June 1994. The dates are significant only because the SIB had no jurisdiction over the industry prior to the first date and after the second it assumed that the practice, once exposed, would not persist. Because personal pensions were being sold for up to two years before the first date, we can safely assume that there were victims in that period too. They have the normal recourse to the law if they wish to pursue the perpetrators. The abuses covered by the review were almost certainly covered by existing law.[16] However, it would probably be difficult and expensive to bring a successful action and I do not know of any. The FSA provides no help in this area.

The total number of claims for a review under both phases is just short of 2 million. When it came to calculating any compensation due, it was found that not all suffered actual loss. That it is not to say the advice was necessarily less negligent. It is safe to assume that virtually all transfers from occupational to personal pension schemes involved a high risk of detrimental outcomes. This is because the pension benefits are usually higher in a company scheme, the employer contributes all or something to your pension, there are often other benefits thrown in like life insurance or sickness cover and because the costs are usually much lower than in personal plans.

Compensation was based on actual outcomes rather then a broader concept of risk that might better measure the negligence of the advice. The compensation due is calculated using a complex procedure based on the cost of restoring the benefits to those that would have been available if they had stayed in their company scheme, based in most cases on actually being taken back into the scheme, or having not contracted out of SERPS. It was as though a reckless driver could only be charged with dangerous driving if he or she actually caused an accident.

What the total number of cases tell us is that between a quarter and one-third of all personal pension plans sold in the measured period were

---

[16] In his 1996 paper, 'Regulating Pensions: Too Many Rules, Too Little Competition' (published by the Institute of Economic Affairs), Standard Life's economic adviser, Professor David Simpson suggests action could have been taken under the Trade Descriptions Act 1968 (misleading descriptions), under the Misrepresentation Act 1967 (right to rescind a contract or claim damages) and under the Insurance Companies Act 1974 (reckless claims or statements made to induce a person to enter into a contract).

suspect. This proportion alone suggests that bad business practice was widespread rather than exceptional.

When we look at the blacklist of companies made to pay compensation and fines under Phase 1, it is plain that relying on blind trust in fine British institutions, which for most victims is exactly what they did rely on, could easily have ended up providing no protection at all. There is barely an insurance company in the life and pensions business that is not on the list. When we know all the facts about Phase 2 we will presumably see the same guilty parties, since the only difference between the two phases is the age of the victims.

Table 7.1 lists the 20 largest offenders, by number of plans sold rather than by size or compensation due. These are based on Treasury figures.[xvii]

Table 7.1 ■ Phase 1 mis-selling cases

Number of cases	Insurance company
Over 40,000	Prudential
30,000–40,000	Pearl
20,000–30,000	CIS, Lloyds TSB
10,000–20,000	Allied Dunbar, Legal & General, Royal London, Sun Life of Canada
8,000–10,000	Abbey Life, Britannic, Lincoln National, NatWest, Royal & SunAlliance, United Assurance
5,000–8,000	Barclays, Commercial Union, GAN, Guardian, London & Manchester, Standard Life

For both phases, it appears that the number of negligent company cases exceeds negligent IFA cases by about 11 to 1.[xviii] We cannot tell much from these numbers about the comparative extent of bad practice as between companies and advisers because we do not know how prevalent it was among the sales staff of the offending companies. Generally, blatant abuse was probably less prevalent amongst IFAs but was nonetheless not exceptional and was as likely to occur with the former national insurance brokers or firms that were members of (and regulated by) big 'networks' as by small independent operations in the high street. On any more general definition of unsuitability that takes into account the conditions of the products sold, going through an intermediary has definitely not assured protection.

This is anyway not a numbers game. Once bad practice becomes this prevalent, both among institutions with their own direct sales force and among IFAs, it is a significant risk for the customer. Because of the lack of regulatory warning and the complexity of the product, it was effectively very difficult for the customer to manage that risk by selecting providers and agents carefully.

What about the actual cost, as assessed by the regulators? Under Phase 1, a total of 717,000 investors were identified and 98 per cent have been informed of the outcome of their review. Of these, compensation totalling nearly £3.6 billion has been due to and accepted by 406,000 investors. The deadline for making claims under the procedure for Phase 2 was June 2000. The FSA's estimate six months later was that out of 1.2 million customers who had asked for a review there were grounds in over 800,000 cases. By that stage, about one-third had been assessed and compensation calculated. Based on experience to that point, the FSA estimated that the total bill for Phase 2 would be about £7.5 billion, making £12 billion in all. To the actual redress must be added the FSA's estimated £2 billion in administrative cost.[xix]

Allowing for the redress due but not pursued for plans mis-sold in the few years prior to the enactment of the regulations, the total cost of this one aspect of mis-selling might be in excess of £15 billion. To put this into perspective, this represents about 3 per cent of the average stock of assets managed by the life and pensions institutions during that period. We will return to this aspect when we look at the costs of personal pension contracts and the losses suffered by people who were unable to maintain their regular contributions. Though they have attracted less attention, the period over which they have been occurring is much longer and the cumulative costs are much higher.

Topping-up schemes

Associated with the scandal of recommending that members of occupational schemes take out private plans was the so-called mis-selling of free-standing additional voluntary contributions (FSAVCs). Additional voluntary contributions (AVCs) refers to the right of members of an occupational scheme to 'top-up' their funded benefits by making additional contributions to a separate fund or family of funds. The company sponsoring the pension plan usually selected a manager for their 'in-house' AVC plan (many selected Equitable Life). Members nonetheless had the right to make their additional contributions to a different scheme of their choosing, hence the FS for Free Standing. Mis-selling occurred when sales staff or advisers recommended FSAVCs in preference to AVC arrangements that provided higher benefits. The most blatant abuse took the form of talking people out of FSAVCs where the employer actually matched the employee's contributions!

The regulators were even slower to cotton on to this one so the period of the mis-selling review is also longer: from 29 April 1988 to 15 August 1999. The FSA has estimated that firms will have to review between 4 per cent and 8 per cent of FSAVCs sold in this period, with potential redress of between £95 million and £200 million.[xx] It stands to reason that the victims of this scam were generally far better off then the typical victim of pension mis-selling, had easier access to advice (including from their employer and in-house AVC manager) and so might be expected to be less vulnerable.

Endowment mortgage mis-selling

About 6 million households have chosen to repay their current mortgages with an endowment policy. That means that all they are paying to their lender on a regular basis is interest on the full amount of the loan. Over the life of the loan they separately pay money regularly into an insurance company investment fund in the expectation that the fund will accumulate to a large enough sum, with investment growth, to pay off the principal due at the end of the mortgage term. This investment plan is called an endowment policy. The insurance company sets the terms for those regular payments (which, naturally, they call premiums).

By definition, the choice of an endowment mortgage is an investment decision. Applying the language of Part I, it is a highly specific personal investment task characterized by a precise target, expressed in money terms (not real terms), at a precise time horizon with particular consequences associated with failure to hit the target at the right time.

Like pension mis-selling, there is both a broad and narrow view that can be taken of the form and scale of bad advice or deception associated with endowment sales in connection with mortgages. The broad view looks at the suitability of the contract, taking into account the same kind of inflexibility and hidden charges as were associated with pension contracts. The narrow view focuses on a technical definition of mis-selling that can in turn be associated with a measurable loss, as in the narrow view of pension mis-selling. However, the endowment mortgage is in a different category from pensions. Whereas pensions and investment are clearly inseparable, there is no requirement to use an investment product when taking out a mortgage. I believe this makes it a special case of institutionalized deception.

There is every reason to suppose that if endowment mortgage customers had understood exactly the nature of the gamble they were taking and the potential consequences, and if the range of potential outcomes had been properly quantified and premiums set appropriately, the vast majority would have opted for a repayment mortgage. This is not to assume they were necessarily risk averse or would in all circumstances avoid equity-type risk. At most levels of risk tolerance it is likely to be irrational to link mortgages and investment risk because the link itself creates specific risk features that are an addition to the normal market risk.

> AT MOST LEVELS OF RISK TOLERANCE IT IS LIKELY TO BE IRRATIONAL TO LINK MORTGAGES AND INVESTMENT RISK BECAUSE THE LINK ITSELF CREATES SPECIFIC RISK FEATURES

These features are the potentially serious and upsetting consequences of a shortfall (possibly including the forced sale of the family home); the dominance of the poorly predictable inflation risk over the more predictable real equity return risk (which we encountered in Part I); the way a shortfall emerges without warning when it is too late to do anything about it and the fact that the policyholder is powerless to manage the risk during the life of the loan.[17] You have to be a very sophisticated investor to be able to assess the gamble, and probably a wealthy one too, to be sure that any shortfall can be met by other assets rather than the sale of the family home. Sophisticated and wealthy is not the profile of the typical endowment policyholder. Yet the endowment mortgage has been by far the most popular form of repayment arrangement until, that is, it all started to go wrong in the last few years. Once the preferred option recommended by IFAs, most advisers now view it as too hot to handle. The proportion of new mortgages linked to an endowment policy

---

[17] We will see when we look at with-profits contracts in Chapter 9 that the option of linking the endowment to a with-profits fund (chosen in almost all cases) has not removed these specific risks and, with so much of the total policy payout coming from the discretionary terminal bonus, investors had very little early warning.

peaked in 1988 at 80 per cent before slumping to under 20 per cent recently.[xxi] Many of the main providers have stopped offering the product and others are likely to follow suit.

If it can so easily go wrong, and if it was always an irrational bet for the customer to make, how come they were so popular for so long? The answer is inextricably linked to the way they have been sold and why.

The endowment approach separates the interest and principal functions of the loan. Of the two, the choice of interest rate calculation, as between fixed and variable rate, will normally make a greater difference to the total cost than the choice of the repayment method. Though important to outcomes, the interest choice is widely assumed by professionals to be a gamble that is best left to the customer.

We may note in passing that any advice about the interest rate gamble is not in fact regulated. However, the additional costs of regulating it would be a bad use of what ultimately is the customer's own money if it is not subject to significant or institutionalized abuse. It is not. The reason there is no abuse is that there is no fee or commission to be earned by professionals for pushing the customer towards one gamble or the other. The agent is financially indifferent to the customer's choice.

Unfortunately, indifference does not apply to the choice of method for repaying the mortgage. This is because a sales person or adviser stands to earn nothing from a repayment mortgage except the small commission on the life insurance policy that most lenders require, whereas an endowment policy can earn them a commission of up to seven times more. Surprise, surprise! Where professionals choose to avoid involvement in one gamble that earns them no commission they have nonetheless universally sought to involve themselves in the other gamble that earns them commission.

For a long time the endowment gamble paid off. For much of the past 25 years endowment policies matured at levels sufficient to cover the loan and to generate a surplus. Achieved surpluses were great for marketing endowment mortgages. They could be presented as a goal in themselves, either as a 'useful little nest egg' or as a means of repaying the mortgage early.

Of course surpluses could have been achieved simply by setting the premiums too high but promotion of the endowment mortgage needed another element in the sales pitch: the premiums had to be low enough to be competitive with the total outgoings of a repayment mortgage. The industry cynically believed that the customer would only buy if there appeared to be a free lunch. Even making the comparison involved deception because for a repayment mortgage the interest rate, and hence total outgoings, was likely to be highly variable unless the borrower had elected for a fixed-rate mortgage and even then it might not remain fixed for the entire term.

For most of the 1980s, when endowment sales were at their peak, this balancing trick worked: past bonuses were good and total outgoings could be kept competitive. However, it was never a permanent basis for a preference for endowments. For the trick to work required particular outcomes for markets, interest rates and inflation. The actual outcomes, both before and after the balancing trick failed, were well within the range of what should have been expected and articulated. Had the full range of potential outcomes been quantified, and had borrowers signalled a preference for near certainty of reaching a minimum outcome in money terms sufficient to repay the mortgage (which would for most have been the rational preference), the required premiums at that level of certainty would have been so much higher as to blow the sales pitch out of the water. That is why we can be so certain that the majority would have turned them down.

The failure to form and communicate sensible expectations of the range of possible outcomes as the basis of risk preferences for each and every investment task is a more general failure of people and techniques that we will look at in Chapter 13. In terms of investment technique, we will see that the guilty parties are both the industry and the regulators, with the PIA having ultimate responsibility for the failure to understand how to calculate meaningful projection rates and how to apply these appropriately to the specific task of endowment mortgages. Once again, the regulator's emphasis on processes instead of products failed to protect, and actually harmed, the customer.

In common law, and in the FSA's interpretation of the regulations in place since 1988, it requires an actual breach of a company's duty of care to demonstrate a case of mis-selling. The fact that the entire endowment concept was fundamentally flawed is not enough. Consistent with common law, the FSA decided that a breach had occurred if the inherent nature of the investment risk had not been made clear to the buyer, if the risk preferences of the buyer had not been examined or if the product was incompatible with the risk preferences expressed by the buyer. Risk deception is the abuse we would expect to encounter if the product is complex and if the commission capacity is biased. In the analogy we used above, this is what would constitute dangerous driving. Whether the outcome of the unwitting gamble was a gain or a loss is equivalent to whether or not the reckless driver caused an accident. Unfortunately, the regulators have found it difficult to determine whether the risk was concealed or misrepresented, both because part of the selling process was verbal and because its own insistence on procedures had not prevented many firms from keeping woeful written records.

Through the FSA's independent body for consumer research, the Financial Services Consumer Panel, endowment policyholders were recently polled on their recollections of how they were sold their policies.[xxii] The Panel reported:

When asked directly what they recalled being told during the sales process, only one in ten policy-holders claimed they were told there was a risk the policy would not cover the mortgage in full. On the other hand only one in ten also claimed that they were told the policy was guaranteed to pay off their mortgage in full, but a further 44 per cent of policy-holders claimed they were told it would definitely pay off their mortgage and probably provide a surplus on top.

The idea that people were led to believe they were likely to achieve a surplus is not fanciful and rings true with all insiders I have discussed this with. It could be argued that the only justifiable basis for recommending an endowment policy is if the expectation was that there would be a surplus. There would be absolutely no point taking the risk relative to the certainty of a repayment mortgage unless there was an expectation of a return to compensate for the systematic investment risk, the specific risk features that characterize debt repayment tasks and the particular dangers of funding using a with-profits policy.

Even a presumption of an excess return, however, would not excuse a failure to draw attention to the range of outcomes around the mean expectation of a surplus, a range which of course includes shortfalls. Unless that is made clear, the customer could be forgiven for assuming that the risk smoothing inherent in a with-profits policy would effectively avoid a shortfall.

It is also consistent with common law that an actual loss must have been incurred for a complaint to be worth making since without it there can be no redress. The basis of redress for customers is immensely complex and undesirably judgemental, both of which are serious disadvantages relative to the pension reviews. The essence is a comparison with what would have occurred had the borrower elected to take the repayment option but judgement may be exercised by the provider in deciding whether the repayment option, as opposed to a different endowment with different terms, was the 'true' alternative. Moreover, in most but not all cases (also based judgementally on 'overall circumstances') the benefits of the repayment amounts being less than the endowment premiums will be offset against the loss arising from a notional switch from endowment to a repayment method.

Offers of compensation based on a customer having complained and the firm having investigated and applied the FSA's guidelines may, because of the elements of judgement involved, end up with the Ombudsman. He is likely to be very busy.

Do not be discouraged about taking your case to the Ombudsman if your complaint has been rejected by a firm quoting the FSA's guidance to firms about the imputation of willingness to bear the investment risk implicit in an endowment policy. This guidance was contained in a consultative paper sent to all firms in November 2000:

Other evidence may tend to shed light on likely attitude to risk. For example, this could include how much investment experience or involvement in the stock market the complainant had at the time. Evidence of holding other investments may suggest that the complainant was experienced in and likely to have understood the risks attached to an endowment or was not risk averse.[xxiii]

This is wrong because it assumes that all investment tasks are equal and hence that risk preferences, including the required certainty of achieving a particular target outcome, can be imputed from one to another. It also ignores the fact that debt repayment has a target that is fixed in money terms and so is highly dependent on the inflation rate. This does not apply to most long-term tasks that individuals fund using equities, where they are more concerned about the purchasing power of the money than in its nominal value – in other words it does not matter if nominal returns are very low provided inflation is also very low. For a mortgage repayment, low inflation and low returns can and did lead to shortfalls.

Though this muddled thinking about the risks was itself a major contributor to the industry's wholesale failure to set premiums correctly, the FSA is perhaps unwilling to impose an additional cost burden on the industry that rightly is the fault of the PIA itself. If so, it is the customer who pays.

The industry can, if it chooses, avoid this unpleasantness and the continuing erosion of consumer trust by making unconditional offers to make good out of their own reserves any shortfalls at maturity. So far the companies taking this route are attaching the condition that the achieved returns should be in excess of a certain level, typically 6 per cent per annum. It is not clear whether the Ombudsman would regard this as mitigating any responsibility to pay redress based on a review at this stage. What is clear is that it still leaves the policyholder exposed to a gamble they cannot easily assess. This unsatisfactory situation is a topic updated on our website.

The FSA's action, though far too late, has at least put in place an early warning system so policyholders will know how their policy stands in relation to the required capital sum. This takes the same form as the 'reprojection' letters sent to all policyholders: these show whether their policy is now projected to meet, fall short of or exceed the sum required to pay off the mortgage, given the investment growth rates laid down by the PIA and the actual expenses. If there is a projected shortfall, however, it is up to the customer to make his or her own arrangements to make up for it in some other way.

The FSA is also warning people to stop and think before they act and consider the merit of taking advice because doing the wrong thing now could easily be worse than the damage done by buying an endowment in the first place. The issues, to do with the nasty contractual terms of the policies and the possible loss of tax benefits, are well explained in the Consumer Help section of the FSA website. The options are not just as simple as selling a policy instead of surrendering it, though that may be good general advice.

▪ Pension income drawdown

THE BROADER CRITERION OF MIS-SELLING CATCHES ANOTHER ABUSE THAT HAS STARTED TO ATTRACT ATTENTION: SO-CALLED 'DRAWDOWN' PLANS IN CONNECTION WITH PERSONAL PENSIONS

The broader criterion of mis-selling that includes an in-built high probability of failure due to the combination of high charges and misrepresentation of the true return uncertainty catches another abuse that has started to attract attention: so-called 'drawdown' plans in connection with personal pensions.

There is nothing inherently wrong with taking advantage of the relatively recent right to postpone the conversion of your pension fund into an income stream at retirement via the mechanics of an annuity. In Part III we set out the advantages and a self-protection code for people opting for drawdown. Unfortunately, many flawed contracts have already been sold.

The essence of any drawdown task is that the fund has to grow by enough after withdrawing from it regularly to ensure that the balance does not run out before your need for income expires, such as at the completion of school fees or at your death. For pension drawdown, under the current legislation, you have to buy an annuity before or at age 75 so the target for the balance of the fund is whatever capital sum is likely to secure the annuity income you need at your required certainty.

When we look in Chapter 11 at the cost wedge that product charges drive into market returns, we will see that even typical charges consume a high proportion of the expected return. In the case of a pension drawdown, the target return is also eaten into by the increasing deterioration in annuity terms, known in the industry by the ugly phrase 'mortality drag'. This refers to a phenomenon many readers will be generally familiar with which is that as you live longer so at each point your expected date of death is later than it would have been at the earlier stage. All the incidents of earlier death drop out of the new sample and so it has marginally better survival prospects.

If you have entered into a pension income drawdown contract with an insurance company, as many have, which takes say 4 per cent or even more off the capital for setting it up, in addition to an annual charge, there is a high probability of a shortfall. This means that there is insufficient to achieve your target annuity income at age 75 or, if the annuity requirement is lifted, the capital may run out well before your death.

Such contracts are perfectly legitimate under the regulations. The rules only require that the commissions and other charges be disclosed. They also require disclosure of the implied market return that would cover the charges and mortality drag. Look for the so-called 'critical yield'. But the information you really need is the probability of achieving that yield and the associated risk of a shortfall. Otherwise, it is just a number and yet another confusing bit of jargon.

One of the reasons why insurance companies were able to get away with plan-breaking charges is the inflexibility of the contract. Until February 2001 you were unable to escape the clutches of whichever company provided your drawdown. Once again, the regulators were slow to spot the association between inflexible terms and charging rip-offs.

▨ Learning the lessons

There are at least eight lessons from the sorry story of product mis-selling.

1 It is unsafe to assume that just because financial institutions are selling something it must be safe.

2 Just because lots of other people are buying something does not make it right.

3 It is unsafe to be unaware of the nature and dynamics of market risk.

4 It is vital to relate market risk to the specific nature of a task and to think about consequences directly relevant to the task.

5 It is dangerous to trust sales representatives, particularly when masquerading as advisers.

6 It is naïve to deal with sales representatives or advisers without understanding their own agenda and motivation.

7 Relying on the regulators to put things right after they have gone wrong may not get you back everything you think you have lost.

8 Cutting corners at the point of purchase could tie up even more of your time trying to work out later what went wrong and what you can do about it.

8

The agenda benders

Advice and sales

Pulling over to the side of the road on Clifton Down above Bristol a few years ago, I made a quick call to the office of one of the country's better known and frequently quoted IFAs to get close-quarters directions. 'Oh,' said his secretary, 'you don't seem to have paid a fee. You can't see him without paying a fee.'

Excellent, I thought. Here is a man who knows that the price of independence is a fee not a commission – although it seemed a little strange to be asked to pay up front. I explained that actually I was not a client or even a prospective client. 'Oh no,' she said, 'it's providers who pay the fee.' It seems she had assumed I was representing an investment company and was coming to demonstrate why he should recommend my products to his clients. Had this been the case, I would have had to pay him first for the privilege of him even considering them. When I explained the purpose of our meeting she apologized and gave me the directions I needed.

I had just received a little reminder that it is impossible to know every trick in the book. Creative minds will always dream up a new one. As I dropped down the hill from the heights of Clifton for a series of meetings with IFAs, I wondered in how many respects I was leaving the high ground.

The fact is, the industry has long been mired in the conflicts of interest that arise from trying to be both salesmen and advisers. It is a peculiar feature of the retail investment industry that the functions of advice and selling are bundled together. It does not arise in many businesses and the two are universally seen as incompatible. When they are combined, deliberate misrepresentation and mistaken assumptions can both easily occur. In the investment industry it has always been seen as undesirable but it was considered unavoidable because separation of the two would otherwise push the total cost of investment products beyond the reach of many buyers. What this analysis failed to anticipate is that by bundling the two and lowering the customer's resistance to conflicting agenda, companies would end up getting away with even higher charges than if the two functions had been encouraged to grow separately. It would also have helped if the regulatory emphasis been on product design, furthering the goal of a low requirement for customized as opposed to generic advice.

Let us explore a simple analogy. If you think you have a medical need, you go to a doctor for a diagnosis and prescription for suitable treatment. You do not go direct to the drug companies. Neither do you imagine your doctor is in the pay of the drug companies – even if the surgery appears to be full of coffee mugs and calendars with drug brands emblazoned on them. You take it for granted that the drug companies are in the business of selling and doctors of advising. Unfortunately, in investment it is not as simple as choosing between two routes, like the drug companies or a doctor. Bear in mind that we saw that the majority of pension mis-selling abuses were perpetrated by company representatives, the equivalent of the drug companies. Yet many IFAs, whom you would hope were advisers like your doctor, mis-sold pensions. Most are also financially dependent on the product companies for much more than mugs and calendars. The companies calculate and collect their revenues and pay them over, provide marketing materials and other sales aids, offer conferences and training and we are even beginning to see them offering turn-key 'back-office' support for customer accounts.

> THE RESEARCHERS CAME UP WITH EVIDENCE THAT ONLY 14 PER CENT HAD USED AN IFA, YET OVER 56 PER CENT THOUGHT THEY SHOULD USE ONE FOR 'COMPLICATED' PRODUCTS

In 1999 the FSA commissioned a market research report of consumer attitudes among household 'decision makers' for financial services.[xxiv] The answers show that people are confused and put off by the different guises of the firms they can deal with and this leads to self-evident inconsistencies. The researchers came up with evidence that only 14 per cent had used an IFA, yet over 56 per cent thought they should use one for 'complicated' products, and even 41 per cent thought they should use one for any products. Of those who had used an IFA, one-third did not shop around – but then they did not shop around when selecting companies to buy from direct either. Buyers are behaving as if the differences between selling and advising are not detectable or not important. We could interpret this as an enlightened appreciation that IFAs are themselves tainted by the same selling culture as product companies but I believe that is not consistent with the indicated awareness of the merit of using an IFA. It is also too rational to be consistent with the general impression given by the survey, which points to confusion, laziness and annoyance at complexity rather than genuine attempts to understand and exploit the system.

At the heart of the problem of combining advice and sales are commissions: the one big difference between the typical IFA and your doctor.

Commissions

Commission conflicts are as old as time. From their origins as the sole gateway to capital markets, stockbrokers have had to balance their clients' expectations of regular and watchful advice over a personal portfolio of holdings against their own earnings arising from the individual trades they can successfully recommend.

The best recommendation for a stock portfolio might be to do nothing for long periods of time – what Benjamin Graham, doyen of securities analysis and portfolio management in the 1950s, described as 'inactivity bordering on lethargy'. But Graham was not a broker and if he had been he might have starved without persuading his clients of the merit of activity since it was only on the purchase or sale of a security that he would have earned a commission. This conflict has been partly resolved by stockbrokers increasingly moving to asset-based fees instead of relying on brokerage – although they may of course be benefiting now from both!

The conflict between advice and sales is nowhere more acute than in the world of products rather than portfolios. It is a conflict that exists whether products are sold direct or through agents. A survey of companies selling direct to the public undertaken in 1997 by the trade journal *Financial Adviser* found that nine out of ten of their sales representatives relied on selling commissions for part of their earnings. Even Equitable Life, often held up as being above the commission fray because it would not pay commissions to IFAs, paid them to its own sales staff.

We have already seen that selling commissions contributed to the mis-selling of pensions and mortgage endowments by rewarding quantity irrespective of quality. In the case of pensions, selling incentives interfered with judgement about what action (or inaction) was in the best interests of the customer. In the case of endowment mortgages, the ability to earn a commission that was not otherwise available led to large-scale preference for an unnecessary and irrational product. It is a logical extension of these commission distortions that differences in rates of commission paid by different providers to agents for essentially the same product should also influence the recommendations of those agents. It would be naïve to assume any different.

The Myners Report to the Treasury on institutional investment called for a similar review of the retail investment industry and the government quickly conceded. One of the most persuasive reasons was that when undertaking his review Paul Myners (Chairman of Gartmore Investment Management which itself straddles both retail and institutional business) was repeatedly told that sales of essentially common retail products were distorted by commission differences. That is to say that where product attributes are essentially the same, sales volumes appear to be associated with the different amounts of commission they pay. He was right to highlight any such association as being a distortion of an efficient market in investment products. He is also right to highlight the essential commonality of products that means that any patterns of association with commission differences can reliably be interpreted as proof of bias.

The idea that different versions of the same product are essentially common is one that buyers may at first resist. The industry has done everything in its power to conceal commonality and attach significance to product-specific attributes. The reason is that if we thought they were readily substitutable one for another without making any significant difference we would then expect lower prices and different channels of distribution – in much the same way that we have particular expectations about how baked beans or cornflakes should be sold.

Though the regulators would have protected us better by encouraging us to see that products are really commodities, instead they came up with a process called 'best advice'. This requires advisers to justify the products they recommend. Justification is essentially by their 'suitability' for the client but the process inevitably implies that the research effort and hard-nosed selection criteria that advisers describe in their 'reasons why' letters are meaningful. The very process gives an official stamp of approval to the pretence that product attributes are different and the differences meaningful. It explains why companies continue to invest heavily in brand promotion, a cost that is inevitably passed on to the customer. This charade applies particularly to past performance differences, whether it is the track record of a unit trust or the total policy payout record of with-profits contracts. We go on to expose this charade in later chapters.

IF COMMISSIONS DID NOT INFLUENCE MONEY FLOWS, WHY ELSE WOULD PRODUCT COMPANIES OFFER ADVISERS SPECIAL TERMS TO SELL THEIR PRODUCTS

If commissions did not influence money flows, why else would product companies offer advisers special terms to sell their products, often to compensate for other disincentives to sell, such as a poor performance patch or a less well recognized consumer brand? Why wouldn't some advisers be influenced by an uplift of commission from the standard 3 per cent to say 4 per cent or even more? A 1 per cent difference becomes a 33 per cent increment! Why else do the larger IFAs, particularly the big networks, try to extract higher commission rates on their business unless they plan to concentrate their business on those products?

▨ Whose money is it anyway?

The commission distortion always used to be a function of front-end-loaded sales charges and this remains a widespread practice even though competition is finally increasing customer resistance to loads. It has taken a new twist in recent years with what is called renewal or 'trail' commissions. This means that an adviser will continue to be paid a commission, usually at a rate of 0.5 per cent per annum, for as long as the client holds the product and for as long as the adviser retains the agency for that client. Unlike front-end loads, that come out of the client's money as it passes from client to company, trails are paid to the adviser as a rebate of part of the product company's annual management charge.

However, you should not read too much into this distinction as many companies offering trails will also be charging front-end loads and retaining the full amount instead of paying most of it to the selling agent. They are making an accounting switch between two types of charge but it is still your money your agent is being bribed with.

Many product companies offer IFAs trails but the terms are not universal and this is why they are an important addition to the distortions in the marketplace. Some do not pay trails at all and if it is a low-cost product the trail will not be as much as for a higher-cost product. This can clearly interfere with an IFA's judgement about the merit of recommending low-cost index funds, for instance. Different companies will also vary the trade-off they offer between front-end commissions and trail commissions, as an IFA has to choose between them or to mix them. What they cannot have is the full benefit of both.

Trail commissions are profit maximizers for IFAs provided they assume they can retain the customer's agency for long enough. It is a simple discounted cash flow calculation. They have other advantages. They were demanded by IFAs partly as a response to the regulators' keener eye on commission 'churning', where IFAs could maximize profits by recommending clients sell funds on which they had already paid a front-end load and then buy something else that also paid another load. They could fall back on any number of pretences, under the misnomer of 'best advice', to justify this in each case. If they were doing it too often, however, the regulator could impose heavy fines. Trail commissions meant they could spin out an income stream from the same fund without having to risk an accusation of churning.

Trail commissions have also been preferred because they are more opaque. Most customers are not even aware of them. If they are aware, the IFA may be tempted to reassure them that they are better value because they come out of the company's annual management charge not out of the customer's money. Besides, it is only half a per cent. In Chapter 11, The Cost Wedge, we will see that costs that may appear to be very small actually consume a significant proportion of the systematic market reward. Every half per cent counts.

Selling the customer

One of the ways customers come to deal with an IFA is by referral from their solicitor or accountant. Such referrals are a major source of new business for IFAs and courting introductions from professional firms is a major thrust of most IFAs' marketing approach. What is not widely appreciated is that the professional who effects the introduction may well be taking a share of the commissions generated by the IFA on your business. The Law Society has effectively prevented this practice by its overriding requirement that solicitors account to clients for every specific commission received. Most accountants who do not have their own financial planning practice are willing to sell your business for commissions, without you realizing or being offered the commission because commissions are not treated by their Institutes as belonging to the customer.

This not only distorts efficient markets in financial advice but also helps to perpetuate the practice of living off commissions instead of fees since many accountants appear to prefer initial commissions because they are easier to account for. The FSA seems wisely to want to apply the Law Society's approach to all introducers. If introducers want to pocket any commissions or share of fees from fund managers or product producers they will have to tell the customer it is his or her money and ask them each time, specific to the amount, if they can instead retain it. That should ensure that in future money has to be earned, for a proper service provided.

▧ Economic conflicts

In the investment-management industry profit maximization is typically about getting people to buy what you want them to buy. Profits are highly sensitive to economies of scale. If you can sell more of the same, it is much more profitable than selling something different. This economic reality is fundamentally opposed to the customer's need for customized investment strategies, particularly at the level of asset allocation.

In many cases, such as with-profits funds and large unit trusts, the disadvantage of standardization does not even lead to offsetting cost savings to the customer as firms realize that in large pools the further asset gain from lowering price is negligible.

Business risk affects the behaviour of companies in other ways that clash with clients' interests. Readers may already have noticed that in the area of equity management the competition takes the form of a race between firms in which the customer can appear little more than spectator. This is the impression given by the way funds are marketed but it is also true of the portfolio-management approach. How the manager runs the race is dictated more by the commercial risks associated with different outcomes than it is by the customer's expectations.

In a large unit trust, it has been shown that new business is not particularly sensitive to excess performance (perhaps because advisers and the public both think that it is easier for a small and flexible fund to outperform). Profit maximization therefore leads to the avoidance of relative performance bets because the priority is to retain the existing unit holders. Risking messing up their position in the league table is not very sensible if they stand to lose more assets if it goes wrong than they can expect to gain if it goes right. This business risk leads to the 'herding' tendency that is also common in institutional fund management and which was one of the reasons why the Myners Report was commissioned.

Applying the same logic but with different observed payoffs, managers will typically take bigger investment risks with new funds. If it goes right, they stand to gather a very large amount of additional assets but if it goes badly, they do not risk much current income (there is not much to risk) and in due course the fund can be quietly closed down or merged with another.

It is not only firm risks that can interfere with the client's agenda. Individual portfolio managers can also act on the basis of how they perceive their career risk, hence treating bets made with clients' money as their own career bets.

What are known as 'agency conflicts' have become a serious area for academic research involving light-hearted themes such as 'game theory' and 'tournaments'. Though the detail is beyond the scope of this book, for those who are interested in the behavioural dimensions of finance there is more on the website under the heading Agency Conflicts.

9

With-profits: broken contract

Fit for all or fit for none?

The dodo was done for before the seventeenth century was out. Friendly and approachable, its survival was handicapped by its clumsiness and stupidity. In Australia the with-profits fund, also friendly but clumsy, was killed off before the twentieth century was out. In Britain, where its numbers suggest the with-profits species continues to thrive, man nonetheless threatens its extinction and few outside the breeding community are left to defend it.

INVESTING THROUGH THE VEHICLE OF A WITH-PROFITS POLICY FROM AN INSURANCE COMPANY BRINGS TOGETHER THE WORST FEATURES OF INSURANCE FIRMS

Investing through the vehicle of a with-profits policy from an insurance company brings together the worst features of insurance firms that make them the wrong people to put between your money and the markets. They bring all the ugly features of confusion marketing, concealed charges, inflexibility and swingeing penalties for early surrender that we encountered in previous chapters. The unbridled discretion that life companies operate with gives them unparalleled opportunities to put their own commercial agenda above the interests of customers. They are riddled with agenda conflicts between different classes of policyholders and, in firms with shareholders, between policyholders and owners. They operate with a culture of 'deceit by numbers' and the biggest target of their deceit is gullible IFAs. They introduce elements of principal risk that are rarely if ever properly appreciated until something goes wrong and it is too late. They work against the customization of market exposure and risk tolerances. They make it all too easy for naïve or unscrupulous sales people and financial advisers to misrepresent the nature of the risks of stock market investment. This bird is begging for extinction.

We are not alone. The FSA had already undertaken to carry out a review of with-profits contracts when the Myners Report on institutional investment made problems associated with this widely sold product a key reason for urging on the chancellor a full review of personal investment products. The well-respected 'independent expert' Ned Cazalet was responsible for many of the observations that Myners made. He has made a business out of analyzing and restating life company and with-profits financial statements to get behind the gamesmanship they play with regulators, advisers and policyholders. The Consumers' Association, publishers of *Which?*, produced a highly critical review early in 2001, stung into action partly by the loss of a law suit it had supported against AXA over how excess reserves should be shared between policyholders and shareholders. The Institute and Faculty of Actuaries, the professional body for the people who manage the financial mathematics of with-profits funds, has acted as a forum for reasoned criticism, as well as for proposals for reform. At an actuarial conference in 2000, 75 per cent of attendees thought with-profits had 'no future in their current form'.[xxv]

The problems of the Equitable Life have also done much to drag the entire with-profits concept into disrepute, although ironically Equitable is not representative of the typical with-profits company. Having tried to escape the image of the pedestrian dodo and substitute that of a soaring swift, Equitable's demise was specifically self-inflicted, the product of a fatal combination of errors of judgement and extreme under-reserving. As a highly public failure, Equitable has nonetheless served to let the light in on a sector that has preferred to remain in the dark. The book's website will cover issues affecting equitable policyholders as well as lessons for with-profits investors generally.

The grip of with-profits on the existing stock of wealth is impressive. In 1999 life insurance companies managed £900 billion of assets of which three-quarters were for individuals. Their share of total personal sector holdings of long-term savings and investments was about 40 per cent. Half of that, £400 billion in total, was through their with-profits funds, the rest being in unit trusts or unit-linked products. The number of policies written on the assets of the with-profits funds was around 10 million.[xxvi]

Any product that accounts for 20 per cent of the stock of personal investments has by definition to be popular. Yet with-profits are also non-exclusive, with policyholders ranging from people who might have felt drawn to the humble social origins of the Prudential's first customers to accountants and lawyers who were drawn to the Equitable's focus on high-earning clients in the professions. The popularity of the product in the last 30 years reflects the fact it has been packaged to fulfil three different roles: as a vehicle for personal pensions, as a way of paying off a mortgage and as a free-standing investment for no particular task, in which guise it is often called an 'investment bond'.

The connection between with-profits and each of these purposes is not an obvious one and reflects an industry-serving focus on maximizing product sales and simplifying choice rather than genuine suitability or universality. As we shall see, the features specific to with-profits contracts are not obviously valuable in the particular uses to which they have been put. To be able to position the product as universally appealing for as long as it did, the industry had to make every use of its commission-fuelled distribution channels and institutionalize a false description of their risks relative to alternative investments.

The upside and downside of principal risk

What makes a with-profits policy different from other pooled investment vehicles is that a financial institution inserts itself between you and the markets, not just as agent but as principal. As we shall see, this makes a big difference.

The upside of risking your capital with a life company rather than directly in the markets is that the life company offers you some risk protection. This takes three forms:

1 The company engineers a 'smooth' emergence of the investment return over the life of the policy, in contrast to the volatile 'real world' path of investment returns. This takes the form of declared 'reversionary' (usually annual) bonuses added to the policy 'value'. Reversionary bonuses do not normally alter by large amounts from

year to year, whereas the actual return path for equities and bonds often does.

2 To give more than hollow significance to this bookkeeping emergence of returns, it actually guarantees each new level of the cumulative policy return. Bonuses, once declared, cannot be withdrawn (provided the policy is held to maturity).

3 When the policy matures, the company may also smooth the impact of any sharp movement in the underlying asset value, cushioning those who would otherwise have seen a loss of market value at the expense of those who would otherwise have enjoyed a greater gain.

Rather than seeing the life company as the generous provider of this risk cushion, it is more realistic to see it as a mutual sharing of market risk between policyholders. It is to engineer these bookkeeping 'transfers', or 'cross-subsidies', that the company has to act as the principal between the owner and the markets. The pool of money that can be used to make them comes partly from shareholders' funds and mainly from policyholders' funds or, in the case of the mutual companies, solely from policyholders' funds. If the pool is to remain roughly constant over time, the cross-subsidies must balance out. Companies cannot keep running down or building reserves indefinitely.

There is another historical aspect of the principal role that is often overlooked. Traditionally, a with-profits policy return was not limited to the return on the invested capital but also benefited from profits (or losses) in the business of the life company that was conducted for the 'without-profits' investors, such as pure life business, annuities, or even some general insurance business. This entrepreneurial role explains, for example, why with-profits policyholders have ended up meeting nearly all the bill for pensions mis-selling even in the shareholder-owned companies. It may be annoying to discover that management's errors are mainly borne by the policyholders instead of the shareholders (or even the managers themselves), but it goes with the territory.

The downside of investing in a with-profits business instead of having direct exposure to the markets takes several forms:

1 It leads to a lack of clarity over legal rights, accountability and the limits of discretion. Though this does not necessarily lead to abuse, it requires a high level of trust. It can also entail conflicts that are difficult or impractical to reconcile.

2   Risk sharing and offering guarantees puts the company at risk and so to protect the public from the possibility of insolvency the authorities impose a regulatory framework. The permanent effect is to lower the expected systematic investment return but in particular circumstances it may also interfere with the market dynamics in a way that further lowers returns.

3   The company adopts an asset mix that is both generally unsuitable for most tasks and specifically vulnerable to distortion by the solvency regulations.

4   By promoting the false concept of a universal product with a universally suitable investment strategy, with-profits contracts do nothing to address investors' limited education in investment matters and actively discourage individual responsibility for personal investment decisions and the management of personal risks.

5   The complex economics of smoothing provide a smokescreen for misleading investors about the true level of investment risk.

6   Exposure to principal risk needs to be diversified (as many Equitable policyholders have found out the hard way).

A key characteristic of both sets of features is that they depend on trust: first, that the risk reduction benefits are significant and dependable and, second, that the companies and intermediaries will not exploit the smoke-screen to act unfairly or further their own interests. Is there a basis for that trust?

▨ 'Where mystery begins, justice ends'

I do not believe the political philosopher Edmund Burke had life companies in mind with this remark but the application is perhaps less controversial than the analogy he actually made, which was with religion. The mysteries of faith are probably not mutually exclusive but in the case of life companies it has proved difficult in practice to equate opaqueness with public confidence in fairness.

It may be that this is just a sign of the times and that the modern consumer values individual entitlements more than the collective pooling of entitlements that were part of the original spirit of the life companies, particularly the mutuals. It could be that the erosion of trust in financial institutions generally makes the wide discretion of the life companies inappropriate, as consumers today are likely to assume wide discretion is being abused, even if it is not. It could even be that we were all happy when we were completely in the dark, but as soon as some light was let in we needed to see everything.

The mystery begins in a with-profits policy because your investment return is at the discretion of the life company rather than a direct and enforceable function of the return on the money they have invested for you. Not only is the company not required to tell you how the money has been invested or what it has earned, but it also does not tell you what else has led to your policy return.

The suspicion is that it has been marketing objectives, not the original risk pooling purpose, that have explained the way pay-outs have been decided. This is what we should expect as competition for new business takes place largely on the basis of comparisons of standard policy types for common maturities, such as 10-, 15- or 25-year policies. This means the companies can manipulate pay-outs on maturing policies to suit whatever they currently want to promote. Benefiting from risk sharing then takes the form of a lottery based on events beyond your control and irrelevant, you would think, to your money. The discretion written into the companies' rules (and to which individual contracts refer) is not typically constrained as to the purpose of the cross-subsidies. Nor is it constrained as to their extent, such as between members of the current 'generation' of policyholders or between different generations.

The question of 'justice' is more complex than just fairness. As the Equitable case has shown, there are likely to be conflicts between the contractual rights of individual policyholders or classes of policyholders and the exercise of well-intentioned principles of fairness. Trying to resolve just such an issue took the Equitable and its representative policy-holder, Mr Hyman, to three courts before it was finally resolved: the High Court, the Court of Appeal and the House of Lords. In the end the definitive judgment turned on a 'necessary' interpretation of an 'implied term'. Narrowly technical and highly complex in its logic, the judgment will not easily command respect not just because it did not turn on a principle but also because, by the law lords' own admission, it actually implied a less fair outcome than the one the directors had preferred. Inherently unsatisfactory as 'the last word', it may not even be much help resolving similar conflicts in other life offices where the contractual terms are not identical.

What the three hearings show, even if you accept the final judgment and ignore the disagreements, is that you cannot properly condemn any single guilty party (notwithstanding the lynch-mob mentality of many financial journalists and policyholders) because the problem of insoluble conflict is intrinsic to the with-profits contract and is truly institutionalized. This is so because life companies use a single fund to construct many different product contracts and because the essential feature of smoothing, when combined with tough reserve requirements on enforceable entitlements, requires both wide management discretion and the avoidance of tightly defining, let alone quantifying, the basis of their discretion.

There is a movement afoot within the insurance industry to rescue the reputation of with-profits policies by full disclosure of each individual's 'asset share'. This is normally understood to mean the policyholders' 'unit' value or fair share based on the underlying investment performance of their own investments, before smoothing and before all other forms of transfer of value between different policyholders (although the House of Lords judgment curiously referred to it as the value of premiums paid plus the investment return *after* smoothing).

You can think of it as equivalent to the value of your units in a unit trust. But will removing the smoke and mirrors make people more likely to accept the gamble of whether differences relative to fair share are in their favour or run against them? Might it not be a recipe for making the divisions that now scar the Equitable's policyholders a permanent feature of the entire industry? Maybe with-profits only work if you know you cannot find out whether you won or lost.

The real risks of risk sharing

It is time to apply the understanding of market behaviour and the decision hierarchy that we gained in Part I. A life company's with-profits fund is typically invested in equities (about 80–90 per cent which in some cases may include some property) with a small allocation to conventional fixed income investments. This is 100 per cent investment in risky assets, suitable for people with long-term horizons and willing to accept a wide range of potential outcomes.

Knowing this asset allocation, think about this description of with-profits bonds from one of the largest discount brokers: 'They are cautious investments which should be compared to deposit accounts or National Savings: if you are willing to accept a higher level of risk over a long duration of time then you may be better off in a conventional stock market fund such as a unit trust or OEIC.' For such a statement to be honest, whatever it is the directors are doing to transform stock market risk into something much less risky, it must have the effect of making the range of policy pay-outs much narrower than it would be through direct exposure to markets. The pretence that smoothing the annual bonuses reduces risk is not enough. This has long since been undone by the greater proportional importance, and uncertainty surrounding, the terminal bonus. This reached about 60 per cent of the total pay-out. The typical emergence of return should not be described as less volatile just because 40 per cent of the total is nice and linear!

Advisers may have been fooled by the change in design of with-profits since the 1980s which means many now include in their terms the right to apply a 'market value adjustment' (MVA) even to reversionary bonuses. This means that these declared bonuses are not actually guaranteed and can be clawed back via the MVA to prevent a policyholder cashing in and taking much more out of the fund than can be justified by their asset share. These so-called 'unitized' policies enable the life company to hold smaller reserves against declared bonuses because they are not in fact guaranteed, invest more in equities and keep the apparent value of the policy much closer to the path of the underlying investments. All three can be used as good selling points. The notional path of returns can still be presented as nice and linear, but it does not actually reduce risk because it can be taken away again. In modern unitized policies the ability of the life office to protect policyholders from adverse outcomes by not implementing MVAs depends on the scale of reserves and how the directors choose to use them. In that sense they are not fundamentally different from traditional policies.

In both cases, the potential to protect investors from stock market risk has been widely misundestood or deliberately misrepresented. The correct position is this:

1 With-profits cannot turn equity-type risks into National Savings-type risks.

2 They may not reduce the range of outcomes relative to direct investment at all, particularly in those circumstances where risk reduction will be most prized.

3 There are possible circumstances in which the range of outcomes will actually be widened.

These three statements flow logically from the proportional relationship between reserves and invested funds and from the dynamics of that relationship in light of the characteristics of market and inflation behaviour we observed in Part I. It would be going too far to say that they were common sense but they certainly follow from a sound understanding of investment principles. Any idea that equity-type returns can be achieved without equity-type risk is also one that should immediately offend the streetwise investor's instincts.

The assumption that risk will be reduced is based on a simplistic interpretation of how the life companies use their smoothing power and how markets behave. Both are better suited to the days when life companies mainly held fixed income bonds. The idea is that in a good year they hold back and in a bad year they cushion losses.

But in Part I we saw that the profile of equity market returns is not as simple as that. We know, first, that returns are not just volatile but may also show either short-lived swings or long runs of good or bad years and we cannot predict which. We know, second, that changes in inflation, also poorly predictable, make a big difference to the typical size of investment returns in any period and may overwhelm any predictable trend of returns in real terms. These features have very different consequences for the economic risk and fairness of the smoothing process.

During the 1980s rising markets were only briefly punctuated by periods of falls and so smoothing led to a build-up of reserves above fair or prudent levels. During the 1990s lower inflation reduced nominal returns but we escaped any long bear markets. It is long bear markets that run down reserves and the combination of bear markets and falling inflation that runs them down fastest. There is no natural law in the behaviour of stock markets that suggests the profile of up and down markets will conveniently permit either a meaningful level of risk-sharing or fairness in risk-sharing.

The problem of the particular profile over time of changes in market and inflation trends is magnified when reserves have also been used to achieve marketing purposes. This is an obvious temptation, particularly when benevolent markets have led to high reserves. It shows up in strings of good years when maturing policies for almost all time periods have been excellent by historical standards yet pay-outs still benefit from additions from reserves. This can easily mean there is no cushion left to protect policyholders from any subsequent string of bad years.

It is also perfectly possible for the cushion in a bad market to lead quite quickly to incidents of lower returns, not higher returns, than if the policy-holders had been direct investors. This is most likely to arise where reserves start out being low, where pressure to cushion terminal bonus declarations is high, bad equity markets persist and interest rates stay low. What then happens is that reserves have to be rebuilt at a time of market weakness.

Just because this has not arisen often does not mean it cannot or will not happen. It is entirely consistent with the recent history of market behaviour, inflation and bonus policies.

The adverse impact of low inflation on bonuses and solvency risk is already taxing the minds of the actuarial profession. In 1999 a working party was set up by the Institute and Faculty of Actuaries to analyze the broad implications of low inflation on investment products. They constructed a model of life-company profitability and tested what would happen in different low inflation scenarios to 'statutory solvency', the litmus test for a life company to continue to trade.[18]

THE ADVERSE IMPACT OF LOW INFLATION ON BONUSES AND SOLVENCY RISK IS ALREADY TAXING THE MINDS OF THE ACTUARIAL PROFESSION

The actuaries categorized firms as strong, average or weak (based on their 'free assets' or smoothing pool), assumed a bonus policy that firms would feel under pressure to adhere to because of policyholders' reasonable expectations and projected positive outcomes over ten years.

Their model showed there was at least a 60 per cent probability of statutory insolvency for weak companies, even with inflation no lower than 4.7 per cent. Average companies faced a 22.4 per cent probability of insolvency at 2.5 per cent inflation, rising to 36.4 per cent at –0.5 per cent inflation. Strong companies faced a 6 per cent probability at 2.5 per cent inflation rising to 15 per cent at –0.5 per cent inflation. Without smoothing, though, the insolvency risk for all companies was negligible (at under 7 per cent at all levels of inflation tested).

The actuaries make several comments that customers (and certainly their advisers) should be aware of. They concluded that 'this work shows that very low inflation could cause significant problems for with-profits offices'. They recommended that 'it would be preferable to align long-

---

[18] In practice, the regulation of British life assurance companies, which closely monitors their solvency, has prevented failures. When companies are at risk, they tend to be merged or the funds closed and run off, as we saw when Equitable was at risk. Solvency protection nonetheless carries a cost, as the effect of being forced to strengthen reserves will tend to weaken long-term returns.

term policy pay-out to asset share rather than overpaying' but conceded this might conflict with 'reasonable expectations'. They cautioned that projections made at the time a policy was taken out might still prove to be over-optimistic. For new policies, with realistic projections, they note that charges 'at current levels based on this type of investment might not look attractive to the potential policyholder'. Bonuses are not the only aspect of with-profits that look exposed when returns are low!

In spite of the risks of overpaying, the evidence points towards a continued pattern of pay-outs in excess of asset share since the working party reported. The magazine *Money Management* regularly reviews with-profits pay-outs by comparing them with the underlying returns of the life companies' own managed, balanced funds (which are unit trusts with quite similar asset-allocation strategies). The comparative pattern has, they maintain, acted as a good proxy of whether reserves are being run down or built up. Their analysis points to a string of overpayments since 1995, briefly reduced for policies maturing in 1998 but with policies maturing as recently as July 2000 again overpaying. This is arising in spite of steady cuts in reversionary bonuses, in line with interest rates, throughout the period and in spite of markets mostly them being near record levels in both nominal and real terms.

Risk and holding period outcomes

Even if we believed that smoothing does reduce the range of policy outcomes at maturity, it would only apply if the policy were held until maturity. What we have seen in previous chapters is that policies are not normally held to maturity. In those cases, the risk-reduction benefits are lost completely. This is a major plank of the Consumers' Association's argument against with-profits:

Most consumers on long-term contracts, however, will never benefit from high terminal rates or smoothing – the key features of with-profits – as they are only realised at the end of the contract. It is estimated that on 25-year contracts, only 30 percent of policyholders maintain payments until maturity. Nearly half of these endowments are surrendered within ten years, yet policyholders face huge penalties if they surrender or transfer their fund in the early years.[xxvii]

For unitized policies, the same applies. Policyholders will be able to cash in early more easily but there will not be the reserves to allow more than a few quick or lucky ones to take out more than their fair share.

▨ Mismatching the asset mix

In Part I, we identified asset allocation as the key to organizing efficient and customized task-based investment plans. With-profits policies impose an 'average' asset mix on all policyholders, regardless of purpose, targets, time horizon or personal risk preferences. This mix is partly a historical accident and partly a function of the changing financial strength of a company, itself reflecting both the actions of its board and whatever happens to markets and inflation. Thus differences in financial strength between companies at any time will also tend to show up as differences at that time in the asset mix. Strong companies can invest more in equities and less in fixed income.

The solvency regulations have also prevented companies from diversifying fully abroad and from obtaining part of that diversification from exposure to foreign currencies. Portfolio theory treats international investing as a good thing but solvency rules treat it as a dangerous mismatch of assets and liabilities.

The inflexibility of the with-profits contract means that the investor has no way of managing risk exposure during the life of the contract. You are stuck with whatever asset mix the fund chooses and you cannot alter the total exposure to that mix (such as by switching to a different company) without risking penalties under your contract. Unitized policies do increase your flexibilty, however, allowing you to salvage more of your fair share of the fund than the early surrender or even sale of an older policy. However, ease of exit also means the stability of the funds is less: more could leave the fund as a result of Equitable-type scares, fear of further market falls or a general distrust of with-profits. So while unitized policies use their freedom to hold more in equities, they may find themselves, like any unit trust, forced to sell them prematurely to meet redemptions. Matching is not so easy when you insert agents between investors and the markets. If the investment environment and the policyholders both become more awkward this will be a regular nightmare for life company fund managers and will surely carry a cost.

▨ The value of information

We can take it as a sign of a healthy product market if there is information available that allows us to make rational selection choice. In 1999 I researched with-profits fund published data to see if I could find any relationships that would allow an individual or their financial adviser to predict with any confidence whose policies would do well and whose badly.

If I were an IFA advising on with-profits policies, analysis of historical figures is the sort of work that customers would expect me to perform. The regulators might also want to check that I had done some detailed analysis before making any recommendation of a particular life company, to demonstrate 'best advice'. In my 'reasons why' letter to my client, I would refer to the analysis that supported my selection of one or more companies.

It might look impressive but it would be a meaningless sham. I found no reliable basis for predicting future relative policy pay-outs. The implication was that the research is a waste of time and, for those who buy in insurance company data and research services, a waste of money.[19]

The bankruptcy of the published data stems from the combination of three factors:

1 the fact that the underlying relative investment performance is itself a lottery (as we shall see in the next chapter)

2 the excessive discretion of life-company actuaries

3 the very long-term view (10 to 25 years) that is required for with-profits outcomes.

I found no predictability in the information available about past policy pay-outs and financial strength measures. These two feature most prominently in IFAs' research. Certainly there was evidence that some offices that do well in one period do badly in the next – unhappy outcomes for most IFAs – but unfortunately they are just as likely to do well again or move towards the average: another lottery.

Whereas the policy pay-outs are at least hard numbers, there is considerable freedom for companies to massage their financial ratios – freedom they readily seize. There is also scope over the term of a policy for any genuine advantage of financial strength to be blown by grand management schemes to boost new business or enter new markets or by poor management of the assets. The biggest threat to industry financial

---

[19] See With-profits on the website for some of the output of this analysis. I hope that people in the industry will respond, via the website, to the challenge in this chapter to the practical value of analysis of with-profits funds.

strength is that with-profits funds will be providing much of the risk capital for companies wishing to play the stakeholder pensions game. According to Cazalet, only about eight companies will make money out of stakeholder pensions but there are 48 planning to compete.[xxviii] If he is right, a lot of policyholder's capital will be destroyed and the numbers are far from trivial – Standard Life is committing £1 billion, for instance.

I also found no relationship between the pay-outs and asset mix – until, that is, it was too late to do anything about it (remember that these are both long-term and highly inflexible products). I found no relationship between life company costs and performance.

It is not only the information about the company as a whole that is of little value. When existing policyholders are trying to decide whether to add to their policies or stop them they are totally dependent on unverifiable information provided by the company. This has to be taken on trust. But there has already been a run on the reserves of trust in the entire with-profits concept and it is far from clear that anything can, or should, be done to rebuild them.

10

The performance lie

Stars in their eyes

Looking down on the City of London and across the sweep of Westminster, your eye following the line of the Thames snaking towards a hazy horizon, it was easy to imagine how the directors of NatWest, in this very room or one close to it, could have believed totally in their designs to be the biggest in this, the best in that. Even the view exuded privilege and power. But this was 1999, NatWest's plans had gone awry once too often, their landmark tower had been sold and the view from the 42nd floor now belonged to a catering company.

Jupiter Asset Management were renting the room that bright January day. Their lunch guests were mainly IFAs who supported Jupiter's funds by recommending them to their clients. They were there to hear William Littlewood, manager of their flagship income fund, talk about what he was doing with the fund's assets. As all invited knew, he was an 'active manager', a 'stock picker', who by selecting individual equity or bond investments and altering his selection over time sought to outperform a benchmark index and other funds in his peer group. As an income fund manager, his performance would also be judged in terms of the yield produced. As all invited also knew, he had been doing all of these things well and for several years. If anyone deserved to be rated a 'star' manager, it was Littlewood.

The favoured guests placed at either side of the slight, bespectacled and youthful figure of Littlewood at one end of the table had perhaps found during the first two courses the confirmation they were looking for of the broad sweep and penetration of this man's discernment. Everyone else had to wait until the dessert arrived and the luncheon was opened up to questions and answers.

Halfway down the long table a woman of about Littlewood's age asked what had happened to the fund's 'tracking error' a year or so before. If an inaudible groan can be visible, this one certainly was. Littlewood politely but firmly dismissed this pedestrian enquiry. You do not get to achieve the performance record of the Jupiter Income Trust worrying about its tracking error. As the young woman lowered her head and toyed with her dessert, the subject passed to the 20 per cent of the fund Littlewood had recently staked on US-government inflation-linked bonds, American cousin to our index-linked gilts. This was more like it. Here was his global vision on show. Moving on through the latent value in some high-yielding small companies in the old industrial heartland of Britain, he hinted at the depth of his reach as well as its breadth.

Littlewood was totally plausible. Had his fellow director that day told us, as he brought the proceedings to a close, that Littlewood would soon be directing in Westminster Abbey a performance of Tallis's *Spem in alium*, a fantastically complex motet for eight five-part choirs, it would have seemed the most natural thing in the world.

In the investment business, 'plausibility' is a coveted business asset. 'Since active managers are marketing their services on a basis of being smarter than their competitors, it is essential for active managers to attract and retain personnel who can convince the marketplace of their superiority.' This comes from the OFT's report on the 1997 Pensions Enquiry.[xxix]

The combination of an outstanding track record and personal plausibility contributes powerfully to the generality of the belief that some managers have the skill that it takes to beat the market and defy the odds, and that we can and must make the effort to find them and then stick with them. This notion nonetheless runs counter to a substantial and irrefutable body of evidence, supported by a very persuasive theory, that the active management of portfolios of selected securities, different from a market index that captures the systematic features, is in fact a lottery. The rewards to active management are a myth perpetuated by the industry but sustained also with the help of the customers' 'willing suspension of disbelief'.

In this chapter we look at the theory and the evidence in terms of the plausibility that really matters: how plausible is it that *we* will beat the odds, whether by luck or judgement? In the next chapter we will look at what it costs to play, which in turn dramatically affects the odds. As the longest chapter in the book, this might seem to be giving importance to the subject of selection performance that is out of all proportion to its role in the decision hierarchy identified in Chapter 3. This is true, but it is also fundamental to investor self-protection that individuals free themselves from the tyranny of the industry's obsession with performance and that they are able to turn the whole investment process the other way up.

For reasons that will become clear, it will not be possible to reach a specific conclusion about the highly plausible William Littlewood but our purpose is to put the industry in the dock, not judge individuals.

If the rewards to stock picking are a myth and active management is the alternative National Lottery, when does the myth become a lie? The answer is implicit in that seemingly harmless quotation from the OFT report. It is when an industry, knowing full well the evidence, brushes it under the carpet and sets about how to market the myth to a gullible public. Seemingly harmless lunches for IFAs to meet and listen to a successful active fund manager are just one small cog in that marketing machine.[xxx]

Back to earth with the theory of efficient markets

Like the tobacco industry, investment professionals might be held responsible from the point at which they knew the evidence and ignored it, or possibly from when they should have known it. Either way, this goes back a long way. The opening shots, like much of the later munition, came from academia. It began with a theory which was the investment industry equivalent of claiming that the earth was a sphere: The Efficient Market Hypothesis.

Eugene Fama, a tenured professor before turning 30, began teaching modern portfolio theory at the University of Chicago in the 1960s. This was after Harry Markovitz had established the fundamental trade-off between risk and return that formed the foundation of modern finance but still before it was an established field. Fama's PhD thesis, 'The Behavior of Stock Market Prices', took up an entire issue of the University's *Journal of Business*. In 1965 a version of the paper titled 'Random Walks in Stock Market Prices' was published in the *Financial*

Analysts Journal which, as the most widely read investment journal for both the industry and academia, ensured that flat-earthers knew about the challenge.[20]

The challenge was that, in a stock market that was efficient in terms of the dissemination of information effecting share prices, no information or analysis could be expected to result in outperformance of an appropriate benchmark:

An 'efficient' market is defined as a market where there are large numbers of rational, profit-maximizers actively competing, with each trying to predict future market values of individual securities, and where important current information is almost freely available to all participants. In an efficient market, competition among the many intelligent participants leads to a situation where, at any point in time, actual prices of individual securities already reflect the effects of information based both on events that have already occurred and on events which, as of now, the market expects to take place in the future. In other words, in an efficient market at any point in time the actual price of a security will be a good estimate of its intrinsic value.[xxi]

In the 1960s and for a long time after, Markovitz's portfolio theory required such complex science and massive computing power to implement it in the day-to-day work of a manager as to make it truly 'academic'. Fama's logic, however, implied immediate redundancy to the activities that engaged almost every practitioner, be it in bonds or stocks, in broking or fund management.

Though there was strong circumstantial evidence suggesting markets were 'information efficient', both in the structure, workings and regulation of capital markets and in the presence of many features we associate with randomness, it required analysis of actual portfolios to demonstrate real redundancy. Fund analysis could either confirm that markets are efficient or demonstrate that, if in a few important respects they are not, active managers are nonetheless unable to take advantage of those inefficiencies. This might be because of costs or because the portfolios are all so diversified as to diminish the significance of any benefits. Either way, active management of diversified portfolios is then shown to be a waste of time and money.

---

[20] The story of the theory has been well told in a number of books and on several websites; lists and links to useful websites for readers interested to know more are included on our website under this chapter heading.

Such analyses began to be published in the 1970s in the USA based on publicly available performance data for American mutual funds. The flow of research spread to UK funds in the 1980s, based on unit trust data. The pace picked up in the 1990s. Between 1998 and 2000 there were three authoritative analyses published in the UK, including one commissioned by Virgin Direct and one carried out by the FSA itself.

The problem of proof

How come, you may wonder, after all this time and research we are still having this debate? Why has neither side been able to land a knock-out blow? The answer has to do with the problem of proof which in turn has to do with the length of data required for absolute certainty. It is this little scientific inconvenience that allows the investment industry to fight on, not so much by answering the challenge as brushing it under the carpet and maintaining 'business as usual'.

Business as usual enjoys the advantage of the public's perception of the facts. Is not the record of Littlewood's tenure as manager of the Jupiter Income Trust evidence that a manager can be superior, that he or she can outperform the market and competing funds, by a large margin and over a long period? If you take any sample of funds or managers, in any period, and see that some have managed to pull off the same feat, is that not evidence of a skill? Or even simpler, if half of the sample beat the other half, is one half not smarter than the other?

However you would answer these questions yourself, be assured that your answers will lie within the range of responses that investment professionals would themselves make, such is the diversity of familiarity with statistics, for this is indeed a problem of statistics. But it is not a very complex one. Even so, it is a reasonable question whether the minimum standards of streetwise self-protection require individual investors to be familiar with the nature of the statistical issues and the way to interpret evidence offered them. Because the myth is so pervasive and cancerous throughout the industry's relationships with customers, I am convinced it is. To ignore it on the basis that it might be too complicated for the reader is to talk down to you. I have decided that some maths need to make an appearance in this central chapter of the book but most of the explanation also appeals to common sense and uses graphs and charts as a way of presenting the evidence. If you really do not want to see how conclusions were reached, you can skip the workings.

The statistical approach to testing for the presence of a skill involves seeking to reject the hypothesis that the results are consistent with randomness and chance alone. Charles Darwin had a useful insight into the convention of turning the burden of proof this way round: 'I always make special notes about evidence that contradicts me: supportive evidence I can remember without trying!' The scientific reason has to do with the amount of historical performance data needed to eliminate with certainty the possibility that a result could have arisen by chance alone.

How much data is enough? The statistical approach says there is a connection between the number of observations and the standard deviation or spread of results. This ties in with our everyday appreciation of chance. Even without knowing the exact probabilities, we react with very different levels of surprise if double six is thrown twice or three times in a row. It is common sense that if a manager takes a few occasional but very large bets we will need to wait longer to collect enough evidence of the distribution of the gains and losses to exclude luck from the results.

If we take the manager with a typical standard deviation of returns relative to the index, it would require more history than his or her working life to be able to prove their results were the result of skill, whether the skill is theirs alone or down to a team. This is clearly quite a practical problem. It is unusual for individual managers, a team or a consistent style of management to stay in place even for as long as a decade.

In Littlewood's case this was demonstrated even sooner. After taking a six-month sabbatical from Jupiter pleading exhaustion, he then retired from the City altogether to look after his health. We may never have enough data to know how good or how lucky he was as a portfolio manager even if, with his health hopefully and happily restored, he chooses at some point to return to challenge the odds again.

Randomness shows itself in the observation that roughly half do better than the other half. This is simply noting that in the familiar 'bell curve' shape of a normal distribution the median (or any other measure of central tendency like mean) divides the bell into two equal halves. If we adjust active managers' returns for costs, which bias the contest in favour of the index, we would also expect the median manager return to be equal to the index return.

Thinking through a little more carefully, however, there may be other features that push the whole population of active managers away from the index, though not necessarily, like costs, in one direction only. Possible features are a lower concentration in the largest stocks; less difference generally between the smaller and larger holding size than between the smaller and larger index constituents; less concentration in particular industrial sectors.

Some of these portfolio construction effects can be roughly captured by comparing the performance of an index whose constituents are weighted by market capitalization (the 'sheep') with a notional index with the same constituents but equally weighted (the 'monkey').[21] The reality for most managers is that though they broadly follow the sheep they place some of their bets more equally as an intelligent monkey would. It is clear that the deviations in the relative return (monkey divided by sheep) are large, that they persist for some time, that they appear to revert to a mean but that degrees of deviation and timing of reversion are both unpredictable. What is not clear is whether there is a slight upward or downward drift to the mean, or even why there should be (though for the last few decades in the UK the intelligent monkey seems to have had the advantage over the sheep).

The monkey/sheep effect and any other passive and shared portfolio construction differences are best seen as an unpredictable tide that can carry the relative performance of active managers collectively in one direction or another, randomly. This effect is unlike costs that bias results in only one direction. Thus, the fact that most managers outperform for a period does not necessarily mean they have got better at picking stocks. Likewise, the fact that most managers underperformed in the second half of the 1990s, even with adjustment for costs, does not indicate a general lack of skill or a deterioration in the general level of skill compared with an earlier period in which the cost-adjusted returns were normally distributed around the index return.

▨ Alpha: the stuff of stars

So how do the academics look at past performance data? We can start with a report that comes from the efficient market school. In a paper titled

---

[21] The terminology and the methodology itself came from former colleague Peter Hart (at Valu-Trac Investment Management) about ten years ago. We were testing models for computer-based stock selection and wanted to isolate the most basic element of selection skill: the ability for some set of rules or criteria to separate before the event good and bad stocks, for which purpose a simple average of all stocks was far superior as a control to an index complicated by different weights in its construction.

'The Performance of UK Equity Unit Trusts', American academics Garrett Quigley and Rex Sinquefield examined the performance of all UK unit trusts that concentrate on UK equities, covering the period January 1978 through December 1997. They adopted a 'risk model' approach.

A risk model uses factors that 'explain' as much as possible of the variance in returns, that is the behaviour of the fund, in the same way that in Chapter 3 we considered the explanatory power of different types of decision. The risk model approach allows for the calculation of 'risk-adjusted excess return', known as alpha. I could write this chapter without referring to alpha but because it is increasingly being dropped into professionals' language with customers it is worth being familiar, if not intimate, with it. Do not be misled by the term 'excess' – alpha can be positive or negative. Consistent with the theory, this approach recognizes that excess return against a benchmark may have been achieved not by skill but by exposing the portfolio to stocks with a higher level of risk than the benchmark. In the language we used in Chapter 2, it takes from the manager and gives to the market any attributes that are *systematic* rather than specific to the manager's selection.

Alpha can be calculated with only one risk factor, beta, that is, the relative risk against the market index.[22] The better the specification of the risk factors, however, the more significance we can place on the resulting alpha number. This explains the authors' preference for a three-factor model for the UK. The factors are beta, a size factor (a function of the excess returns of the Hoare Govett Smaller Companies Index relative to the FTSE All Share Index) and a value factor (based on the excess return to the highest ratios of market value to 'book' or balance sheet value). The authors' conclusions were as follows:

This examination of UK equity unit trusts says that UK money managers are unable to outperform markets in any meaningful sense, that is, once we take into account their exposure to market, value and size risk … Contrary to the notion that small-company shares offer abundant 'beat-the-market' opportunities, we find that small-company unit trusts are the worst performers. In fact, their performance failure is persistent and reliable … Overall, this study like all mutual fund studies does not enlighten us about what kinds of

---

[22] Beta is a measure of the association between the return of an individual investment and the return of its 'host' market. A beta of 1 means it should move up or down in line with the market whereas a beta of 1.2, for instance, implies that in a rising maket it will rise by 20 per cent more than the market and will also fall by 20 per cent more if the market falls.

market failures occur. It does say that if there are any, UK equity managers do not exploit them.

According to Eugene Fama, we can be grateful to Rex Sinquefield for one of the most succinct observations on the performance myth: 'There are three classes of people who don't think markets work: the Cubans, the North Koreans and active managers.'[xxxii] Ouch!

Persistency as a test for skill

You do not have to start with a theory to establish the predictive value of past performance: there are purely empirical methods. Most widely used are tests of the persistency of active managers' performance between periods to see whether the changes in relative return or rank order, equivalent to the movements up or down a sporting league table, are different from those that would occur through chance alone.

Persistency is intuitively sensible because it mirrors the way we are being asked to use past performance as a predictor of the future. So it is relevant and we can relate to it. Excellent!

There is no point buying a fund with a good three- or five-year record unless we think that record can be extended into the future. There is no point trying to decide whether recent poor performance should cause us to switch funds unless it can tell us something about what will happen next. There is no point using progress to date as a guide to the outcome at some future goal-specific time horizon if past performance is not predictive. Persistency is the approach taken by the three other analyses of UK active managers' returns that I plan to refer to, including my own.

In 1999 Virgin Direct commissioned a comparative analysis of active and passive management of UK equity funds from one of the two top performance measurement firms in the UK, The WM Company.[xxxiii] Virgin's entry into the personal investment marketplace famously promoted the 'cheap and cheerful', so they had a vested interest in the use of tracker funds. The WM Company's analysis looked at the performance of unit trusts in the UK growth and income sector over the 20 years to the end of 1998, with comparisons made with the FTSE All Share Index. Their conclusion about persistency is as follows.

Over five years, the chance of an active fund beating a passive fund is around one in four. The issue is how much this can be used to predict the fund's future performance. Overall the probability of a trust achieving top-quartile performance in a five-year period would repeat this in a subsequent period was no better than random. There was stronger evidence that investing in a bottom-quartile fund would give a better than random chance of achieving top quartile in the subsequent period. The key to benefiting from active management is the identification of superior managers before their superiority shows. Past performance figures would appear to have a limited role in this process.[xxxiv]

The question of the odds of making up the extra cost of active funds is an important one we address in the next chapter. The observation that movements through the league table are consistent with randomness confirms Quigley and Sinquefield. The observation that poor performers tend to repeat their poor performance, which is not consistent with the general pattern (and also conflicts with one of Quigley and Sinquefield's suggestions), may be specific to the period or sample.

In some analysis of my own I looked at the persistency of rankings between three distinct periods. This formed part of a consulting project for a firm of IFAs who were concerned that their 'best advice' process for recommending funds, though perfectly compliant from the point of view of the regulators, was not actually 'best' from the point of view of investment theory and evidence. My clients were typical in that they were using a combination of analysis of past performance and 'soft' evidence of skills, such as the 'culture' of a firm, any research advantages, whether their managers tend to stay in place or move on, whether they have offices in foreign centres. I was able to persuade them of the logic that if these soft factors had any predictive value it would show up in non-random patterns in the data for past returns.[23]

The analysis was based on data (from Lipper) for what were then three AUTIF[xxxv] categories: Growth, Income and Growth & Income – at 262 funds a much larger group than WM's 81 funds. These three categories have since been amalgamated into a single category called All Companies. For my sample I excluded smaller companies unit trusts and passive funds and limited it to funds with complete data from the start of 1990 to the end of 1998, offering three separate periods of three years. Each fund in each period was assigned to a decile (a decile representing 10 per cent of the sample) on the basis of its return. If we plot the movements of a fund from one rank in the first period to another in the

---

[23] Thanks to James Baxter & Co for allowing me to extract from this report and to carry it in full on the website (under this chapter heading).

Figure 10.1 ▨ **Changes in decile rank order in consecutive three-year periods**

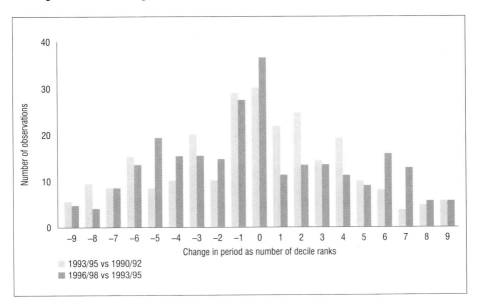

next period, and do this for each subsequent period, the distribution of all the rank order changes is essentially consistent with the familiar bell curve of a normal distribution (bearing in mind that there is some loss of information from the ranking approach). This is shown in Figure 10.1.

▨ What about top performers?

This is the obvious question. The one thing everyone agrees on is that money flows into past top performers. Even if the evidence across the entire league table of active fund managers, such as in Figure 10.1, is that movement is essentially random, it does not exclude the possibility that there exists an exceptional few. This can also be tested for by singling out the best past performers and watching what happens to their subsequent league table position. Using the same approach as before, the next chart shows the results for the first and second decile in each earlier period, representing the best 20 per cent, so slightly more demanding than the typical 'top quartile' category (or the best 25 per cent).

Because we have extracted two deciles, the familiar bell curve is no longer the shape to use to interpret the results. In the top decile, funds can stay the same or fall as many as nine deciles. In the second decile, funds can move between up one and down eight. By chance alone 17.5 per cent of the sample can be expected to remain within the band of up or down one decile, equivalent to a run of good luck. In Figure 10.2 the broken lines are a simplification of the shape were the movement consistent with randomness, mean reversion or trend persistence.

A skill would show up as a bunching of the distribution to the right of the chart, pushing the number of observations at the left well below the random level. If, on the other hand, good past performance was due to a particular market environment that then reverses, like an ebbing and flowing tide, the best performers would then be carried down towards the bottom of the table, showing up as a bunching to the left at the expense of the number of observations to the right.

Between the first and second periods, the distribution of the light grey bars suggests the pattern is purely random. Do not be misled by the peak value of nine funds out of 53 remaining in the same place: this is offset by a smaller than 'expected' number of small changes, that is down two deciles and up one decile.

Figure 10.2 ▨ **Changes in decile rank order in consecutive three-year periods**
Top-performing funds: deciles 1 and 2

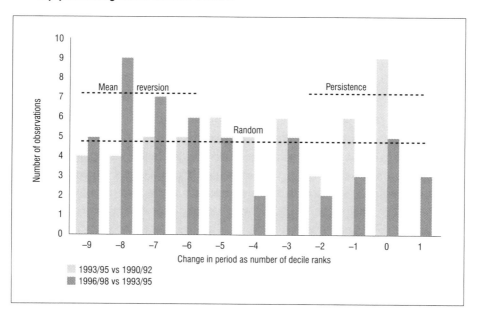

Between the second and third periods, the distribution of the dark grey bars is bunched to the left, consistent with a bias towards mean reversion. Far from suggesting the presence of skill, this implies that those managers who floated to the top in the earlier period were simply riding a tide in the market that suited their own investment style – a tide that then turned against them.

In interpreting these results I believe it is dangerous to assume the presence of mean reversion as an anomaly capable of being exploited as it may be due to the random tidal effects of those passive structural differences. If we could predict their timing, we would know when to abandon past top performers but if we knew that much then surely managers would themselves know how to play those same tides, and that would show up as persistence.

On this evidence, buyers of top-performing funds must be regularly disappointed, so why do they keep doing it? Disappointment may be cushioned for a while if they keep seeing references to past cumulative returns that include some benefit of the earlier good performance: the glow of stardom fades slowly on a cumulative basis. Even if performance droops soon after investing, awareness that the fund is still a top-quartile fund over a longer period can keep the belief alive.

This erosion of cumulative performance was analyzed in the WM paper, using a five-year past performance window to select the top-quartile funds. In samples for three different periods, moving forwards to two years later they noted that between one- and two-thirds of the funds initially in the top quartile were still top quartile over the trailing five years. These new five-year periods of course include three years that were in the original data sample. By year six, when all of the past data has dropped out of the sample, between zero and 12 per cent were still top quartile, which is actually worse than random (25 per cent). By then, there could have been no illusions for most holders of most 'hot' funds! Yet still, under the bombardment of industry propaganda, investors choose to ignore their own experience.

⬛ The FSA's position

The third source of persistency analysis is an FSA occasional paper.[xxxvi] This is part of the analytical basis of the FSA's well-publicized decision that past performance should not form a part of the 'official' comparative information tables for packaged products, a point we will return to. The paper commands authority both because of its sponsor, the regulator, and because of the thoroughness of its approach which goes well beyond that of my own and even WM's. Its author, Mark Rhodes, is an associate in the Economics of Financial Regulation Department (Central Policy) at the FSA.

The paper starts with a review of the literature and then addresses the evidence of persistency based on the same approaches as mine and WM's. However, Rhodes argues that the traditional methodologies fail to make the most of the data, for several reasons:

1 When you establish samples of funds with complete data in the test periods, you lose information about funds that were only around for part of the period (including the poor ones that get closed down).

2 If a fund moves out of a particular rank order and then back again during the two periods, it will still show up as consistent between the two.

3 The approach typically adopted in the literature arbitrarily establishes holding periods (for example, five years in the WM analysis, three in mine) whereas in reality the investor does not know what their holding period will be.

Rhodes suggests that the investor has a different view of consistency or risk from that implied by the normal statistical approach, one characterized by particular risk preferences and reflecting their flexibility to switch funds.[24] He proposes a new methodology that makes allowance for all of these factors and then applies the same tests of normality to the resulting distributions. His conclusions are as follows:

The literature on the performance of UK funds has failed to find evidence that information on past investment performance can be used to good effect by retail investors in choosing funds. The general pattern is one in which investment performance does not persist. Small groups of funds may show some repeat performance over a short period of time, particularly poorly performing funds. However, the size of this effect and the fact that it is only very short lived means

---

[24] In the jargon, he adds a 'utility function' – which Rhodes tabulates thus: 'i) investors dislike risk; ii) higher performance is preferred but at a diminishing rate (an individual, call him Bert), would prefer performance that was twice as high but not by twice as much (this is closely related to i)); iii) dislike of risk does not change with the performance of the fund that Bert is invested in.'

that there is no investment strategy for retail investors that could usefully be employed …

The development of a novel methodological approach allowed for a more consistent examination of performance over the longer term. This also provides an opportunity to examine further the apparent end in the relationship between past and subsequent investment performance. The results concurred with the earlier analyses in finding that there was no persistency in the performance of managed funds after 1987. There was evidence of repeat performance before this point but it would be misleading to suggest that retail investors could use this finding in the present day. The weight of evidence is that information on past performance cannot be exploited usefully by retail investors.

What about risk?

One of the reasons why advisers and product providers stress the value to investors of past performance data is that it allows them to understand the risks taken to achieve their returns. Since the 'no free lunch' tenet of modern portfolio theory is definitely streetwise, this seems fair.

ONE OF THE REASONS WHY ADVISERS AND PRODUCT PROVIDERS STRESS THE VALUE TO INVESTORS OF PAST PERFORMANCE DATA IS THAT IT ALLOWS THEM TO UNDERSTAND THE RISKS TAKEN TO ACHIEVE THEIR RETURNS

Unfortunately, the relationship between risk and return within an equity portfolio is not in fact consistent with the theory. Trying harder to earn your active manager fees by taking bigger bets relative to the index does not systematically produce higher returns. There is no premium to harvest.

This is an inescapable conclusion from UK unit trust data and the only issue is whether bigger bets tend to be losing bets. The WM Company claimed, 'There is a noticeable pattern of high deviations (from the index) being associated with lower returns.' I found the same. From all the funds with nine years of consistent data I extracted the quartiles with the highest and lowest standard deviation of monthly returns relative to the FTSE All Share Index and looked at the distribution of each in terms of their relative return by deciles (Figure 10.3).

Again, to interpret this information it helps to think about what the chart would look like if the theory held and higher risk was rewarded by higher return. This would cause the riskiest quartile, marked by the dark grey lines, to bunch to the left of the return deciles, as the most successful.

Figure 10.3 ▪ **Frequency distribution of quartile ranks for standard deviation of relative return and decile ranks for relative return (nine years ending May 1998)**

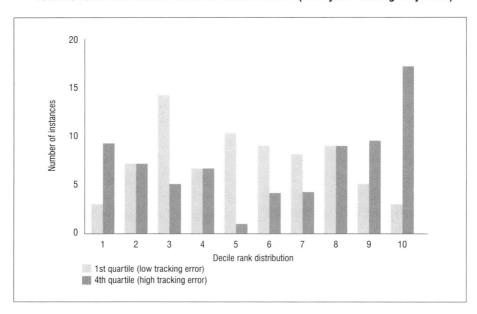

The lowest quartile, marked by the light grey lines, should bunch in the centre since it has avoided the size of bets that will either cause the funds to sink or soar.

What we actually see is that riskier funds are more likely to sink, hence the higher number of observations to the right, in deciles eight, nine and ten, where holders are certain to be disappointed, than the number in deciles one or two, or even three, which was perhaps their minimum expectation. Less risky funds are more evenly distributed than a cluster in the centre and there is a bias in fact to the left, to better returns. Lower risk, higher reward – the opposite of the theory! This does not necessarily mean most holders would have been satisfied. The mean relative return of lower risk managers could itself have been below the index, either because of costs or because of a general tendency for active managers to be dragged down by one of those unpredictable tidal factors.

This is the Catch 22 for supporters of active funds. If you pick a manager who tightly controls the tracking error, you significantly reduce your chances of outperforming by enough to recover the additional cost relative to a tracker. But if you therefore seek out a manager who takes bigger bets, you are as likely – or even more likely – to sink than soar. We return to this in Part III when we offer some practical rules for selecting products. Do not hold your breath hoping for a winning formula. There is none.

The evidence for foreign equity funds

What investors need to know about the performance of UK managers of equity portfolios in foreign markets also has to do with risk and reward trade-offs. As part of my 'best advice' project I analyzed the performance of actively managed UK funds that invest in Europe, Japan and the USA.[25] I found that UK managers took much bigger bets relative to the local index than they do in the UK – they are relaxed about tracking error in much the same way as Littlewood was.

In my experience this systematically reflects both greater concentration and greater exposure to the monkey/sheep effect. However, I can offer no explanation why there should be such cultural differences between domestic and foreign equity management. Though the risks are higher I found no evidence they have been rewarded, except in Japan where it was specific to two brief periods, about ten years apart. Because the international bets are larger it also requires more time to determine whether higher risk is associated with a bias to underperformance, even taking costs into account. I found no evidence of persistency in relative returns, just as in the UK. Considering the extent and unanimity of the academic research on US securities, my conclusion that active performance for British managers of US portfolios is random is hardly astounding.

Hedge funds: where the stars go

If there is genuine skill amongst some elite of the money management business, where better to look for it than in the market that attracts many of the most plausible managers in the world: hedge funds. These are the funds where alpha should be most concentrated because the managers can earn far more out of performance fees than managers of public funds

---

[25] In the case of European funds that exclude the UK it has not been possible to isolate the effect of country bets from stock-picking bets and it is likely that this has been a changing effect as the convergence of economies and currencies will have reduced the explanatory power of a fund's market allocations within Europe.

or institutional portfolios.[26] It is a global market, with many funds sold across borders, so it attracts alpha merchants from every corner of the globe and from every discipline: equity, fixed income, commodities, currencies, options and futures.

For our purpose here, we want to be able to take this very broad church of many different styles of fund and apply the same tests of persistency for individual manager returns. I believe the best source of research is Narayan Naik at the London Business School and his co-author on two papers, Vikas Agarwal, who drew on the database of hedge fund returns provided by Hedge Fund Research in Chicago to test for persistency.[xxxvii]

IF THERE IS GENUINE SKILL AMONGST SOME ELITE OF THE MONEY MANAGEMENT BUSINESS, WHERE BETTER TO LOOK FOR IT THAN IN HEDGE FUNDS

Their first paper looked at short-period returns but this was not really appropriate to asset strategies for funds that often involve lock-ins, preventing trading in the funds themselves. A shortage of history prevented them looking at discrete three- or five-year period as we have done for unit trusts but in their second paper they analyzed year-to-year persistency. The authors applied two different measures of performance. They analyzed individual results in two categories: 'directional' (which are associated with the return path of an asset class because their bets include exposure to a market or class return, like a geared bond fund, for instance); and 'non-directional' (which neutralize much or all of the market exposure to leave bets on relationships between securities, such as a 'market neutral' equity fund or a 'convertible arbitrage' fund). Each of these two categories were in turn subdivided into types by the nature of their bets, such as long, short or arbitrage, and by asset specialization, such as equity or fixed income. The authors found no statistically significant difference from random outcomes. This applies to both categories and to each of the subcategories. No matter what the specialization, no matter what the type of bet, there was no convincing evidence of skill for these giants among men.

---

[26] Hedge fund managers typically structure their fees as a combination of a base fee, as a percentage of assets, that they earn regardless of their performance and a performance fee, as a percentage of the profit they earn. Some only earn the performance fee if cumulative returns are above a benchmark rate, such as the return on cash. The typical combination is 1 per cent and 20 per cent, that is, a base fee of 1 per cent per annum of assets and a performance fee equivalent to 20 per cent of the positive or excess return. Performance fees allowed some of the top-performing managers, including George Soros, to string together fees of over 20 per cent per annum (versus the average unit trust fee of, say, 1.4 per cent) for a number of years before the good times came to an end!

A further analysis of hedge fund performance was published by two academics at the ISMA Centre at Reading University, which specializes in financial economics. Gaurav Amin and Harry Kat observed that the way most hedge funds are marketed and selected requires an assumption that returns are 'normally distributed' – including, incidentally, the calculation of our friend alpha – but the whole point about many hedge fund strategies, which have 'option' features, is that returns are likely to be skewed.

They analyzed the risk-adjusted returns of 77 hedge funds over a ten-year period ending April 2000 using an approach that did not require any assumption about how returns were distributed. They found that 72 had 'inefficient' risk versus return trade-offs. Though the universe is dominated by funds marketed in the USA it covers the entire range of types of hedge fund strategy. As the authors admit, their dismal conclusions are likely to be an understatement. Risk is likely to be biased downwards and reward upwards by the fact that the worst losers drop out of the game, flattering the average of the remaining funds.

If there is genuine skill at work in hedge funds and this branch of the industry is indeed creaming off the best of the active manager breed, it is not able to overwhelm the greed of the breed. High management charges and performance fees that bite into returns even when they are inefficient in terms of the risks are proving to be an insurmountable obstacle. This problem is merely exacerbated when the typical private client product, a fund of funds, loads an extra layer of charges.

▦ Stars in their ads

One of the ways funds are promoted by fund managers, IFAs and on websites is by pointing to awards and medals they have won. These are conferred on funds (and in some cases on management groups) by independent agencies. The leading agencies and the currency of their accolades are: Micropal stars (up to * * * * *), Fund Research ratings (up to AAA) and Lipper ARC medals (from bronze to platinum). Micropal and Fund Research are owned by the American data publishing house Standard & Poors and Lipper by Reuters. One of the leading US ranking sources, Morningstar, also launched a star approach (up to * * * * *) in the UK in 2001.

If these were awarded purely for past performance, we now know enough to say with certainty they would be useless as anything other than a measure of the past. However, the wider acceptance of modern portfolio theory shows up in the adoption by all the rating services of quantitative measures of risk. As a crude form of risk adjustment, what they do is divide the absolute or relative measure of return in a particular period by the standard deviation for the same period.[xxxviii]

It is common sense that, for these awards to be valuable as a guide to the future, the quantitative risk measures have to be stable over time. Let me explain why.

We use the benefit of hindsight, knowledge of all the past period information, when deciding how to make selection choices. Drawing on the evidence about active manager risk and return we have now seen, hindsight might lead us to prefer to fish in a particular pool. We might, for instance, choose the one containing only those managers that have earned a risk premium appropriate to their level of risk (whatever that level was), or we might prefer only those with a level of risk, say, close to average. Hindsight will only be helpful in framing our criteria if the managers who we find in those particular pools tend to stay there. If they swim off somewhere else, the criteria will fail to do their job.

The evidence shows that risk and return relationships are in fact unstable. Their instability stems not only from the return randomness we have already seen but also from changes in the risk characteristics themselves. Unstable fund risk is a problem for all the main criteria applied by the industry in fund selection: risk-adjusted past performance, suitability by active manager risk and suitability by absolute levels of risk.

As part of my 'best advice' report, I demonstrated this instability using beta, or the sensitivity to market movements, as a risk measure but the results are significant enough not to be affected by the measure of relative risk chosen. Taking the same three discrete periods, I defined a group with betas in the first period between 0.95 and 1.05 (in other words they were barely more risky or less risky than the index which by definition has a beta of 1).

In Figure 10.4, the area the sample occupied at the outset, and would have stayed in if consistent, is defined by the box.

After three years, the group's range of betas had expanded to 0.8 to 1.13 and by the end of the third period it had expanded further to 0.44 to 1.14. This wider range was indistinguishable from the range of betas in the third period of the entire population. Well over half had swum off to another pool. Examples in this period include several widely promoted UK equity funds whose riskiness was almost certainly inadvertently mis-

Figure 10.4 ▨ **Change in beta for all UK growth funds with nine years of data
Beta in 1st three-year period vs beta in 3rd three-year period**

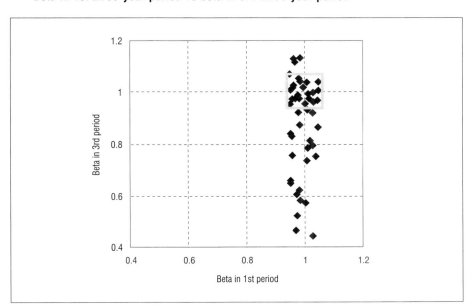

specified by IFAs, such as ABN-Amro UK Growth, Fidelity UK Growth, Friends Provident Stewardship (the popular 'green' fund) and Schröder Enterprise.

Most customers buying products partly on the strength of their rankings are being bamboozled. They will not understand how they have been arrived at or what their significance is.

Unless we are very streetwise about statistics, a typical error is to exaggerate the importance of ranking differences. The difference between two funds that lie either side of some artificial breakpoint, such as for a measure of risk-adjusted return, could be infinitesimal. The significance attached could be enormous, if, for example, one wins the coveted Lipper ARC platinum award (which only 2 per cent of funds achieve) and the other is merely gold. The very maths of the risk-adjusted observations, dividing a return measure by a risk measure which is both relatively large and unstable, makes the answers highly sensitive to even small differences in the risk measure. That is also streetwise maths.

Stars and medals are very useful to the marketing departments of the fund management groups but do not help customers. It is the fund managers, incidentally, not advisers, from whom Reuters and Standard &

Poors receive most of their income for fund data services. This is not just because the manufacturers of products are the biggest consumers of information about competitors' performance. It is also because the fund managers pay to have their funds analyzed by these independent agencies. Once again in this industry the label 'independent' turns out not to be quite what it implies.

Performance claims by portfolio managers

Statements about past returns in marketing literature for products are controlled by tight financial service regulations, not just advertising standards. We can assume that what companies say about past returns or about some third-party award is not itself a lie. There is nonetheless a systematic general intention to mislead evidenced by the machinery put in place to perpetuate the performance myth. There are also systematic specific attempts to mislead, characterized by the generality of the industry's use of selective past performance periods and selective bases of comparison.

There is currently no regulation or even convention that prevents managers from selecting whatever past performance period shows them in the most favourable light, such as performance since launch, for the past ten years, five years or even a shorter period. There is nothing to stop them selecting a cumulative return without showing the individual years. This can and is used to disguise recent upsets or very high volatility in the path of returns. They can even quote numbers for a period in which a fund has been merged with another, or the manager changed, perhaps even several times, even if those changes in turn led to changes in the style of management or the focus of the fund's investments.

Advisers too can be selective to suit their own agenda, be it as devious as seeking to justify buying a fund paying high commissions or switching funds to generate commission or as harmless as supporting a recommendation to hang on to a fund that has had some bad recent numbers. Likewise, managers are free to select the benchmark against which they invite comparison. This they also do so as to cast themselves in the best light, such as by highlighting either a peer group of other funds or an index. Combining both selective period and selective basis of comparison multiplies the opportunities for marketing departments to mine the data to extract flattering numbers. Advisers can also play this game if they want to lead their clients to a particular conclusion.

Even worse, yet even more commonplace, is to compare the performance of a fund that takes equity-type risk with the lowly return of a building society deposit, grabbing for the manager the systematic risk premium accorded by the market. Chapter 2 established that this belongs to the investor, for choosing to expose their money to the market, not to the manager.

Take even a small market risk premium and compound it for, say, ten years (or even a longer period since a fund's launch) and a manager can appear very smart to a less than streetwise customer. I clipped a little piece from the FT a while back when Simon London was writing his excellent 'Serious Money' column:

Recently, my wife and I acquired a nearly new Ford Mondeo. Buying it involved running the gauntlet of countless salesmen. But none, as I recall, informed us that it accelerates faster than a lawn mower. So why do purveyors of unit trusts and investment trusts feel obliged to point out that their high yield Latin American equities fund – to take a hypothetical example – has performed better than a deposit account? The two things are no more comparable than a Ford and a Flymo.

The scope for misleading selectivity is even greater for the managers of customized portfolios, whether investing in securities or in packaged products. For a start, a single fund is replaced by many separate portfolios. These need to be categorized on the basis of commonality (plenty of scope for selectivity there) and then the results within each category weighted somehow. Since the members of each category will show some dispersion of results for any period, weightings matter. If the manager is offering any genuine customization, it should show up at the level of asset-allocation differences. Since these have a greater influence on returns than differences in security returns within a market (the hierarchy effect), customization should cause meaningful dispersion of portfolio returns – it is good thing, not a bad thing. Weightings then matter a lot – perhaps so much that even categorizing them at all is misleading.

Unless a prospective customer or their agent can examine the data for the all the firm's clients (which is unrealistic) they will not be able to place much reliance on the stated historical performance as a true representation of actual results.

Individual portfolios also offer more scope than packaged products to use past performance numbers to shape the customers' expectations about how bright a future the relationship holds. Regulated firms are careful to avoid anything that smacks of guarantees but that still allows them to hold out misleading expectations. Maybe this happens because of the professionals' own limited grasp of probabilities but that is hardly an excuse.

A typical recent example in my own experience is a telephone conversation with a member of the client service team in one of the 'private banks' that offers a personal wealth-management service in the popular market segment known as the 'mass affluent'.

His call to me followed my request, via their website, for a brochure. During the conversation it was suggested, unprompted, that a reasonable performance target was '2–3 per cent per annum outperformance net of fees'. He claimed that they had achieved 3 per cent per annum for clients since launch three years before, so I asked how long they could keep it up. His reply was along the lines of 'indefinitely' – in other words he did not pick up the implication in my question that the odds against a particular margin of outperformance rise with the length of time it is sustained, just like repeating double sixes.

We did not explore the related question of how he could quote either an achieved or target rate if the bank claimed to offer portfolios fully customized to personal needs and risk preferences. I certainly had not mentioned mine.

His selling approach had been misleading in another typical respect. He had sought both to encourage high hopes for performance and to reassure me that there are tight risk controls in place. He could anticipate that I would want to see both and might have assumed (at that stage in the conversation) that I was not cute enough to understand the conflict between them.

It was time to get cute. I pointed him in the direction of The WM Company report, specifically the chart showing that out of 81 UK unit trust managers in the ten years to 1998 only one beat the index by 2 per cent per annum after expenses and only three beat it by any margin. I also pointed out that the three funds out of 81 that had beaten the index had all taken much bigger bets than the index. Though we have seen that taking bigger bets at the security level is not systematically rewarded by a risk premium and seems likely to fail, this is still the price you have to pay if you wish to shoot for a high target.

I have no doubt that the risk control framework that the bank's salesman described to me was inconsistent with the relative return target

I was being encouraged to aspire to. In this cloud-cuckoo-land, I was not sure either was genuine.

The FSA's lead on performance claims

Discuss performance issues with the FSA and you quickly recognize that it is acutely sensitive to the consumer protection angle and is not merely taking a narrow, legalistic view of what is said about past performance or implied about future performance. Once the FSA gets its teeth into an area of consumer protection, it will come up with something. However, in this case it is severely limited by the legal impracticality of trying to gag statements that are factually accurate even if deceptive.

The institutional market solved the same problem with a 'standards convention', a set of voluntary rules covering treatment of expenses, period selection, bases of comparison, the categorization of separate portfolios and verification by an independent third party. Beginning in the USA a version was quickly adopted in the UK and is now emerging as an international standard. Though not legally enforceable, peer group and customer pressure soon ensured that if managers want to compete, they have to play by these rules. The cost of all this for managers is very high. Of course, if performance is random then having better information may not improve the customer's decisions but at least it stopped business going for the wrong reasons to the most 'creative' marketing teams.

The FSA may go down the same route of standards. It could encourage their uptake by a combination of consumer education (for which it has a budget) and the marketing reward to advisers and managers who comply – by offering them what amounts to the advantage of the moral high ground.

The FSA is contributing to consumer education in another way: the introduction of 'official' league tables. With the objective of being widely published, they include comparative analysis on a consistent basis as determined by the FSA. The regulator caused a storm when it floated in a consultative paper the idea that the league tables should exclude past performance altogether. You can imagine how the consultation went! Yet the FSA, as we have seen, is totally sure of its ground and did indeed decide to go ahead without past performance. Instead, the tables collate such facts as charges, flexibility and minimum payments.

It is difficult for the FSA to take such an enlightened step without also addressing the nonsense of the 'best advice' process for IFAs. Though the policing of these regulations focuses more on the presence of procedures and proper documentation, the regulator cannot ignore the qualitative criteria implied by the name, 'best advice'. If the FSA follows its own logic about the performance lottery, a set of darts would constitute an adequate selection tool. If the darts were aimed only at funds with low cost and high flexibility, what could be better?

Should we also anticipate at some point new and prominent health warnings? The statutory warning that 'the value of your investments could rise or fall' hardly has the subversive potency to worry the industry. How about using Mark Rhodes's own words, for display on all actively managed products and services, taken from another part of his paper but replacing the conditional 'if there is no significant link ...' with a simple determination of fact, as follows:

[There is] no significant link between past investment performance and future outcomes [and] consumers should not take heed of any information on past performance. To the extent that they nevertheless use such information they could be led into error and give inadequate weight to the features of the product that do matter.

High on the FSA's list of what matters is cost. As we shall see in the next chapter, the performance lie is not just paid for in random outcomes: the customer also pays for the full cost of the marketing machine that maintains it.

11
The cost wedge

Getting between you and the market return

Streetwise investors see the industry as providing a gateway to exposing their money to 'the system', and hence to market returns and risk premiums, yet also as placing in their way a series of obstacles. Their aim is to exploit the gateway and avoid being exploited themselves, which means minimizing the obstacles. One of the hardest to recognize yet simplest to minimize is the cost wedge that the people in between come armed with. They have a number of tricks to make you think this is a harmless little weapon, that it really will not hurt at all. For decades the consumer has bought this version but whereas surveys show many investors are still unaware of the costs they incur, let alone their implications, there is a growing band of switched-on people who either suspect a rip-off or have worked out what is really going on.

In this chapter we look at all the different forms that the cost wedge takes, quantify them, add them all up and check their impact in terms of measures of the market return, that is, how deep the wedge goes. This involves understanding how sensitive the damage is to the market return assumed and to the investor's time horizon and switching activity. When we relate this information to what we have already learnt about the lottery nature of active management, we will see how high the house stacks the odds against us. This is enough to demonstrate that the self-protection code is vital.

We will see that it is active management of securities portfolios that dictates the majority of the cost of the industry's services, acting like a tax on privately held wealth and falling most heavily on those who can least afford it. Unlike real taxes, it has virtually no benefits for the national economy. The retail investment industry could perform its desired economic functions – namely, as a gateway to markets and as a marginal contributor (along with institutions) to market efficiency – at a fraction of the cost that private individuals are typically being asked to pay. This is a story about the collective failure of an industry, rather than about the excesses of a few bad firms.

The law of small numbers

You are conditioned by the industry to view investment costs as small numbers compared with big numbers. If you are investing £10,000 the fact that a few percentage points are skimmed off the top before it gets exposed to markets may look like small change. When investment returns are about 20 per cent a year, how can you begrudge the wizards harvesting these rich returns taking a few percentage points out of your pot? This is an illusion that suits the industry well.

The streetwise investor looks at costs as big numbers compared with small numbers. In Part I we saw that funding long-term goals is hard graft: the systematic dynamics that drive the accumulation of *real* wealth and carry our capital and savings towards our personal goals are small numbers. We identified a normal market real return of just 6 per cent per annum and a normal risk premium relative to a safe-harbour asset of 3 per cent per annum. These are the drivers that costs need to be compared with.

We will see that an actively managed equity product with typical charges and trading activity takes *half* the normal market return and *all* of the normal risk premium! If this is not a broken system, what is?

In the last chapter we saw that if we hold an active product for as long as ten years even a 1 per cent per annum margin of cumulative outperformance against other active funds is quite exceptional and probably only arises by chance. The additional costs of active management that we analyze in this chapter drive the chance of achieving a better return than a low-cost tracker below one in four, possibly as low as one in ten. For a high-cost product, the chance is insignificant.

We will start with unit trusts, then look at some costs specific to pension contracts and finally try to penetrate the fog of with-profits contracts.

The unit trusts cost wedge

Defining the different costs of a unit trust:

1 the government's stamp duty on the purchase cost of units

2 up-front sales commission – a percentage of the value of the new funds invested in the fund deducted by the manager as the money goes in; sales commissions are also known by the American terminology, 'loads'; 'front-end' charges may be replaced by a back-end charge which is usually only levied when an investor redeems in the first few years and is usually applied on a sliding scale to penalize the fastest exits

3 the annual management charge – the percentage of the value of the portfolio taken by the fund-management company for providing their service

4 other third-party expenses – mostly custody charges paid to the banks who physically hold the assets, fees to the trustee and accountancy fees, most of which are fixed rather than calculated as a percentage of the assets; these are not usually a large addition to the management charge unless the fund is very small, is administered offshore or if the assets are held in more expensive international markets

5 the 'total expense ratio' is an American term for the sum of the management charge and third-party fees, expressed as a percentage of the fund value, and captures the ongoing cost of running the fund; the total expense ratio can be calculated from the fund's accounts but does not yet have to be disclosed

6 transaction costs borne by the fund – what it costs to buy and sell securities in the market and so largely a function of the level of activity or 'turnover' the manager chooses to engage in. The costs are made up of the difference between the price to a buyer and the price to a seller, known as 'the dealing spread'; any market impact

(if the unit trust's activity is on a scale such as to cause the buying or selling price to alter) which is known as 'market impact'; stamp duty on all purchases in the UK market; broker's commissions for acting as agent in the buying or selling of securities on behalf of the fund (which may be wrapped up in the spread and market impact if the manager deals through a 'market maker' or principal).

The thin end of the unit trust wedge

The thin end of the wedge is the minimum or unavoidable cost of exposure to the UK equity market systematic return. This minimum can be taken as about 0.6 per cent per annum, being the sum of the total expense ratio of a low cost tracking fund and allowance for transaction costs.

In time, with more competition from index fund managers and from Exchange Traded Funds[27] and with larger economies of scale in index tracking, this is likely to come down to about 0.4 per cent per annum, with transaction costs proving the most sticky. Since most of the transaction costs in a tracker are due to unit holders buying and selling rather than rebalancing the constituents, it is possible the cost of providing this liquidity will be a separate charge borne by the buyer and seller and not by other passive holders. This is fairer and will lower the cost over long holding periods to, say, 0.3 per cent per annum.

International trackers can be expected to cost more and a good working assumption is 0.7 per cent for now falling to 0.5 per cent per annum later. Many smaller trackers are not yet achieving scale economies and have total expense ratios over 1 per cent per annum.

Generally, trackers will not charge sales commissions or up-front charges but the tracker buyer cannot avoid the government's own 'front-end load', the 0.5 per cent stamp duty. On a lump sum investment assumed to be held for a long period (more likely to the case if trackers are being used) the duty written off over that holding period will be insignificant as an annualized cost.

---

[27] We will not know the true cost of Exchange Traded Funds until we can see what happens to liquidity and trading costs but their explicit costs are likely to be set lower than index trackers for marketing purposes.

Estimating explicit active unit trust management costs

The average annual management charge for actively managed unit trusts is about 1.3 per cent per annum.[xxxix] There are clusters at 1 per cent, 1.25 per cent and 1.5 per cent. The 1 per cent group is boosted by a large number of income funds where there is pressure to keep costs from eating into distributable income. 1.25 per cent used to be a fairly standard rate for funds aiming at capital growth but the number charging 1.5 per cent has grown steadily (even though institutional management charges have been coming down). This is partly because managers have had to pay IFAs the 'trail' or 'renewal' commissions we met in Chapter 10, these being paid by the fund managers to the intermediaries out of the annual management charge. Whether front-end load or trail, the customer gets to pay part of the commission bill. The most actively promoted funds, heavily backed by advertising, have charges at the upper end of the range. Other than in unitized pension products there has been little noticeable downward pressure on fund managers' fee rates as a result of the stake-holder pension or the growing market share of trackers. Allowing for these factors, the average of 1.3 per cent is possibly on the low side. The average often quoted for growth funds is 1.4 per cent.

Because other charges are typically fixed money amounts, they are lowest in the bigger funds where most private client assets are concentrated. Fitzrovia International[xl] have estimated the average annualized cost at 0.3 per cent for all onshore funds but allowing for lower costs for large UK equity funds the figure may be half that. Fitzrovia's observations about offshore funds, however, are important. They pointed to an average of 0.53 per cent which they did not think was affected mainly by fund size.

Estimating trading costs in an actively managed unit trust

To play the active management lottery you have to pay twice: you pay for the active manager's time and resources and you pay the market costs the manager incurs by trading an actively managed portfolio. These trading costs do not have to be disclosed by managers. They are a function of both explicit charges, such as stamp duty and brokers' commissions on trades, and implicit costs, such as market spreads. To estimate the effect of trading costs, we need an assumption about the typical cost of a trade and a further assumption about the percentage of the portfolio turned over each year so we can multiply the two to get at the likely annual cost.

In a research paper in February 2000 in the FSA's Occasional Paper series, 'The Price of Retail Investment in the UK', Kevin James summarized various sources of estimates of trading costs.[xli] James estimated a typical turnover rate as being 66 per cent (in other words the typical active manager replaces two-thirds of the holdings each year). It is not well researched and does not differentiate between the effect of switching positions and providing liquidity to buyers and sellers of units. Because of the lack of data and the differences between funds and over time in the net flows into and out of unit trusts, I prefer to assume a range of annual activity from 25 per cent up to 66 per cent and look at the cost wedge in terms of different combinations of *all* the cost variables.

James estimates the explicit and implicit trading costs as 1.8 per cent per 'round trip', in other words, for a sale plus matching purchase. Applying a cost of 1.8–25 per cent of the portfolio value gives a trading cost of 0.45 per cent per annum on the entire portfolio value, rising to 1.2 per cent if the higher rate of activity is assumed.

Estimating the impact of sales commissions

Annual costs are not necessarily the only costs as there may be sales commissions as well. Part or all of the commission may be applied by advisers as a fee for general financial planning rather than just to researching a fund recommendation. Either way, commissions are still an industry cost and part of the wedge and we need to gauge their scale and impact. This requires assumptions about both the level and the frequency of their occurrence.

WHEREAS PASSIVE MANAGEMENT WILL ALWAYS BE THE SOURCE OF SOME DISAPPOINTMENT THAT THE WELL-PUBLICIZED RETURNS OF SOME ACTIVE FUNDS WERE PASSED OVER, ACTIVE MANAGEMENT BRINGS *REGRET*

There is plenty of industry evidence of high turnover in front-end loaded funds. It is in fact a logical consequence of preferring active management. Whereas passive management will always be the source of some disappointment that the well-publicized returns of some active funds were passed over, active management brings *regret*. The tracker cannot do much about the lost opportunities and knows it is a case of being wise after the event. When an active fund performs poorly, the holder or his or her adviser has an actual problem and, not being rational about the vagaries of random relative returns, feels a decision is needed. The effect of regret at past investment decisions is to increase switching activity.

Regret is subtle. It is not merely provoked by the general tendency of active funds to underperform, which is perfectly rational given the cost disadvantage. It is not just that money is too easily seduced into once hot funds that, as we have seen, have either a random 25 per cent chance of remaining in the top quartile after five years or, worse, carry a greater than random risk of disappointing. It is both of those but it is also the fact that even the best performing long-term investments (with the benefit of hindsight) will be indistinguishable from a dog somewhere along the way. This is simply a function of the standard deviation of active manager's relative returns: it is a statistical phenomenon. It is not realistic to assume that when your imagined star starts to look like a dog you will be able to stick with it.

Fund turnover allows the government of the day, advisers and fund managers to take another bite at the capital. This is why I choose to assume that the standard 5 per cent sales commission should be written off over a holding period of just five years to arrive at a realistic annual cost.

Adding up the wedge

The total annual cost of unit trusts is shown in Figure 11.1 as a representative range of possible combinations, starting with the thin end of 0.6 per cent and rising to as much as 3.85 per cent per annum for the highest assumptions. These estimates ignore the impact of stamp duty on the investor's own trading in units.

What this table makes clear is that the annual management charge is not alone a good guide to the cost-wedge specific to an individual fund, as the combination of portfolio manager turnover and how often a sales commission is incurred will alter relationships based on explicit charges alone.

The notion that a fund could offer the deadly combination at the extreme right in the chart (an annual management charge of 1.5 per cent, high turnover and a full sales commission of 5 per cent) is not fanciful. Indeed, these are exactly the sort of numbers that a star manager might be expected to show. High turnover is 'macho', high charges are 'worth it' and why discount sales commissions if the money is flowing in regardless? Plausible perhaps, but it is costing nearly 4 per cent per annum. Even if the sales commission is written off over a ten-year holding period, the annualized cost is still over 3 per cent.

Figure 11.1 ▪ **Estimated total cost combinations for UK equity unit trusts**

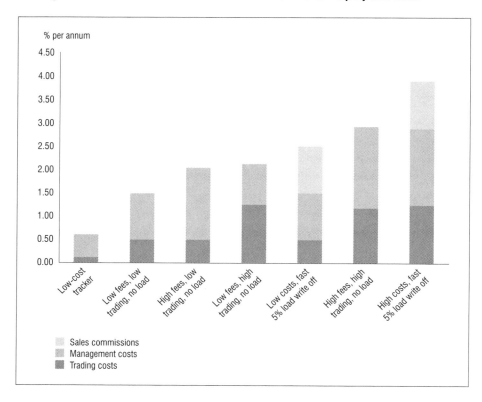

The cluster of combinations around 2 per cent to 2.5 per cent gives a clue to how difficult it is to avoid high costs even if no front end commissions are being charged. The addition of commissions takes a fund with average charges and mid-range turnover to a level over 3 per cent per annum. On this basis, a figure of 2.85 per cent, however alarming, seems quite representative of the cost of actively managed unit trusts in today's not very streetwise marketplace.

How deep is the wedge driven?

Bearing in mind the warning about the law of *small* numbers, we can now take these examples and see how much of the market return measures the industry is taking for itself. Table 11.1 summarizes several examples of total costs, including the tracker option, and calculates the percentage each represents of the different measures. These are the exceptional outperformance targets and the systematic market return measures when market conditions are normal or exceptionally high or low in relation to the bands defined in Part I. Where the industry takes more than 100 per cent, the proportion is in bold type.

Table 11.1 ■ Percentage of the return measure taken by the industry at different levels of total costs

	1% pa outperformance target	High market return	Ave market return	Low market return	High-risk premium	Ave-risk premium	Low-risk premium
Costs % pa							
3.85	**385**	43	64	**128**	92	**140**	**385**
2.85	**285**	32	48	95	68	**104**	**285**
1.50	**150**	17	25	50	36	55	**150**
0.60	60	7	10	20	14	22	60

At 2.85 per cent (line 2), for example, the typical fund costs are absorbing 48 per cent of the normal market return (column 3) but when markets are high in real terms (column 4) future returns could be all but wiped out by that level of costs (95 per cent). This is highly relevant after an exceptionally long and powerful bull market. Other than when the expected risk premium is very high, industry costs are taking over 100 per cent of the investor's reward for risk (column 6), forcing him or her into unwittingly irrational choices. If the risk premium is low (column 7), almost no cost level for an active fund appears to be rational by comparison with a tracker. To get away with this, they have to make you believe the lie.

However, even the lowest charges overwhelm a slim but sustained margin of outperformance of 1 per cent per annum (column 1) that might be all we should hope for, on the evidence of the previous chapter. Only chance, and that at very long odds, can come to the rescue by delivering an even better margin of outperformance. For the market return measures (columns 2–4), it is inflation that comes to the rescue by concealing the actual erosion of real wealth implied by a ratio over 100 per cent or, when it is 50 per cent, the erosion of the real growth rate of wealth.

The illusion that inflation increases the investor's return margin over costs is partly created by the PIA assumptions which are the only projections or assumptions the typical customer gets to see. These are only expressed in nominal or money terms. No attempt is made to separate the inflation element and the real return element. As we noted in Part I, money illusion has tripped up far too many people in the history of retail investment, from my grandmother and her War Loan to the actuaries at Equitable Life. If we could all see the effect of charges set out in real terms as in this table, we would surely think again about paying them.

It is high time the FSA took a lead in shattering the money illusion, but in the mean time falling inflation is helping by reducing the highest nominal return rate that the FSA allows. So when an adviser or product provider quotes a 'reduction in yield', it will look like a bigger hit if the provider is taking 2 per cent from 7 per cent than if it is taking 2 per cent from 12 per cent. Even that assumes the investor actually looks at the 'reduction in yield' figure and knows what it means, which many surveys suggest is unlikely.[28]

A type of funding task that is particularly vulnerable to excessive costs is the conversion of a capital sum to a finite stream of income (such as pension income drawdown, school fees funding, the requirement to live off a divorce settlement or meet regular expenses out of a damages settlement). As the fund is drawn down the balance is also subject to investment growth, the key being to ensure that the relationship between them keeps enough money in the pot for as long as it is needed. It must not run out!

For a drawdown phase of, say, 15 years, paying 2 per cent costs instead of 1 per cent costs could shorten the life of the capital for a given rate of withdrawal by two years and adding in a front-end load of, say, 5 per cent could be another year of income. For some plans, high costs could make the entire approach an irrational choice with a high proba-bility of failure.

The cost wedge in personal pensions

Packaged personal pension contracts invest either in unit trusts or with-profits funds of life insurance companies. If they are investing in unit trusts, they expose the investor to the same cost sources and same range

---

[28] Because reduction in yield ignores the trading costs, it is not even a good measure of the true cost drag for an active product and not a fair comparison with the reduction in yield quoted for a product based on tracking an index.

of cost combinations. However, there are a number of additional and largely unseen costs that have a particularly bruising impact on a pension plan. These include:

1 the higher costs of collecting and administering a stream of potentially small monthly contributions

2 the penalties that pension companies have typically applied to customers who stop making payments or switch provider

3 the cost of purchasing an annuity to convert the final sum into a stream of retirement income payments.

All three were analyzed in a report by pension experts connected with Birkbeck College, University of London. The authors estimated the total plan costs at 45 per cent of the capital value of a fund![xlii] In other words, the final value of the plan will typically be 45 per cent less than it would have been without those plan costs. This is the cumulative impact on wealth of attaching a ball and chain to the wealth driver, month after month for the expected duration of a career.

This is made up of about 5 per cent for the annuity purchase, 25 per cent as the total cost of management and 15 per cent as the typical cost of stopping contributions. The 25 per cent management cost roughly corresponds in the table above to a charge level of 1.5 per cent per annum (however it is made up). These proportions exclude the impact of trading costs within the funds so we should assume that if they cannot be translated into additional return the 25 per cent and 45 per cent figures understate the real drag.

The cost of a with-profits policy

As we saw in Chapter 9, almost everything to do with life office with-profits funds is as clear as mud. That includes costs. However, the Birkbeck paper's authors estimated the total expense ratio, as a measure of fund-management costs, as 1.3 per cent of funds under management (an average for 146 offices in 1997, all being open funds with active marketing).[xliii] In earlier years costs were evidently substantially higher, which is worrying. The point about the underlying cost to an investor in a life fund is that it is not fixed as a percentage of the assets. The with-profits name itself derives from the fact that the life fund is itself a business which like any other has fixed and variable business costs and can make profits or losses. This makes the relationship between the running costs and the market value of the assets highly unstable.

The aspect of Birkbeck's estimates that is of concern is that the 1.3 per cent figure that suggest comparability with the explicit charges of unit trusts arises only at a time when market values had risen strongly and so it might therefore normally be higher. While some of the largest life offices claim to be able to run their life funds for less than 1 per cent of assets, this reflects lasting benefits of scale economies but also less dependable benefits of high market values. You should not for a minute believe that a with-profits product is generally a low-cost product.

As many customers of the industry will have noticed, life offices are not very efficient and need heavy investment in IT systems. Against this background, the recent trend of consolidation of the industry through mergers and acquisitions and the demutualization initiatives to bring in additional capital all make sense.

Double charging: double trouble?

Double charging refers to products or services that require the customer to pay explicit fund-management charges and then expose them to another set of fund-management charges within the portfolio contents, typically because the contents are other funds. There could be two layers of management expenses and two layers of sales commissions, or other combinations. Double charging arises in a 'fund of funds' or in portfolios of funds.

MOST DOUBLE CHARGING DOES TAKE THE CUSTOMER HIGH UP THE WEDGE

Having two layers of management charge is not necessarily a disaster for the consumer: it all depends where it takes you on the wedge. A portfolio service that customized an asset allocation and then used tracker funds, which is very streetwise, could involve two lots of charges and still come out less expensive than a typical active unit trust.

Most double charging does take the customer high up the wedge. Typical examples are the funds of funds promoted by Portfolio Fund Management Ltd and the portfolio of funds service provided by Rothschild Asset Management, both of which invest in other managers' funds. Double charging is on the increase. Funds investing in hedge funds inevitably combine two sets of high basic charges as well as conditional performance fees. Double charging is an inherent element of most of the personal wealth-management services being offered to the mass affluent because these mostly need to use existing products as portfolio contents. It is also inherent in the widely used insurance 'bond' structure provided, as a wrapper, by companies such as Skandia and Clerical & Medical.

The cost of a personal portfolio

Traditionally, if you had a personal portfolio managed for you it was made up of individual securities and the chances are it was managed for you by a stockbroker, and often it was on an advisory rather than fully discretionary basis. All of their income came from brokerage commissions. Though some still operate on this basis, brokers are moving to discretionary management contracts with fees calculated as a percentage of the portfolio value, recognizing that the service being provided is no different from that of a private bank or specialist money management firm.

Asset-based fees bring a number of advantages but not least is that private client managers can then mirror the charging structure of funds, so as to compete with their asset-gathering machine on the same terms. Most now charge around 1.5 per cent and are willing to pay away to IFAs or other introducing agents up to 0.5 per cent per annum as a trail commission. Of course, if they are stockbrokers, they may also have the benefit of some if not all of the brokerage they generate. The level of trading activity is not necessarily higher just because they also broke stocks, however. Some private client money under the management or advice of stockbrokers is more passive than a tracker (the index constituents are at least altered from time to time)!

As private client managers may also use unit trusts or investment trusts as well as (or instead of) individual securities, there is likely to be a degree of double charging at the level of management fees and there may also be sales commissions that are not fully rebated to customers.

Customized portfolios are increasingly managed on an asset-based fee basis by IFAs. They too view regular income as better than irregular selling commissions and recognize that the productivity of an advisory practice is dragged down by the process of making recommendations to clients and chasing up replies when as discretionary managers they just call a fund group and place the order. Fee levels and commission rebating practices appear to vary considerably.

Though personal portfolios generally lie in the middle area of the cost wedge, they may cost more but are unlikely to cost less except for very large portfolios where institutional-style fees can be negotiated.

The odds against making up the cost wedge

Knowing that active management is a lottery and knowing the costs of playing the lottery, the logical thing to do next is to put the two together to calculate the odds of winning. Winning means at the very least clearing the hurdle of high costs through achieved fund returns (which common sense tells us should be a minimum expectation) but it should really mean exceeding the hurdle by a clear margin.

If we know the odds they will give us an idea of whether we want to play at all (or just stick to index trackers and minimize costs). If we want to play and we know the odds, we will know how important it is to be aware of the cost differences between different active products and managers. Simple though it sounds, the calculation is complicated by the fact that the data for achieved fund returns does not allow for the individual running costs (as distinct from selling commissions) within each fund. Therefore we cannot tell the extent to which past relative returns have been influenced by costs rather than by chance, skill or stupidity.

One piece of analysis has attempted to isolate the impact of individual fund costs to try to arrive at 'clean' results. This is an article titled 'The Charges of the Pensions Brigade' by John Chapman which appeared in *Money Management* in September 1998. A former researcher at the OFT, Chapman is an acknowledged authority on the life and pensions industry although his penetrating research and trenchant views have not endeared him to company bosses. He writes regularly in *Money Management* magazine and other journals.

Though the analysis was specific to pensions I believe it is representative enough of the entire population of unit trust managers to allow us to draw some general conclusions about the odds of making enough extra return to cover different incremental costs as you move up the wedge.

Chapman took 36 pension fund unit trusts investing in UK equities and after adding back charges to identify charge-free performance, used frequency analysis applied to different holding periods to calculate the odds of making up cost differences through 'pure' performance. He could not adjust for trading activity within the funds, however. He chose to categorize funds by bands of charges. By fitting in with his cost bands, we can calculate the chances of surmounting two examples of cost hurdles, 1 per cent per annum and 2 per cent per annum.

As we have seen, 1 per cent is a good indication of the additional cost relative to a tracker of a a active fund with low annual charges and high activity and no load, or of an active fund with high charges but low activity and no load. A 1 per cent hurdle also approximates a 5 per cent load written off over five years.

Chapman calculated the odds of making up a 1 per cent difference after 15 years as just 25 per cent or one in four. The closest charges gap to 1 per cent at ten years was 0.8 per cent which offered a chance of 30 per cent, so, much the same.

The 2 per cent gap is appropriate for making up the costs of the more expensive products at the upper end of the wedge, including double charging products. It is also appropriate if we want to assess the chance of getting over a 1 per cent cost difference and earning a 1 per cent per annum clear profit. For a ten-year holding period Chapman calculated the chance of making up a 2 per cent difference as just 9 per cent or near enough one in ten! However, at 15 years it is 25 per cent, which is better than the ten-year comparison would suggest. The distribution of charge-free returns at each interval is probably only different because of random return influences in the period of market history analyzed and the lower chance for a larger gap is more likely to be representative of the gamble.

These odds assume the holding is in fact retained. As we have noted already, and as Chapman points out in his article, very few are retained as long as ten, let alone 15, years. He suggests that after ten years, just 49 per cent of pension policies sold by IFAs and 37 per cent sold by company representatives will still be running and that after 15 years it will only be 35 per cent for IFAs and 24 per cent for companies.

Even if we take the view that a rational investor will stick with his or her active fund selection for a long period, a chance of one in four or one in ten underestimates the true odds for decision making. There is a strong case in portfolio theory for arguing that there should be a risk premium for the additional uncertainty associated with active management. Even if a manager or customer managed to clear these two hurdles, cost and the risk premium, it does not mean they have truly beaten the system, only matched the reward to the risk.

Applying this to Chapman's analysis, a low-cost product may have one chance in four of matching the return of a tracker but closer to one in ten of matching the efficiency of a tracker, in other words by earning enough extra to justify the extra risk. A mid-range product may therefore have less than one chance in ten of matching the efficiency of a tracker and a very small chance of achieving a clear profit (which in portfolio theory terms we could call an excess return). For more expensive products, the chance of achieving an excess return may effectively be negligible.

There is no doubt that investors are for the most part completely unaware of these probabilities. Confronted with high industry charges, they are not consciously gambling to overcome the obstacle. Drawing people into hopelessly irrational bets on the sly is an important proof of a system corrupted. If they know the odds and still choose to gamble, that is another matter.

If we are being systematically exploited, someone must be getting rich at our expense. We are about to see that the riches are not spread around quite how we might have expected.

12

Who gets the cream?

A subtle sort of rip-off

Retail investment costs are higher in the UK than in the USA but industry profit margins are lower here than there. This is the first indication that the situation is more complex than a straightforward industry rip-off. So where is the money going? Where are the fat cats?

What we find is that most of the cost wedge is tied up with the performance lie, including bribing us with our own money, and that people working in the industry closest to the lie can justify taking out very high salaries and bonuses. Shareholders of most firms in the industry are left with good but not exceptionally high profit margins and return on capital: industry profitability surveys show no sign of a smoking gun.

The securities trading business is competitive and the investment-management business is highly fragmented so neither is where we would expect to see old-fashioned robber barons. We have already discovered that blatantly unethical behaviour often goes hand in hand with excessive charges. Yet the same charging structures and commission flows have been operated by firms who regard themselves as fundamentally ethical and whose own profitability in no way speaks of a rip-off.

We see a system that perpetuates itself precisely because even mediocre firms can keep large numbers of employees happy while shareholders earn reasonable returns. This is not the Darwinian system we are familiar with in a market economy. Good investment firms rarely drive bad firms out of business and investment companies seem not to be able to establish skill, resource or technology advantages that they can exploit consistently. If the fundamental driver of asset growth and profitability is essentially a lottery, this is exactly the industry system we should expect to see.

It may not look like the straightforward rip-off that headline journalism portrays but it is perhaps all the more pernicious for being so subtle, so institutionalized. These are the symptoms of a system if not corrupt then corrupted.

Four-way split

In the previous chapter we identified two major sets of costs of investing: direct charges and trading costs. We saw that most of the direct charges are a function of the additional cost of providing active management and that most of the trading costs are associated with active management.

The industry's revenue stream from trading can be thought of as the first claim on the cost wedge. It is widely dispersed through investment banks and securities houses, most of which now operate on a global scale. The market in securities trading is efficient and for the most part competitive so while we may question the point of paying high trading costs, whether as broker's commission or in the form of market spreads, they are not the product of anti-competitive practice.

CUSTOMERS OF THE INDUSTRY MIGHT ASSUME THAT FUND MANAGERS ARE DRIVEN TO PRODUCE GOOD PERFORMANCE

We have seen that the fund-management industry collects its revenue stream in the form of the annual management charges, the gross commissions it collects from customers when they buy their products and, in some cases, various other administrative policy, wrapper, product or service charges it levies on particular functions.

A ridiculously high proportion of this gross income is redistributed to oil the wheels of the industry marketing machine. The proportion of the industry charges spent on promoting growth of assets rather than delivering performance is possibly as much as two-thirds and selling incentives of one form or another are the greater part of this. Marketing (or 'distribution' as the industry often calls it) is the second claim on the cost wedge.

Customers of the industry might assume that fund managers are driven to produce good performance. But what they are actually driven to produce is growth of the asset base to which they fix their charges. After all, business managers know they do not control the market returns that influence the value of assets under management and they mostly know they have very little actual control over the contribution of relative performance, so it is logical to make marketing the key focus of their business strategy. Note this from the horse's mouth (from a 1995 research report from securities brokers Goldman Sachs – also big players in the fund management business):

Managing money is not the true business of the money management industry. Rather, it is gathering and retaining assets. Good money management skills are only one of many important tools essential to the business of attracting and retaining assets.[xliv]

The third and fourth claims on the cost wedge are represented by the split of the remaining fund-management revenue between two groups: shareholders of the businesses and employees of the businesses. There is always a competitive tension between them. There is good evidence that employees are doing substantially better than shareholders. If true, it is in a long tradition of City firms and is consistent with the dominant modern model which is American.

▩ Paying for the marketing machine

If two-thirds of the industry revenue goes on promoting asset growth, most of that can only be justified in terms of the performance myth. If there was no pretence about the predictive value of past performance and products were presented simply as commodities, differentiated by a few functional features and by costs, there would be neither need nor justification for an expensive marketing machine.

The Treasury has understood this for a long time and the charges cap on a stakeholder pension is much more about forcing reductions in the costs of distribution and administration than about lowering the expense of the portfolio management. Standing back and looking at the industry as a whole, it makes no difference what the balance is between each firm's spending on advertising and commissions, or if the selling incentives are paid to a product company's own sales staff, to tied agents or to IFAs.

These are just different approaches to distribution. It is the collective cost of running the industry machine that matters.

Estimates of how much the industry spends on marketing are not entirely hazardous. For life insurance company pension products we can use the same DTI information gathered by the Birkbeck College authors referred to in the previous chapter. They found that for a typical company the proportion of the total expenses related to marketing in selected years was 73 per cent in 1989, 69 per cent in 1994 and 65 per cent in 1997. In each year, roughly half was accounted for by commissions. Most, incidentally, do pay commissions externally rather than paying selling incentives to their own sales force although some of the exceptions are firms with large individual market shares, such as the pensions business of Equitable and Legal & General. Of the balance of the expenses, the authors speculated that around half each was accounted for by administration and the fund management itself. In other words, the ratio of the cost of marketing their performance to the cost of achieving it is about four to one!

The marketing claim on the income of a unit trust group is unlikely to be substantially different although the profile will vary between firms if they rely heavily on a distribution channel that is not typical. I suspect that the clearing banks spend relatively little on promoting their products, not many of which will have outstanding performance at any one time, and rely instead on responding to the selling opportunities that present themselves in the branches. A firm like Jupiter and Aberdeen Asset Management, on the other hand, seeks to build its business by promoting itself heavily both in the press and to IFAs, using the commission currency to the full. In 2000, Aberdeen might well have recycled a staggering £60 million of customers' own money to harvest net inflows of nearly £3 billion![xlv]

The main difference between unit trusts and insurance funds is the lower exposure to collecting small regular savings. Allowing for this, it is likely that the ratio of marketing to management is about three to one in a unit trust group.

The real fat cats

Though commissions or equivalent selling incentives account for most of the cost of marketing, they are spread across a highly fragmented advisory industry. So while it is true that commission incentives have made some exceptionally talented or unscrupulous salespeople very well off, most of the insurance company 'consultants' (that is, sales persons) or IFAs you meet are unlikely to be very high earners. As we saw in Chapter 6, there are not enough hours in the day for a super-salesperson to make a killing out of commissions unless he or she is sitting at the top of a pyramid structure of commission-sharing agents.

The biggest individual beneficiaries of high retail investment costs work as fund managers or as business managers in portfolio management firms. Managers' power to extract superior salaries and bonuses comes from us, the customers. Their power only works if we go along with the industry obsession with performance and are willing to take at face value, as presented to us by the marketing machine, the plausibility of the superior skill or intelligence of a manager or of an entire team of managers.

It is ironic that as commoditization is increasing, the cult of the individual is actually being more heavily promoted. You might think that with financial journalists thinking and writing far more independently, greater public awareness of discounting of sales commissions and easier public access to performance data, we would be less susceptible to the idea that each individual product might be 'special'. But something else is also going on. The more information we have and the less convinced we are that we have the right information, the harder the problem of reaching conclusions becomes. Brand distinctiveness is no longer powerful enough to act as a decision short-cut. So it is very tempting to fall back on another version of blind trust: so-and-so has the 'x factor' that will make our money outperform.

As pinning faith on individuals takes a stronger hold, it also meets a growing social phenomenon: the *OK* magazine appetite for the glitzy superficiality of stardom. In the glamour stakes, British investment professionals have a lot of catching up to do compared with Wall Street's top fund managers and stockbrokers, but they are on the way.

Gender has done much to flavour the growing British trend of public salivation over the high salaries of fund managers. Portfolio management is an activity in which women have for a long time flourished. If we view relative performance as a lottery, men and women must have an equal chance, although American research suggests that women give themselves an edge over men by trading less.[xlvi] Machismo does not pay! Though the performance edge may not be the reason, there is no doubt the combination of a good track record and fabulous earnings is more likely to catch the headlines if it's a woman.

Combining the gender factor with youth means being a hot shot in the day and plain mum in the morning and at night. This was the angle that helped propel 'Superwoman' Nicola Horlick to *OK* status. Sacked by Morgan Grenfell for secretly negotiating with another firm to transfer herself and a team, she reappeared a little later running a new investment team at Société Générale. The public's interest in her, though sustained more by advertisements than editorial, has tended to be sympathetic.

Youth plays another role in the cult of the individual as it is more likely, statistically, to be associated with an unblemished track record. A young manager can have a string of good years, possibly explained by the results of only a few bets, and look really smart, until randomness catches up with him or her and some of those bets turn out to be losers. In Chapter 10 we saw that a run of winners can last several years or it can be overturned in just two or three, depending on the nature of the bets and the way the market environment alters.

The statistical advantage of youth that helped Horlick has also been maximized by Aberdeen's new chief investment officer, Katherine Garret-Cox. She was a star manager of US portfolios at Hill Samuel before being recruited in that capacity by Aberdeen. Both under 40, Horlick and Garret-Cox are reported in the newspapers (possibly too glibly) to be earning over £1 million.[29]

I have often heard it said that the advantage of age is also a cyclical factor because bull markets temporarily reward the bigger risk takers and these tend to be younger. This implies that with the passage of time we acquire lower betas as well as higher hairlines. However, some of the industry's highest-earning fund managers are also mature men with their betas as macho as the next man's.

Money management, like many City activities, has always involved inherent tension between shareholders and employees: they contest for a share of the spoils but they both need each other. For the most part, individuals have correctly judged how far they can push boards of management to maximize their own earnings and the very public hubris of Nicola Horlick is unusual.

---

[29] Whatever their actual earnings, it is surely not surprising that they should be as high as for men of a similar age for similar degrees of plausibility. In fact, it is unlikely that the top executives and best-paid portfolio managers in the industry will be earning basic salaries of much more than a quarter of that headline figure but bonuses, contingent on achieved success, could just about bring the total up to £1 million.

Even the less gilded actors in the performance game can turn the machine to their advantage by exploiting the importance to the business of continuity. It is very bad to lose a star manager but any manager who has a decent following from IFAs or who is associated publicly with a firm or a product can seriously disrupt sales by jumping ship. It was ever thus but there has been a definite tendency for individuals to increase their bargaining power by acting in concert, as a team. That increases their value to both the current and prospective employer. The star culture, heavy ISA advertising and the bull market carried this to the point where the risks for individuals could appear negligible. In reality they never are negligible and we will no doubt be hearing some more hubris stories before long.

The prize for chutzpah goes to the Jupiter team, whose boardroom dramas managed even to eclipse the impact of Littlewood's departure. Jupiter stands out as the only investment team to have sold themselves three times to the same buyer in five years.

In 1995 Jupiter sold 75 per cent of itself to German bankers, Commerzbank, for £175 million – terms that reflected an already high profile in PEP sales based on a broad stable of funds with competitive performance. Under their flamboyant founder, John Duffield, Jupiter had encouraged the individual flair and creativity that Littlewood had taken advantage of successfully. They showed the same entrepreneurial spirit in negotiating terms of an option to sell the 25 per cent share of the equity they retained. Exercising this option in January 2000 the Jupiter team collected a further £500 million, a near tenfold increase in their price tag.

These terms nonetheless rankled with the Jupiter team. After bubbling disputes with Commerzbank, the Germans' patience finally ran out and they fired Duffield and four other directors. The star manager of their special situations fund went with Duffield to establish a rival firm with the less than modest name of New Star Asset Management. The dispute was settled out of court for a reported £5 million.[xlvii]

With IFAs and self-directed investors uneasy about the bust up, coming so soon after the loss of high-profile Littlewood, Commerzbank found itself negotiating incentives with the remaining (and newly recruited) managers at Jupiter: round three. If it was too tight-fisted it could lose the team but if it gave up too much it could end up with a derisory return on the £680 million already invested. Salaries at the top end of the industry scale are a given in this situation and the issue is the share of the profits or equivalent equity rights that can be won for the team.

When Brian Ashford-Russell and Tim Woolley, stars in the once bright firmament of technology investment, announced late in 2000 they were leaving Henderson to set up their own 'boutique', they were part of an entrepreneurial trend that includes a number of managers wanting to run their own hedge funds.

Each market environment brings new manifestations of the battle between shareholders and portfolio managers. Technology managers have been the hottest properties in recent years but not many years ago it was emerging market specialists who could call the shots, such was the popularity of the sector and the desire of unit trust groups to have a product to offer. In the late 1980s one of the biggest challenges for business managers was recruiting and hanging on to Japanese equity managers! Perhaps in a few years' time we will again be reading about a shortage of Japanese managers.

THE SOMETIMES PUBLIC COMPETITION BETWEEN SHAREHOLDERS AND EMPLOYEES MAKES THE INDUSTRY MORE INTERESTING BUT IT DOES NOT IN FACT GO FAR IN DIRECTLY EXPLAINING HIGH COSTS

The sometimes public competition between shareholders and employees makes the industry more interesting and might even inflame passions but it does not in fact go far in directly explaining high costs. However, it may contribute indirectly to the myth, and hence to the high cost, by encouraging the belief that if individuals can make this kind of money they must be very special.

Portfolio managers are acting rationally in seeking to exploit their own relative performance and the fluctuations in the fashions for their own areas of expertise. Business managers, representing the shareholders, are acting rationally in playing the game because they can hardly change the rules after building a marketing machine that promoted and now feeds a public appetite for the person not the commodity. The only irrational party here is the customer, by not trying to understand what the professionals' game is and how the professionals are likely to want to play it.

13

Madness in their methods

Intelligence failures

This is not an unintelligent industry. There are a lot of very clever people working in it and regulating it. However, in the light of what we have learnt in earlier chapters, we may wonder what good the industry's intelligence has done customers.

There is no question that the intellectual capital of the industry has been efficiently directed to furthering its own interests, but these are not the same as ours. As we have seen, the way both portfolio management and so-called independent advice are organized as a business is a rational and, therefore, intelligent response to the way the financial rewards are structured. This applies to the way individual practitioners act in their best interests, as we saw in the previous chapter. It applies to the way businesses as a whole see their financial interests, as we saw when we looked at the economics of investment management and the risk posed by the public wising up to the commodity nature of products. It even applies to the way the industry organizes itself to defend its collective interests.

When we looked at the essential premise the industry seeks to sell, the performance myth, we found that our willingness to accept it is likely to be a function of how plausible we judge the claims to exceptional intelligence. We do not follow people because they tend to be lucky or have good contacts, even though these might have been admirable criteria for the nineteenth-century stockbroker! Now it is what they know, not who they know.

Though we seem to need the comfort of institutional brands, we tend to associate success in investment with intellectual equipment and not knowing any better we associate this in turn with individual judgement rather than with collective resources or the application of technical methods. Yet the implication of the preceding chapters, set against the introduction in Part I to what really matters, is that there is a fundamental mismatch between the intelligence the industry seeks to maximize and the skills that the customer would be best served by.

From the customers' point of view, there is madness in the industry's methods. From the industry's point of view, there is method in that madness, but only for as long as their business agenda is served by keeping customers in the dark about what really matters. Any change has to come from customers being more enlightened and rewarding businesses that come over to their side.

TECHNOLOGY TYPICALLY REPLICATES THE WRONG TYPE OF SKILL AND APPLIES IT TO THE KIND OF DECISION THAT SUITS THE INDUSTRY RATHER THAN THE CUSTOMER

The fundamental industry problem has to do with the *type* of skills: the kind of decision on which they are focused and the technical methods that they apply. When we examine the type of skills needed to provide individual investors with wise counsel, we find that they are much more agnostic and intellectually humble than the mindset the industry would have us believe is required. The skills are also ones that depend much more on the use of centralized, high-level technology than on personal judgement or intellect.

There is also a fundamental problem of the typical *level* of skills, in an activity where the public's access is via tens of thousands of individuals, be they IFAs, private client stockbrokers or sales staff in the institutions. The challenge of raising technical competence across such large numbers of people contributes to this problem. It is a challenge that desperately cries out for distributed technology as the solution.

Though there are some signs that technology is being used more effectively to raise standards at the point of sale, that technology typically replicates the wrong type of skill and applies it to the kind of decision that suits the industry rather than the customer.

In advisory firms the focus is on centralizing the fundamentally flawed 'best advice' process. In private client portfolio-management firms the focus is on centralizing and regimenting standardized decisions, like a set of templates. There is little evidence that investment technology is being used to raise the standards and integrity of resource planning and asset allocation, or to inject discipline and consistency into decision making or to promote greater customization. Any of these would be more valuable to individual investors.

As to the type of skills that matter, these must be related to the decision hierarchy we introduced in Part I. The key to the outcomes of investment tasks, and therefore personal involvement in choices about how money is managed, is asset allocation, or the exposure to markets. We saw that the essential feature of markets is that the range of outcomes is highly uncertain, even if those uncertainties are in some way bounded. Within those bounds, exactly what will happen is not predictable. Most of us will interpret this as meaning that markets compel intellectual humility. We are likely to assume that the skill required is in measuring and determining the appropriate probabilities, not in correctly forecasting a particular outcome within the probable range.

Likewise, when we looked at the performance myth, we found overwhelming evidence that attempts to make the right forecast and outsmart other market participants are flawed and that relative return outcomes are essentially random.

With few exceptions, however, the industry equates skill with making the correct bet or the correct forecast: 'the market is going to 6,000 by Christmas', or 'now that Joe has left the Joe Technology Fund it will underperform'. Not only that, but it also typically makes its forecast independently of any probable range of potential outcomes, as though even admitting to the uncertainty would itself undermine their own confidence in the forecast, let alone anyone else's. In terms of the psychology of a macho, gnostic investment manager or adviser, this may very well be the case.

We could debate whether machismo is a position practitioners feel forced to adopt, either to perpetuate the myth or to pander to the expectations of clients who already believe it, or one they feel genuinely comfortable with. I know some practitioners who are fundamentally uncomfortable with it but I feel sure that most are actively seeking to make fools of the market and prove their own superiority even if by doing so they are actually likely to make themselves look foolish.

In this chapter we will see how the industry's methods fail the customer through a combination of:

1 a lack of respect for investment theories

2 the absence of an intellectually independent advisory function

3 focus on management at the expense of investment planning

4 resistance to investment decision technology

5 the unintended consequence of regulations that institutionalize unsound investment assumptions

6 inadequate training and competence.

Though these weaknesses are prevalent throughout the industry, it is possible to avoid them and in Part III we offer practical guidance to finding the minority of professionals who have the right resources, are using the right methods and are applying them to a customer-centric agenda.

The absence of theory

In the skills department, the principal failure of the industry is a lack of familiarity with or respect for any underpinning theory. I single this out because basing the service provided to customers on widely accepted investment theories would do more than anything else to raise standards, reduce the regret caused by false certainty and improve customer participation and control. I also single it out because it is the most glaring difference between the services used by most institutional investors and those made available to individual investors.

What is it that institutions benefit from that individual investors do not? First, they are more likely to encounter the decision hierarchy that we presented in Part I as the key to organizing investment planning and investment management. The '90 per cent rule' that we introduced in Chapter 3, based on where portfolio returns come from, is one that trustees of most pension funds would be aware of.

When I was talking to an IFA about the importance of asset allocation a while ago, he protested, 'I know what you mean by asset allocation but 90 per cent of my clients wouldn't know what I was talking about.' This is not the right version of the 90 per cent rule! His comment is revealing because most IFAs simply do not see themselves as being in the business of educating customers or communicating simplifying structures that help clients participate in the decision process. You cannot structure portfolios to meet goals specific to the individual investor without explaining asset allocation. It is the medium by which the assets in the plan are determined to 'match' all the features that define a planning goal: the Three Ts we met in Part I.

To analyze both the needs and the assets of an individual investor in a 'matching' framework takes significant resources, appropriate to the task. It calls for particular technology, as well as a certain intellectual approach. The way both are applied should also admit the participation of the client. All of this compromises the way people run their business. For instance, getting clients to articulate their goals takes time. Customizing asset allocations to match all these different sets of goal definitions also takes more time, even with sophisticated technology, and runs counter to the need for standardized portfolio results to use in marketing.

The second feature of a theoretical underpinning that institutional investors benefit from is 'portfolio theory'. This helps them see that what counts is the behaviour of portfolio contents when combined, not the behaviour of the contents individually. Hence they are also more likely to realize that what counts is the suitability of a portfolio, rather than the suitability of individual managers or products. This is inconvenient for most investment advisers, who have some limited means of assessing the merits of individual products but no means of assessing combinations in a portfolio. In practice, they mostly avoid this limitation by only generating activity at the margin, relating recommendations to the specifics of a fund rather than the more complex concept of the overall portfolio integrity.

The third aspect of investment theory that influences institutional trustees is market efficiency: the idea that beating a representative benchmark for an individual asset class or market, through the exercise of selection skills rather than by luck, and beating it after all expenses, is implausible. This shows up in the greater use of index tracking among institutional portfolios. However, it also shows in differences in the approach to the selection of active managers and a greater awareness of the importance of costs. Just because institutional trustees choose to take a gamble on active managers with some or all of their money does not mean they are no different from most private clients. The difference is likely to be that they have made a conscious decision to take a controlled gamble in full knowledge of the odds. It may be less than fully rational but it is not in ignorance nor is it blindly dependent on people who have a vested interest in the business of active managers.

Independent advice: the actuarial model

The actions of trustees are underpinned by formal investment theory not because of the role of investment managers but because of the role of consulting actuaries. Most institutional funds benefit from advice from actuaries, as independent technical experts. Very few individual investors are advised by actuaries.

How actuaries perform their function is quite different from how IFAs perform them, even though the functions themselves are directly comparable. Both are engaged in task-based resource planning. Both should be recommending asset allocations. Both may also advise on the implementation options for those asset-allocation strategies, down to picking managers or funds. They may both be relatively dynamic, as part of a continuous stewardship role. To perform the same functions, the intellectual resources of the half dozen or so dominant consulting actuaries, the technology they have at their disposal and their customers' access to high-level skills are in a completely different league from the IFA industry.

TIME AND AGAIN I HAVE HEARD IFAS SAY THAT THEY CAN GET CLIENTS TO DO WHATEVER THEY WANT THEM TO DO

In this sense alone actuaries are independent: they have control of all the resources they need to perform their function. This is a definition of independence I attach a lot of importance to. Actuaries are also financially independent, charging fees for their service rather than depending on commissions from third parties. Time and again I have heard IFAs say that they can get clients to do whatever they want them to do. That is only because they have an interest in getting them to do something in particular. It should never arise if advice is independent and there is no motivation to sell.

The actuaries' culture is one of advice, not selling. They do see themselves as being in the business of communicating essential principles and of educating their customers. They are by training and instinct unwilling to take decisions in the place of their customers, even if (as quite often happens) trustees seek to load that responsibility onto anyone but themselves! Actuaries' response to that problem is to try to present the choices in a clearer way, such as by simplifying the principles, quantifying probabilities or using graphical aids, so as to facilitate not just participation but actual control by their client.

Planning versus management

Virtually all portfolio managers and most investment planners believe they should apply their skills to a particular 'decision time frame', probably no longer than five years, rather than to the (usually) much longer horizon of the owner of the money, which is related to the task the money is performing. This mismatch between decision and planning horizons is a peculiar but very common feature of private clients' investment arrangements. How did it come about and what is its impact?

It is perfectly feasible to divide up a planning horizon into shorter intervals if there is good reason for doing so. One reason would be if the short term was much more predictable than the long term. Then it would make sense to view the journey as a series of short independent periods and navigate from mark to mark rather than keep a fix on the ultimate goal. What we find is that there is no additional visibility over short horizons and no advantage from mean reversion. Another reason would be if the intention was to hire and fire managers on the basis of their progress over some period long enough for their skills to be tested. As we saw in Chapter 10, three and five years are popular intervals for assessing the skills of an active manager but it is futile to assess active manager relative returns and risks over a short time period. On both counts, the industry convention of dividing the long term into a series of short decision horizons is not supported by evidence of the link between time and predictability.

The industry tends to view the impact of short decision time frames as helpful to its own business agenda, and hence an intelligent response to available rewards. I am not so sure. For most firms that have already acquired a critical mass of assets, the benefits of successfully managing their clients' expectations, as part of a sustainable relationship based on service, could well be greater than the lottery of chasing competitive short-term track records. Live by the sword and you die by the sword. The statistical evidence of the value of a long-term customer and the high cost of each new customer using the precarious lottery approach suggests management have got it wrong.

The key to the alternative and more enlightened customer relationship is planning, not management. Management is merely the implementation of a dynamic plan. Dynamism simply means the planning process is continuous rather than once and for all, at the outset.

Planning is different because it is always focused on the client's own horizon. It is not about navigating from mark to mark as though the different legs of the course were independent one from the other. As we saw in Part I, the language of planning investment tasks based on personal life goals is very different from the language of investment management. This gives us a clue to the real difference, which is the techniques themselves. By putting the intellectual capital of the industry to work with the wrong techniques, most of it is being wasted.

Investment technology

Just as consulting actuaries apply mathematical techniques residing in computer programmes to perform most of their goal-based planning function, so private clients should expect to see the same technology lying behind whatever relationships they have with the industry. At present, it is highly unlikely that they will. They may well hear claims made about the appliance of science. They may sound impressive but they are likely to be deliberately misleading, pandering to the public's growing awareness of computer-based decision tools but taking advantage also of the ease with which non-technicians can be bamboozled.

Investment technology should be applied in each of the areas we have already addressed in the context of theory-based processes. It is a key part of the planning of resources for a task, which involves the complex modelling of the different sources of risk or uncertainty and the relationships between them. It is also fundamental to the process of asset allocation.

Let us walk through an example of a pension planning task, mindful as we go of how best we might deal with the calculations required. Imagine a range of tools: the back of an envelope, a calculator and a computer programme. There is no attempt here to overcomplicate the task. The list that follows is a genuine account of the components of a typical private client pension task:

1 It will definitely involve exposure to inflation. Unless investment risk is modelled directly in terms of real outcomes, it will be necessary to model inflation uncertainty. This has to capture both its dynamics as a function of the length of the planning horizon and its dynamics in terms of its relationship with market risk.

2 We will certainly need to specify expected stock market returns. As we saw in Part I, these are specific to individual markets and assets,

to actual market conditions in each and also to the time horizon. The sensitivity to market conditions is also different as between existing capital and future contributions. This is logical: the first cannot escape today as the starting point for future projections whereas the second will be invested in a series of tomorrows when market conditions will vary and may 'average out'.

3   If the portfolio is to be diversified geographically, there will also be some currency risk. The effect of diversifying the market risk and combining it with currency uncertainty has to be specified. These elements of investment uncertainty are also sensitive to the time horizon.

4   The horizon could be a single target year, such as the expected retirement date, or, if a drawdown is being planned, there is effectively a series of time horizons, such as one for each year of drawdown.

5   Drawing down capital has the opposite impact to contributions on the balance of the fund. The dynamic effects of shifting market conditions during drawdown cannot be ignored because if you make a mistake there may not be enough capital left to buy the required annuity.

6   Whether planning for an immediate annuity or drawdown, there is still (as the law stands) a requirement at some stage to purchase an annuity so the plan must make an allowance for mortality uncertainty, possibly for both husband and wife. Either the annuity terms must be based on contractual inflation protection or the inflation risk inherent in a level annuity must also be specified.

7   The conversion of a capital sum into a stream of annuity income payments itself introduces uncertainty. This uncertainty must be calculated taking into account the likely association between the level of the capital in the portfolio at the end of the programme and the level of interest rates at that time that will determine the level of income an annuity sum will purchase. The two factors are causally related, not independent, and that makes a big difference when the risk is specified.

8   The overall planning uncertainty and the mean expected return should allow from the outset for the fact that the portfolio can be altered during its life, notably as the remaining time horizon

shortens. This approach, increasingly coming to be known as 'lifestyle' investing because it is sensitive to age or stage in life, means that the outcome uncertainty is not a slave to market conditions at the end of the plan. Assume, for instance, that as you approach your planning horizon you choose to hold your desired target-outcome constant and that your risk tolerance is also unaltered. Then, to keep the possible outcomes inside your acceptable bounds, the asset allocation will have to change. The effect of anticipating this dynamism as part of a long-term plan is to lower the mean expected return slightly but the planning benefit comes in the shape of a narrower range of likely outcomes.

9 No plan should ever be made without also taking into account the costs. We have seen in Chapter 11 that how far your resources will go is critically sensitive to the size of the cost wedge. Some realistic cost assumptions are needed as a planning input. These can be generic, appropriate to the style of implementation (such as how much in trackers and how much in active funds) rather than specific to the actual funds used.

It is easy to see that these are calculations that are impossible to perform in the head or on the back of an envelope. They cannot be modelled using a calculator because it is a tool for compounding and discounting at fixed rates and cannot allow for the dynamics of risk or the way different sources of risk combine in a portfolio. They are calculations that can only be done with a computer. Only by using a computer can the probabilities be quantified, enabling the odds to be called. Only then can numbers usefully take the place of woolly flannel as the basis of customer under-standing and involvement in the choices.

So much for the planning process. Next comes the asset-allocation decision. Ideally the two should be integral rather than sequential so that the outcome probabilities are specific to a particular investment strategy. Otherwise there is only a weak link between the planning assumptions and the actual investment programme.

There is more than one way to skin the cat when it comes to asset allocation but the decision process also typically involves quite complex mathematics, based on some kind of 'optimization'. As we saw in Chapter 3, this involves a 'trade-off' type of decision, typically involving three inputs:

1 the expected returns of the different portfolio building blocks in the opportunity set

2 the standard deviations or volatility of each building block

3 the correlation (or co-movement) between them.

Though there are equations that could be laboriously followed to approximate the same type of trade-off, possibly even on the back of a large envelope, it really is a job for a computer programme.

Asset allocation may not just involve calculating some optimal or efficient combination of risky assets (which we defined in Chapter 2 as assets with uncertain outcomes). It can also involve combining an optimal risky-asset portfolio with a risk-free asset (which we defined as one with a certain – or for all practical purposes certain – outcome). This will in turn involve some formal way of characterizing the way the individual customer values different outcomes, such as how they trade off at different levels of portfolio wealth the possibility of additional wealth versus the possibility of loss of wealth. This 'utility function' also needs to be modelled mathematically. This is also a job for a computer.

You would be absolutely right to conclude from this that every one must already be using computers and that, if not, either there is a lot of guesswork going on or else no attempt is even being made to take these decisions formally.

In stockbrokers' offices, in private banks, in IFA practices and certainly in the sales departments of the direct selling institutions, computer-based techniques for these decisions are the exception. We are talking about a tiny minority. But at least it is growing.

Even online investment sites do not yet offer this kind of decision technology, although they are also moving gradually in the direction of interactive planning and management tools that have the essential elements of modelling precisely the different elements of uncertainty, specific to an individual investor's goals. In Chapter 18 we will look at what is already available online and imagine how, with growing sophistication of these early approaches, the internet will become the primary means of access to sophisticated and customized advice, particularly at small portfolio sizes.

The industry's unwillingness to embrace mathematical, computer-based decision techniques is another intelligence failure. Like the obsession with stock selection and active management, it is a symptom of the triumph of intellectual arrogance over all the lessons of market history that compel intellectual humility. Yet in one important respect it is different. Whereas for the industry to admit the performance myth would threaten mass redundancy of method and people and dramatically impact on what it can charge, the adoption of technology for resource planning and asset allocation does not cause the industry to self-destruct. Indeed, it should both raise standards and lower costs. This makes the arrogance of the resistance to it all the more staggering.

Investment assumptions

An investment plan is as good as the assumptions underlying it. The PIA must be held responsible for institutionalizing the use of planning assumptions that are half-baked and amateurish, have already proved highly dangerous and are likely to prove even more so in the future. These are the 'growth rates', as stipulated by the PIA (and now by the FSA), that you see on any recommendation of a packaged product.

The intention was sound: to prevent competition by assumptions, so that one product should not appear a better buy than another simply because it projected outcomes using a higher assumed growth rate. Whatever the intention, it was naïve not to realise that these 'illustrations' would then be used by the industry as the basis for planning tasks and calculating the capital and contributions (or premiums) required to hit a customer's target. This is exactly what happened, even though technically the projections are only binding on product providers and advisers are free to make independent assumptions for planning purposes or even in their 'reasons why' letters.

As planning assumptions, the PIA growth-rate illustrations are flawed because they only appear, by providing a range of rates, to offer realistic and sensible bands of uncertainty. As far as I am aware, at no stage has the PIA attempted to relate these assumptions to any formal model of nominal return uncertainty, such as is regularly used by consulting actuaries in the institutional market, as we noted earlier. If they did, it is not recognizable. Because they are not based on a formal model, there is no confidence level that can be attached to either the high or low number. Without a formal distribution of expected growth rates, even taking an average of the high and low assumptions cannot be presented as a mean expected growth rate, though this is how it is often used and presented in the industry.

Mis-specifying uncertainty is the cardinal sin of investment advice. The PIA has made no attempt to check its specification, describe it or qualify it. The obvious qualifications are fourfold:

1 The same rates are applied to products investing in different asset classes, let alone different markets within an asset class. These cannot be expected to share the same ranges of future return possibilities. (The only allowance the rates make is for tax effects, depending on whether the product is held in a tax-free wrapper.)

2 There has been no formal basis for shifting the range (and the implied mean) upwards or downwards to allow for differences in market conditions, according to whether past returns have been unusually high or low.

3 There are no means of relating the returns to a holding period, although the implication when a product has a maturity (like a pension or endowment) is that the rates shown are appropriate to the maturity.

4 The projection rates are not tied in with costs, which are dealt with by a separate calculation, the 'reduction in yield'.

Had the rates been based on available models, the PIA would have realized that they are less sensitive to the assumed market return than they are to the assumed inflation rate. The true measure of inflation uncertainty for any long holding period is alone much wider than the entire PIA return band from highest to lowest illustration!

The PIA dealt with the inflation contribution to return uncertainty by responding late and at irregular intervals to what appeared to be happening to inflation and then publishing revised rates. The most recent of these revisions shifted the entire range by a massive two percentage points! Any institutional actuary who changed the projections used to calculate funding adequacy by 2 per cent overnight would be rightly shown the door. You cannot make long-term plans with this kind of inconsistency.

During its existence the PIA has directly contributed via these growth rates to the wholly inappropriate sales pitch for mortgage endowments which are highly sensitive to inflation uncertainty, as we saw in Chapter 7. It is also likely that they have contributed to general underfunding of personal pensions, because of the illusion created by postulating high nominal (but not real) growth rates for much of the 1990s. The effect is to underestimate required resources for a given outcome in real or purchasing power terms.

Training and competence

'T&C' is a technical term in the regulations covering the rules and procedures through which the regulators seek to ensure high standards of practice as well as basic consumer protection. At the level of conduct, it is likely that we can sleep more easily in our beds because of the FSA.

The pension mis-selling scandal was encouraged by abysmal training of sales staff, many newly recruited from quite different jobs in order to take advantage of the new opportunities to sell retail investment products. Poor training was then aggravated by remuneration packages that rewarded mis-selling. Such management practices are far less likely to arise across the system as a result of enforceable T&C.

At the level of skills or technical competence, it is now less likely that the people you encounter will be green behind the ears or out of their depth, although you may meet them in the company of a more experienced colleague who is supervising their training. Each element of investment activity is mapped out in the rule book and matched by exam qualifications, on-the-job experience and regular internal or external coursework. At each stage the appropriate levels of supervision versus independence are mapped out.

These measures help but they do not remove the need for self-protection against damage done by the wrong kind of thinking, the wrong focus of skills, the wrong techniques, bad product design, excessive costs or inducement to make bad gambles. We have seen that all of these have become so institutionalized as to corrupt the entire system, even with tougher regulations in place. Indeed, the very fact that a regulatory body prescribes particular T&C procedures, including particular exam qualifications, will tend to give orthodoxy to whatever thinking and techniques, right or wrong, already dominate industry practice. This is a more subtle version of 'unintended consequences' that we saw with the PIA growth-rate illustrations.

As an example, consider the distinction the FSA makes between the qualifications required for advising on packaged products and those required for managing portfolios. The assumption in the regulations is that when investment forms a part of financial planning it requires less investment skill than when it is merely the implementation of a plan or of a particular element of a plan. Only if an IFA's activity extends into portfolio management, such as if they are managing a 'broker bond fund' or managing with discretion (such that they do not need to refer to the client before making transactions), does the FSA require them to take a higher-level investment paper that will give them exposure to the theories and mathematical principles discussed in this book.

It is no wonder the industry has the decision hierarchy upside down! Applying the logic of the '90 per cent rule', the task-based resource planning role and risk-preference selection that IFAs are engaged in are more important to outcomes than the investment selection. Yet the implication of the regulations is that these planning functions require only minimal investment skills. The decisions that are relatively trivial and are determined solely by luck are the ones that the regulator says require a higher level of investment competence. Where is the method in this madness?

Of course, some IFAs try to limit their influence to resource planning and pass on the asset-allocation to a third party, such as by recommending a managed fund or a with-profits fund. This does not excuse the inverted bias in the regulations, however. There is nothing in the regulations to prevent an IFA with the minimum investment qualifications from retaining the asset allocation decision. Even if they delegate it, they obviously need to be aware of the effect of doing so. This should include, for instance, pointing out the possible mismatch between the long planning horizon and inflation exposure of a young person building up a personal pension and the fixed-income content forced upon traditional with-profits funds by the solvency rules.

When the Lords' ruling went against Equitable Life, IFAs were quick to point out the likely cost, in reduced investment returns, of the enforced higher fixed-income content of the with-profits fund. Had these same IFAs taken the trouble to point out the identical impact on outcomes of carrying bond exposure throughout a 25-year mortgage endowment or 30-year pension plan, when they recommended any of these at any stage in the past? I doubt it.

The implication of the regulatory distinction that a 'packaged' investment is somehow different or less risky than any direct investment ends up condoning the practice many IFAs follow of excusing themselves from involvement in investment, even when they recommend products or advise on resource planning. This is incredible! Though I have heard IFAs make this claim in convincing ignorance, in many cases it is a deliberate ploy to try to limit their compliance risk under the regulations.

I have even seen it in the 'terms of business' letter template that forms a key part of an IFA 'business format' that one firm of IFAs sells (as a sideline) to other IFAs. Their sales blurb actually emphasizes the reduction in compliance risk! Any IFA that advises on packaged investment products and tries to disassociate itself from either responsibility or resources is an IFA you should send packing.

Though the techniques best suited to making effective investment-planning choices may be complex, the key principles are not. If you take the time to grasp those principles yourself, and to adopt some simplifying rules, you will not be dependent on trusting blindly to the adequacy of the investment T&C of the people you deal with. Neither will you need to rely on FSA rules as a proxy for the qualifications you know you want to see. How you define those qualifications, where you look for them and how you should test for their presence are described in the next part of the book.

The self-protection code for new relationships

14
Controlling the enemy within

Against our nature

'The investor's chief problem – perhaps even his worst enemy – is likely to be himself.' So wrote Benjamin Graham, American author of the best-selling investment book ever, over 50 years ago.[xlviii] Were he alive today he might well observe that in spite of computers and our advances in investment theory we have learned next to nothing about how to control the strange brew of head, heart and gut that makes us habitually poor investors.

NON-CONFORMITY OF IDEAS HAS ACTUALLY MOST OFTEN PROVED A SURE ROUTE TO EXCOMMUNICATION OR AN EVEN WORSE FATE

Slowness to learn has a long pedigree: millions of years of evolution that have rewarded successful social behaviour rather than exceptional cognitive prowess. In the tiny and most recent fraction of our species' history when superior reasoning might have been a stronger selection criterion, non-conformity of ideas has actually most often proved a sure route to excommunication or an even worse fate. So it is hardly surprising that we have evolved preferences for crowd behaviour and criteria of self-esteem that are conformist and psychologically comforting.[30]

Because neither our survival nor our satisfaction depended on it, our mental equipment is not well honed to making complex calculations or choices in a rigorously logical or clinically correct way. As we have seen, though, this can be a problem when it comes to making investment choices, be they about the people in the industry that we work with, how we manage those relationships or how we take individual investment decisions.

Living with the consequences of problems in all of these areas may now loom larger as a threat to our comfort levels or self-esteem than was once the case. Issues about individual financial responsibility relative to dependence on the state have also moved into the mainstream of social debate. Many consumers are clearly sensitive to this responsibility and many are also angry or confused, all good reasons for wanting to change their ways of working. This suggests that we are not in fact impervious to the costs of mistakes and want to learn from them and that we want to take more control. There is a deep Darwinian instinct to develop our antennae better and sharpen our skills. What is not so obvious is that this is also associated with a desire to become super-rational processors of information.

For a code of practice to have a realistic chance of being adopted and adhered to (on which its real benefits depend), it needs to find some accommodation between the gains from being more rational and the reality of our nature that means we often prefer less than rational choices. We do not behave like the textbooks would have us behave and we probably never will. We mostly prefer to 'grin and chatter' than to master the ability to engage in complex cognitive processes.

The code must be able to lean against the pressures that cause us to make mistakes but cannot be expected to prevent them absolutely. There is in fact no virtue, and certain failure, in trying to free ourselves from

---

[30] The reaction of horrified society to Darwin's theory of evolution itself illustrates the pressures to conform. During a famous debate in Oxford in the summer of 1860, Samuel Wilberforce, Bishop of Oxford, snidely asked the Darwinian T. H. Huxley whether he was descended from an ape on his grandmother's side or grandfather's. Huxley replied: 'If I am asked whether I would choose to be descended from the poor animal of low intelligence and stooping gait, who grins and chatters as we pass, or from a man, endowed with great ability and a splendid position, who should use those gifts to discredit and crush humble seekers after the truth, I hesitate what answer to make'. Touché!

captivity by the industry only to imprison ourselves in the rigour of super-rational information processing and decision making. As soon as the going gets too tough emotionally, we will break free. The chances are that changing course will then do more harm than if a more conformist, emotion-rewarding course had been chosen at the outset.

Working within these practical constraints, I can see four strong foundations for a sustainable code of safe practice that does not expect us to change our natures fundamentally:

1 recognizing characteristic harmful behaviour in ourselves and our agents

2 replacing rules of thumb and decision short-cuts that have a harmful bias with simplifying structures and rules with a constructive bias

3 leaving the tricky thinking to computers

4 using odds and consequences to inform (but not necessarily dictate) our own choices.

In this chapter we confront the most common features of harmful behaviour so we can recognize them when we next meet them. Because the 'enemy within' is inherent in the nature of our species, we can expect to meet it in advisers, sales staff and money managers as well as in ourselves. When it comes to behavioural biases and poor thought processes, we are all in the same boat, whether professional or lay investors.

Many of the features of human behaviour associated with errors are covered by an entirely new branch of finance theory that has grown up since the 1980s based on the evidence of how we actually behave rather than how rational models would have us behave. It is called 'behavioural finance'.[31] It merges economics and psychology to try to improve our understanding of financial markets.

Behavioural theory tends to treat these features as the product of the development of our species. Though no doubt true, it unfortunately suggests that the poor individual wanting to turn the tide is up against

---

[31] Several books have been written on behavioural finance and the psychology of investing, though few are written with the layman in mind. The fact that most are aimed at professional investors underscores my point that silly behaviour is not at all confined to individual investors. The subject is covered, with information about useful sources, on the website.

millions of years of conditioning! This exaggerates their dominance. I prefer to see them as dominant only in the sense of what rushes in to fill a vacuum and I believe that what does most to exclude them is avoiding the vacuum in the first place.

The point about the knowledge and information set out in Part I is that it occupies the space that would otherwise be largely or entirely filled by silly or error-prone thinking. This is the big empty space left in so many investors' minds by the failure to educate themselves about investment and by reliance on blind trust in third parties.

Minimizing regret

When talking about this book casually with people the most frequent response has been, 'Will it tell me how to make a lot of money?' Looking at the titles of most investment books, you would have to assume that this is what people are looking for and that they are ready to believe the stock market is a route to riches. Why bother to look for any other motivation for investing?

In fact, very few investors act consistently with a risk-seeking, profit-maximizing or speculative motivation. Though the presumption in investment theory of a rational, risk-averse investor may seem to be a poor description of people's irrationality, skittishness and greed, it is much closer to the reality than the idea many individuals have of their own motivation. No doubt we all want to satisfy speculative urges or to impress ourselves or others with occasional big successes but this is not representative of how we behave with most of our money.

Saving is typically motivated by the desire to achieve personal life goals that are sensible and realistic. Some of these are probably necessities, some aspirations. Capital not linked to specific tasks is usually invested with a combination of expectation of growth and fear of loss. Even when the consequences of not investing might be dire, it is not undertaken with the aim or expectation of transforming lifestyles in the way, for instance, that lotteries are. Indeed, for risk seekers stock markets are not the best hunting ground as the cost of a fair gamble is almost always higher than alternatives, particularly for high-volume repeat bets. Failure to make a killing is unlikely to be a cause of either surprise or heartache.

In common with the theorists and academics, many seasoned professional investment advisers and some individual investors who think for themselves, I believe that minimizing regret is a better description of what most individuals want from their investment arrangements than maximizing wealth. Does this inconsistency matter? If it sends the wrong signals to sales people or advisers, yes. If it makes us more likely to be gullible, yes. If it raises the chances of regret, yes, it matters a lot.

Regret is intimately related, via feelings of responsibility, with self-esteem. Think of it as a response to outcomes that were potentially within our power but we chose not to exercise that power. Disappointment is then by default reserved for outcomes we could not control or that were within our understood and accepted range of possibilities. We cannot avoid disappointment. It follows from the inherent uncertainties in investing that there will virtually always be some stock or fund that did better than ours, or better timing than that we chose. Even when we do well, we wish that we had invested more.

If we place a bet knowing it is a bet and we lose, we suffer disappointment but not regret. If we lose without realizing that it was a bet or without knowing what the alternatives were, we are likely to experience regret. If we fail to plan ahead and outcomes are unsatisfactory, we will assuredly experience regret as well as disappointment. If we feel cheated or exploited by others, our response is inseparable from how we view our own contribution to our fate, such as by inadequate checking, or repetition of an earlier error.

■ Avoiding gullibility

Is it our own inaccurate description of our motivation that makes us so ready to believe in improbable prospects, prefer a slick sales pitch to factual analysis, be more influenced by the attraction of the messenger than the attractiveness of the message or rely entirely on the good name of organizations? It is difficult otherwise to square the vulnerability to regret catalogued in Part II with the aversion to regret that is our standard motivation.

Being more realistic about what we really want will help us recognize the protective value of a sceptical mindset. We can give it a helping hand by regularly asking ourselves whenever tempted by a course of action: 'Am I being gullible?'

We should know now that in most circumstances growing money is hard graft and takes time. When it gets easier is when markets are cheap, not when we meet a new adviser or see a new product. We know enough about likely returns to spot improbable claims about future prospects. If it sounds improbable it probably is. Because we recognize and accept the ubiquity of randomness we should react against people who claim special or unusual skills or who, by their language, suggest they do not themselves respect the uncertainties of markets. We know in which circumstances reversion to the mean is likely to occur and avoid action that will be made to look stupid by it. We should discourage our chosen agents from thinking we expect or want to see macho thinking and macho behaviour on their part. If we do not understand a proposal, we should resist it.

Taking pride in modesty

Overconfidence is the most common manifestation of biased thinking. A powerful vacuum hater itself, it sucks in with it a whole host of related traits that contribute to investment mistakes. Whether it is our ability to pick our own investments or to pick those professionals we think have skills in picking investments, we tend to assume we are better than we are. Most professionals certainly think they are better than they are. We display here the same kind of bias that makes most of us assess ourselves as above-average drivers, for example, which clearly most of us cannot be!

Overconfidence about the skills of others is particularly silly when we recognize our own limitations. If we know that making good investment decisions is so difficult, why do we assume it is easy for others? If we accept that we may not be able to pick good investments, what makes us so sure we can pick good people?

Mistaken confidence is often related to failures to process evidence correctly, even when it is not particularly complicated. This shows up in drawing conclusions from partial or unrepresentative data, extrapolating recent trends, giving more weight to recent information and thinking we can see meaningful patterns in random data. According to the literature, when the imperfection of the information takes the form either of greater complexity or of ambiguity, instead of increasing our uncertainty about the future or of being more mistrustful of our judgement we apparently err the other way and become even more confident. The implication that certainty is reinforced when most challenged is a particularly alarming one.

Even when we sensibly accept the imperfection of the information available to us, we are inconsistent in interpreting it. We are capable of being healthily sceptical about the next move in the market most of the time and then in some set of circumstances we become totally convinced it will do this or that. We can be instinctively mistrustful most of the time of our ability to spot the adviser who will give us wise counsel yet be completely won over by the charm of one we encounter by chance or by the endorsement of someone we barely know.

Apparently, we attach more credibility to information delivered personally, even by a stranger, rather than remotely or impersonally, such as the output of purely statistical research. As the internet has shown, 'conversations' are critical to the mass popularization of opinions, even when they are as remote and vacuous as chat rooms. We can resist some popular and tempting notion that we keep reading about, like the 'new paradigm' that is supposed to have transformed the performance of the American economy, until we have one real life conversation, if only with a taxi-driver, and we turn on a sixpence from agnostic to believer.

Overconfidence lies behind the tendency of most professional and many private investors to trade too actively. Hard evidence about the costs and random payoffs of trading make this activity irrational and it is a significant contributor to the wedge driving deeply into systematic returns and often overwhelming risk premia.

I have no idea how actively private clients trade stocks when they manage their own portfolios. Research in America into 78,000 households with accounts with a major discount broker over a six-year period ending January 1997[xlix] came up with an average annual turnover rate of 75 per cent of the portfolio. It knocked 7 per cent per annum off net returns, on average! The higher the turnover the worse the net return, whereas gross returns were not significantly affected by different rates of turnover between these households. Assuming these people were aware of the commission costs of trading, they must have been attributing a value to the information they were using out of all proportion to its actual value.

Overconfidence shows in a tendency to underestimate the true extent of uncertainty, even when we recognize its existence. Tests have shown that we assume that the range of uncertain outcomes, at any level of confidence, is much narrower than it really is. This bias is also affected by views already formed. Research shows we ascribe too high a probability to events we think will happen and too low a probability to events we think will not happen. In investment planning this bias shows up in the frequently unrealistic expectations of retiring early, for example.

Our inability to quantify uncertainty realistically, particularly the bias to underestimating the chance of those outcomes we are most likely to associate with regret, argues strongly for basing the advice we receive and the choices we make on a process that uses estimates of probabilities. Adopting a sceptical rather than gullible mindset is a good general defence against overconfident behaviour in ourselves or our agents. Relating decisions to our own feelings about the consequences of different outcomes will also diminish the effect of weaknesses in the way we handle thinking challenges.

For professional firms, the best guarantee of protection from overconfidence (if they can embrace the intellectual modesty this requires) is the use of computer models that bring rational objectivity and consistency to bear on the irrational forces in their nature.

Beware of false accounting

Overconfidence is perhaps so common because we have acquired expert ways of avoiding the lessons of our mistakes. This expertise resides in a number of mental accounting devices. Mental accounting is a general term used in the behavioural finance literature and, as well as being directly about dealing with mistakes, it is related to other traits such as 'framing' and inconsistencies in our aversion to risk.

Mental accounting includes false attribution. We blame misfortune or other people for what are really our own errors of judgement. We also tend to suppress memories of errors in favour of selective recollection of our successes. Successes, of course, we attribute readily to our own skill!

Why do we block out lessons from our mistakes with money when in other areas we typically learn by experience? It is perhaps a proof of the immense destructive power of regret that we think we can 'manage' it more successfully by false accounting than by learning, as though the loss of self-esteem can never be recovered by simply avoiding repetitions. If so, it is surely a privilege of the very affluent. For most families, the loss of self-esteem will be much greater if the consequences of errors have compounded with time and no time is now left to put right the damage done.

How we think about our mistakes is also conditioned by the company we keep. It was Keynes who observed that it was better to fail conventionally (in a crowd) than to fail unconventionally (as a lone maverick). In Part II we saw that this has been taken to heart by the fund-management industry in the form of 'herding', or how to ensure your own errors do not stand out. It is one thing for them: it may actually be a rational response to the commercial risks and rewards that go with investment risk. For the rest of us, a mistake should not carry less force just because everyone else made the same mistake, whether it is taking out endowment mortgages or being sucked into the latest technology boom. In fact, following the crowd increasingly looks like a lazy and error-prone option and so is more likely to be associated with feelings of regret when the crowd is wrong in future.

Ensuring advice is customized to our own needs, such as by the device of the Three Ts and quoting odds on target outcomes, is the best way to ensure that our investment decisions are not effectively taken by the crowd.

Behavioural research offers three linked quirks of mental accounting, to do with loss, that you may recognize. We regret errors resulting from action more than errors resulting from inaction. Hence, lost opportunities cause less disappointment than actual losses. We treat a realized loss as more of a mistake than a paper loss. These are emotive distinctions that get in the way of dealing with disappointment, whether at the asset-allocation or fund or stock level. Not looking forward to planning horizons is what most often creates the vacuum into which rushes the backward-looking focus on the consequences of earlier decisions or the jealous sideways look at what others have done.

Research also indicates that we regard errors differently if they result from actions outside our normal pattern of behaviour, or out of character. This is worth remembering. In several of the examples of overconfidence above, where attitudes to the value of information change or a chance encounter is enough to throw off normal instincts, out-of-character decisions can be expected to magnify feelings of regret.

■ How to use framing

Framing is a term used to describe the context within which we consider decisions. It can apply to the way a question is put or a choice is presented. For instance, salespeople typically choose carefully how to frame proposals or put questions so as to increase the chances of getting the response they want. In behavioural research the effects show up in the way people respond differently to the same choice presented in two different ways, like the half-empty or half-full glass. When considering proposals, think about the motivation of the proposer and how he or she is likely to want to use framing to influence you. Remember from The

Performance Lie the monkey tricks professionals play with selective referencing, particularly with performance.

Money illusion is an example of a common framing error, caused by the failure to think carefully about the terms of reference, real or nominal, that most matter to an objective. Referencing needs to be explicitly addressed in goal-based investment and routines like the Three Ts ensure it is always part of the process.

Framing also applies to whether decisions are presented or viewed as part of a broad context, such as a string of similar decisions, or in a narrow context, such as a one-off choice. Research shows this also conditions our approach to decisions.

Some theorists argue against the separation of wealth into different pockets or tasks, on the basis that an overall attitude to wealth effects would more accurately reflect our personal utility than applying marginal risk aversion. Most investment planners, however, observe that customers are helped by compartmentalizing money by tasks. Thinking about the consequences of specific outcomes makes risk aversion more accurate and more tangible. The sacrifice of deferring spending is easier to commit to when the outcomes and consequences are well articulated. Whatever helps the customer's self-control is good practice but it also follows the lead given by institutional investment planning where the matching of assets and liabilities relies on compartmentalizing the liabilities as if they were separate tasks. But separation of tasks should not get in the way of an overall view, as in the example referred to earlier of having a Rolls-Royce of a pension plan and a programme for school fees that is unlikely to last the course.

Some theorists also think it irrational that many households save for one task (such as school fees) and at the same time borrow for others (such as house purchase or credit-card purchases). Planning that compartmentalizes tasks and time frames will at least prevent unintentional irrational choices. Good planning also identifies the cost and benefits and should not exclude the possibility of 'soft' benefits such as flexibility and liquidity. Bank accounts that offset borrowings and deposits are dramatically lowering the after-tax cost of such flexibility.

Even if many householders regret their reliance on endowment mortgages, the fact is that it will suit others to gear up their overall 'balance sheet' with borrowings. We have seen that trying to take more risk by selecting more volatile assets is not necessarily rewarded and often leads to mistakes. If taking more risk is sensible and deliberate, such as for a young person with good earning prospects seeking to maximize pension growth, then filling all available tax wrappers, pensions and ISAs, to the maximum permitted levels using mortgage debt, possibly even an interest-only loan, is probably the most efficient way.

The idea of 'different pockets' implicit in using a loan associated with one asset to achieve an objective for a different asset, possibly via a wrapper not itself associated with the objective (like an ISA as part of the pension task), is good planning. It is more revealing and relevant for the customer if wealth management is broken down by task rather than by the narrow framing of which agent, who sold the product or what label on the wrapper.

▨ How to use short-cuts

In the literature, mental short-cuts used when information is complex or incomplete are known as 'heuristics' and they embrace a number of different forms of rules, decision-process proxies or habits that make decision making easier or faster.

Rules of thumb are a common manifestation of the use of heuristics in investment and they are particularly relevant to this book because it actively supports their use. However, I see 'golden rules' as helping us remember essential principles, order thoughts, prioritize and encourage self-control. They are not a substitute for complex or sophisticated processing of the information (though the customer does not personally need this equipment if it is 'under the bonnet').

The decision hierarchy is an example of how a simplifying structure can be adopted to assist constructive as well as time-efficient decisions, even if it excludes or diminishes less important but legitimate kinds of decision. The role of the Three Ts (or any similar approach to articulating explicit goal parameters) is to assist planning and risk choices but they continue afterwards to provide the route map for the stewardship of the investments and to keep all parties to it on course. The key tests for such a heuristic are, '*Does it work?*' and '*Is it helpful?*'

In the course of the book we have already encountered a number of popular rules of thumb that are short-cuts to nowhere. For instance, the convention *spend income, conserve capital*, so popular for the conservation of great estates and manifested in trusts with life interests, is irrelevant and misleading for most modern investors' goals. Though the distinction is preserved in the tax code and (often inconveniently) in trust deeds, it may need to be avoided or circumvented in investment planning.

Saving and investment is for the most part the deferral of spending, and the consumption of capital is merely the realization of its purpose. This applies whether it is at the termination of a plan at some date in the future or as a stream of income from day one. This is why the term 'drawdown', usually associated with pensions, is useful in all contexts requiring a stream of 'income', whatever the source. The separation of income from capital in returns also interferes with the quantification of the risks and payoffs of systematic investment. The system's predictability, as we saw in Part I, resides in the delivery of real total returns – 'the bottom line' that does not differentiate between the contribution of income and capital.

We also encountered earlier some different versions of a common selection proxy: companies exhibiting high growth or high profitability will generate better investment returns – as in, 'good companies make good investments'. This myth persists even though a simple extension of the logic leads inevitably to investors bidding up their price and thus lowering their expected returns. A derivative of this mental short-cut combines growth and price, as represented by the catchy 'growth at a reasonable price' tag that Jim Slater gave to his personal stock-selection criteria in his book, *The Zulu Principle*.

Far from being the new philosopher's stone, trying to capture the upside of excellent company performance without the downside of overvaluation has long been the everyday work of many professional fund managers and is part of the population evidence of randomness we found in Chapter 10. In this case, the information being overvalued is earnings estimates. Discovering the fallibility of brokers' earnings estimates in his early experience of selection based on 'screening', Slater later incorporated momentum, or recent share-price performance relative to the market, as an extra, final screen to try to keep the performance up, rather than admit to the inadequacy of the underlying heuristic.[32] Momentum is another heuristic, as in, 'the trend is your friend' and 'don't fight the tape'.

---

[32] My own experience of backtesting predictive models using both valuation and momentum in the UK market showed that momentum is a better predictor and is weakened by combining it with value. Had Slater backtested his momentum screens without first limiting the sample to stocks with 'growth at a reasonable price', he might have found the same. But try selling a research service that only consists of a list of stocks that are up the most! It would also make for a rather short book. Some heuristics 'sell' better than others, regardless of their statistical merit.

Momentum or trend following is popular among some professional investors because sectors and securities appear, contrary to market efficiency, to move through waves of relative return even when there is no new information. As momentum followers who rode the fashion for technology and media stocks up and then down discovered, this is no philosopher's stone either. It can be painful to see momentum profits wiped out when a fashion changes abruptly (as is often the way). It requires immensely strong nerves immediately after accepting heavy losses (or loss of profits) to jump on the next rolling band wagon knowing the same may happen again. If it works, it is only because it is so difficult to stick with it. It is another proof of the best golden rule of the lot: 'There is no such thing as a free lunch'.

We have also seen how the benefits of diversification can be under-valued when applied to stocks and overvalued when applied to asset classes and markets. Contextual differences in the usefulness of rules of thumb can have an unfortunate effect.

Whatever the conventional wisdom about international diversifi-cation, there is also a well-recognized tendency to associate greater famil-iarity with less risk or uncertainty, which in turn can lead to domestic preferences. Though not necessarily dangerous for well-matched portfolios, it excludes opportunities that, as we have seen, are really far more comparable than we think. Within international equity markets, we have also seen that prejudices about the relative risks for different markets or currencies (based, for instance, on familiarity, unrepresen-tative histories, presumption of the dominance of one or other influences in isolation, or failure to think through the implications) are misleading.

The longest catalogue of failed heuristics is of course in Chapter 10, relating to the active management myth. This is no accident, as the selection of individual securities or individual funds involves by far the greatest number of opportunities in the set. Selection is then made easy by processes of elimination, however arbitrary, provided they eliminate enough of the opportunities. Not even statistical screens can necessarily kill off enough of the population to satisfy our urge for a short-cut. It is no wonder we fall back on five stars, a platinum medal or personal 'star quality'.

As we have seen, these are short-cuts leading nowhere in particular (if random) or to poor future performance (if the flowing tide that earned the award is likely to ebb). In the absence of any special information you personally value (but being careful you have not overvalued it), the best decision proxy you could use is cost. Having screened for suitability to implement an asset-allocation strategy and eliminated higher-cost alternatives, if you are still left with a final selection step you can always use the decision device with proven suitability in the presence of randomness: the dart. Try sublimating your emotional biases about decision making to that flawless logic!

The UK individual investor has had a raw deal from the industry but in most cases professionals and sales people have either mimicked or exploited the silly behaviour that they observe in their customers. If you can successfully control the enemy within, that will go a long way to protecting you from the enemy without: agents who misrepresent themselves or their products or who insert their own agenda and excessive costs between your money and the markets.

15

Selecting the right relationships

Using a 'search process'

This book is a wake-up call to anyone who has not yet got round to doing any investment planning. They are not the largest target. Anyone with investment needs can benefit from reviewing their relationship with the investment industry from what is likely to be a new angle of control, customization and cost-effectiveness.

The number of consumers with investment arrangements that look good viewed from this overwhelmingly sensible angle is likely to be infinitesimally small. This is a sweeping generalization but it does follow from what we have already observed. It is likely but not necessary if indeed relationships are mostly based on something other than these criteria since they will then only be met by good fortune. This would apply if most relationships with the industry are the accidents of history, chance encounter, casual recommendations or ill-informed assumptions about fits based on wealth or social background. It follows more certainly, however, from the observation that most of the products and services the industry has sold in the past are redundant, inefficient or downright dangerous – due to product design, cost structures or the inversion of the decision hierarchy. It also follows from the typically abysmal level of investment-planning skills and ignorance or misdirection of investment technology.

Not even growing awareness of the inadequacies of industry relationships has yet done much good, because of the difficulty worried and aware investors encounter when it comes to changing them. It is all too easy whenever you approach the financial services marketplace to be intimidated by its sheer size, diversity and fragmentation and even by something as practical as not being familiar with the means of access. Many of those who thought that DIY was the way out of the trap appear now, judging by the use of internet services, to be having second thoughts.

The way out this book proposes is based on specific but minimal knowledge and information. However, to put it into practice requires a particular style of relationship with the industry and particular forms of investment arrangements. This chapter outlines how to go about the search for these. It describes a process that I believe is highly likely to lead to new arrangements but even if it confirms your existing ones they are likely to be strengthened by the process, probably to the benefit of both parties.

This chapter deals with relationships that are person-to-person, offline, although you may use the internet as part of the search process. Relationships that are entirely or mainly online are dealt with in Chapter 18.

Though the essential principle of customer control is absolute and non-divisible, there are nonetheless a number of ways you can achieve it. The differences in form covered here are in:

- the nature of the relationship (such as advisory or discretionary, a one-off review or continuous stewardship, broad advice or single-task advice)

- the contents of portfolios, (be they products or securities)

- the way you pay (which could be asset-based or time-based fees, possibly involving 'commission offset').

The chapter is divided into five sections:

1 the range of firms which *on paper* can provide what you need

2 ideas about how to access them

3 the individual selection criteria

4 how you choose the form of the relationship that suits you best

5 how you should aim to manage the relationship.

Because the approach is based on what we have learned in earlier parts of the book, the description of the process assumes familiarity with earlier chapters and will not refer in each case to where we first met an idea. However, the index can also be used to pick up those earlier references.

There are no hard and fast rules for organizing your search or using your time but the logical way is to screen using simple questions requiring simple answers that either qualify or disqualify. This initial process could be by telephone or in writing. You should expect to be able to visit personally any firm that meets your initial criteria and to spend at least half an hour discussing your needs and their service without obligation. This second stage will provide you with an opportunity to check the remaining criteria and form a view of the integrity of the agent and their service.

Using the book's own website

Though the search process described here is complete, the website offers an opportunity to develop over time a more powerful and quicker process that incorporates the industry's response to your own distinct voice.

Publicity and user support for both book and website will help to alert the industry to a section of consumers who have taken the trouble to artic-ulate what they want and on what kind of terms. The larger the community of like-minded individual investors appears to be, the more firms will want to position themselves to appeal to that community. Indeed, because there are at present so few genuinely eligible firms, it is highly attractive and efficient for those few to be able to identify themselves. The website offers such a channel.

Only time will tell exactly how this channel might develop and what resources might be applied to it but the intention to facilitate the matching of customer and agent is clear. Also clear is that the channel derives its power from consumers and the responsibility of its editors is to moderate it with independence of mind, rigorous scrutiny and financial impartiality.

The website also carries a more detailed checklist of questions for agents, as part of a formal search process.

Who offers customized investment planning?

Whether you call it investment advice or investment management, the common denominator of the customized service you are entitled to expect is that is based on long-term planning of personal tasks or goals. The levers of control that you are looking for are connected to these goals rather than to abstract or industry-centric properties.

What then mainly divides the possible contenders is the implementation options, because the industry is typically split by a historical fault line with products on one side (IFAs) and securities on the other (stockbrokers and portfolio managers). Exposure to market systems at the lowest cost and least risk of implementation error calls for portfolios of funds not securities, although you may wish to combine the two for different tasks or pockets. You may therefore either need a single firm that is able to cross this fault line or work with more than one firm.

YOU ARE LOOKING FOR THE RIGHT FIRM, NOT THE RIGHT TYPE OF FIRM

You are looking for the right firm, not the right type of firm. Though it is more likely that the right firm will be found within a particular type, type is not a valid proxy. By type, the range includes product providers, such as unit trust groups and insurance companies, private client portfolio managers and portfolio advisers, specialist wealth-management arms of the banks, IFAs and other firms of advisers whom you may not at first recognize as IFAs, such as the advisory arms of accountants and solicitors.

IFAs

The idea that the *management* of goal-based portfolios (whether of products or securities) is actually a form of continuous *planning* obviously fits the planning background of IFAs. On paper, any IFA whose 'permitted business' lines under the regulations include 'advising on packaged investment products' is in the running. However, of the 4,000+ IFA firms that are regulated, most include this as a permitted business, even if the amount of work they do is trivial or limited to with-profits sales (or, in the past, endowment sales). Such is the result of the barmy bias in the regulations that investment planning requires less expertise than investment management! The vast range of actual expertise and resources behind their claims to offer an investment service means they are worthless without a critical search process.

Portfolio managers

IMRO-regulated specialist fund-management firms run about £77 billion in private client assets on a discretionary basis, which is not a large proportion of total wealth.[1] Most firms do not have a planning background and will not genuinely customize, or only if your assets are in the exclusive upper echelons of personal wealth. Most offer securities portfolios with only partial use of funds and their culture tends to be alien to tracking. However, there are exceptions in every market and a few have even grasped the merit of 'active/passive' management: dynamically managing the asset mix but using trackers for implementation. Specialist portfolio managers' own minimum size limit (which is normally £100,000 up but may also take into account likely growth in wealth) is effectively the first criterion.

Stockbrokers

Private client brokers dominate advisory and discretionary management on the securities side of the fault line. They act for around £230 billion of private assets of which only £50 billion are under discretionary agreements.[ii] Advisory channels break down into execution-only broking, at about £70 billion of assets, self-directed and customer-held assets with access to advice, at some £30 billion and lastly advisory portfolios, with securities held by the broker, at £70 billion. Customer-controlled portfolios could straddle either advisory or discretionary arrangements. Execution-only services would depend on the planning and asset-allocation advice coming from some other agency, perhaps online.

The growth areas are execution-only and discretionary. What each says about the customer's desire for control is at first sight very different but both are actually more deliberate than the service that stockbrokers have traditionally relied on, which was haphazardly focused on marginal transactions instead of policy and strategy.

The drive to convert customers from advisory to discretionary portfolios has a commercial logic: to pool portfolios under a small number of managers and manage them collectively and more economically. This may be good business but it is no friend of goal-based customization. Time spent planning, allowing different asset mixes and using different means of implementation are all enemies of the economic drivers of standardization and scale.

However, there is also a trend among some stockbrokers to develop their advisory function in the manner of IFAs, focused on specific tasks, using wrappers specific to different tasks and blending tax and investment advice. On paper, such firms might suit you.

The specific criteria are still very important. It is not easy to adopt the mindset of customized and long-term planning if what you have been doing for most of your working life is selling stocks. You should also remember that customization sells well at the moment so it is more often offered by marketing departments than actually delivered.

Even if you want to use funds rather than securities, stockbrokers can at least offer a transaction platform for those building blocks that could be securities rather than a fund:

- horizon-matched gilts (as safe-harbour assets)
- zero-dividend investment trust preference shares (a tax-efficient way of matching horizons with relatively low risk)
- investment trust shares (as alternatives to unit trusts to provide equity market exposure).

This practical factor should not overwhelm other criteria and, as we will see, other agents should be able to work in conjunction with an execution-only stockbroker.

Institutional 'wealth managers'

Banks and insurance companies are increasingly interested in gathering and managing personal assets. As the new buzz word, 'mass affluent', suggests, their threshold is a much lower level of assets than traditional portfolio management or private banking services. The minimum portfolio size is usually £50,000 though some start as low as £25,000. The catalysts for their new interest in the individual investor are:

- IT investment, which they think will lower the cost of acquiring and managing business at a smaller scale (not yet proven)
- willingness (unheard of a few years ago) to farm out the investment management to firms with a better investment brand.

The chances are that at the lower level of investable assets the personal goals of the investor are relatively straight forward and represent spending deferred rather than surplus or inheritable capital. The targets are also more likely to be resource constrained. Do people in this situation really need a personal investment manager? I doubt it.

They may still want to be aware of what they can achieve with their resources and they may want to understand the risk and return trade-offs available to them by banking or investing capital. They may also need to know what wrappers are most suitable for any investment, if it is not obvious. However, these are classical planning issues that can be bought relatively cheaply on a one-off basis. The cost of a few hours basic planning advice from a decent IFA will make a better contribution to mass affluence than any number of private banking services for the masses.

Where resources will support more complex goal planning, institutional services can be considered along side planners and other portfolio managers: there is no natural advantage or fit. If anything, your bias should be to suspect the sales pitch that emphasises customization and advice. Most of the business models are not compatible with genuinely customised goal-based planning and involve duplication of costs that can carry you way up the cost wedge.

Note also that because of the need for different economies, many of these services depend on the internet as a key or sole medium for the relationship. As we will see in Chapter 18, investors happy to use the internet will have many other options to achieve low cost but high added value customization.

If you have assets available for management (in other words, that someone can attach a fee to) in excess of about £500,000, there are a number of banks which have a service to offer you that is on paper suitable. That is to say, it is customized and operates in a planning framework. Both old-line British merchant banks and new-model global investment banks feature in this market and it is traditionally highly attractive to Swiss private banks and to some other continental European commercial banks.

The fact that asset management and banking services are under one roof is not a particularly relevant selection factor and the concentration of liquid assets with investment assets certainly increases your agency risk and probably reduces cash returns. The integration that does tend to crop up in private banking is between services provided both to companies and to the senior managers or business owners in a personal capacity. If you are in this position, you want to think about whether this should really drive your choice of agent.

The business of looking after so-called high-net-worth individuals thrives on the susceptibility of wealthier customers to thinking they should have more exotic or complex investments. As we have seen, sensible wealth management, like the financial system payoffs themselves, knows no boundaries of class or size. The high-margin products that private bankers delight in selling do not fit naturally in the rational, cost-effective framework of portfolios that this book recommends.

However, it is possible that private banks will take their cue from you and, provided you can agree their fee, they may be perfectly happy to manage low-cost portfolios to implement customized and reasonably dynamic asset-allocation strategies. Note that some place a higher minimum on advisory than discretionary portfolios, which shows that even at very large portfolio sizes standardization and economies of scale are still important commercial drivers – whatever the marketing blurb says about customization!

Product providers

Insurance companies and unit trust groups are essentially manufacturers, some of which also retail direct to the public. To the extent that sales depend on advice, they tend to rely on the IFA channel and it is only as they start to offer direct sales via the internet that they are adding a planning function or generic advice. As we will see in Chapter 18, these are not yet well developed but they are at least more independent and more honest than the pretence that you can call and talk to (or request a visit from) an 'adviser' or 'consultant', both of which are blatant misnomers.

How to access firms

Web users will already be aware of the value of good search facilities and indeed this function is probably the largest single driver of internet use. Most of the organizations suggested here have websites but some you need to telephone or write to. Domain and mail addresses and other contact details are listed at the back of the book.

'Find an IFA'

IFA Promotions Limited runs this on- and offline service whose function is to provide a list of firms (or offices of firms) in your own local area that offer (as defined by the firms themselves) the specific services you request and meet some limited criteria (such as a female adviser). The service sits on various investment websites or can be accessed direct.

The presumption underlying the service has always been that customers look to IFAs because they value their close proximity but there is another agenda behind that: participating IFAs tend to be defensive and like the fact that the marketing 'territories' are effectively kept small. On this basis, the 9,000-odd participating offices is a high proportion of the total market, though not necessarily of the type of firm we are after, which may not want casual or uncontrolled approaches.

Since it is far better to work with a well-resourced firm in the next city than a rotten firm round the corner, you need a little gamesmanship to extend the coverage of the 'find an IFA' search. The online facility works on full postcodes. My own, in London, produced a list ranging to only

1.25 miles, a fraction of the distance I am prepared to travel to buy good groceries, let alone financial advice!

IFA trade associations

Two trade association have carved out most of the IFA industry. The Association of Independent Financial Advisers (AIFA) has no consumer-facing facilities but the Society of Financial Advisers (SOFA) does. SOFA makes play of the fact that it is more discriminating, positioning itself to represent the most professional firms. Its website has a consumer search facility that reflects this by listing individuals, rather than just firms, and showing their professional qualifications. You can search by postcode or city.

Here too you can search by the type of planning area you want to focus on or by areas likely to test investment expertise. The impact of screening investment-qualified firms by eliminating all but fee-based firms is illustrated by one example, where it cuts the list of individual qualifying members in London to a single page from seven.

The Institute of Financial Planning

This is the trade group that most closely fits the culture this book recommends. Its 500 individual members (most of them also SOFA members) have to satisfy the Institute's own exam qualification and meet a number of ethical criteria including 'fee only' services. Its stated objectives include:

... promotion of the profession and practice of financial planning, increasing public awareness for the need for financial planning, creating of recognised professional qualifications for members, ensuring professional standards through a Code of Ethics and screening of new members, encouragement of education in the theory and practice of financial planning and the sharing of knowledge with other professionals.

Though membership is a good proxy for some of our qualifications, the emphasis is on high-quality financial planning and this is not necessarily backed by high-level investment skills. The Institute has a website or you can write or phone.

The Association of Private Client Investment Managers and Stockbrokers

As the name suggests, APCIMS covers both private client stockbrokers and IMRO-regulated portfolio-management firms. Its website is the easiest way to search, offering several criteria that fit ours: 'comprehensive financial planning', 'smaller investors welcome' as well as the conventional distinction between advisory and discretionary arrangements. For example, screening by the first two leads to a list of 29 firms, with their office locations and brief descriptions of their services, including wrapper access. Alternatively you could write in with your own criteria, including obviously your preferred geographical area.

Solicitors

Law firms that offer either financial advice or investment management services tend to use one of two affiliations that help promote them. The Association of Solicitor Investment Managers (ASIM) links some 50 member firms that offer discretionary or advisory portfolio management. Their clients are typically affluent individuals wishing to invest in securities rather than funds and most members are also members of APCIMS. It has a website that includes links to member firms but no search facility. Solicitors for Independent Financial Advice (SIFA) links law firms that offer an IFA-type advisory service using packaged products rather than securities. Its website provides a search facility by town or postcode. Though not an active screen search, areas of planning expertise offered are included with the contact details for each firm.

Though solicitor-IFAs are in theory doing the same job as non-solicitor IFAs, there are differences in practice due to the particular customer profile of law firms, the more rigorous code of ethics that governs solicitors and the overriding principle of the client's 'best interests' (which provides far better protection and means much more to the uninitiated than the narrow IFA requirement to provide 'best advice'). These differences have contributed to a far lower level of complaints against solicitor-IFAs. Product providers also say that solicitor-IFA clients are less prone to terminating contracts that require regular contributions. Both observations imply a culture of advice rather than selling but this does not mean they are the only place you should look for IFA services.

Selection criteria

When you have an industry this large and diverse it helps to think of the selection process, initially at least, as an elimination game. It is quicker and easier to exclude than include. It also ensures that you do not impose irrational or 'soft' criteria at an early stage and allow them to overwhelm the objective and rational attributes of the self-protection code. If you want to start the other way round, perhaps because of the personal attractions of a particular individual within a firm or because of the recommendation of a friend, move quickly to some general or explicit criteria that will determine whether they can deliver what you need.

Though you could have a list ready, the process does not need to be formulaic. Once you get beyond remote screens and are on the telephone or visiting, it is easier to reveal a firm's real thinking and their business agenda if you keep it informal and conversational – as long as you know what you need to achieve.

On your list should be all of the features in Table 15.1, all of which you should now be familiar with from Parts I and II. The list separates several of the criteria as between IFAs and other investment advisers and firms that may also advise but only in the context of a mandate to manage or advise on specific portfolios. Most of the criteria are common to both. There is no particular order but it can save a lot of time if you start with one or two explicit criteria likely to exclude firms quickly. In the table, these suggested initial screens are shown in italics.

Table 15.1 ▓ **Checklist of selection criteria**

Specific to advisers	Specific to managers
Investment expertise	*Customized portfolios*
Fees only or 'commission' offset	Planning expertise
Portfolios of products	Goal-based portfolios
Culture of advice or sales	High level control

Common to both advisers and managers
Technology to calculate outcome probabilities
Language and mindset
Use of the decision hierarchy
Asset-allocation expertise
Coverage of required building blocks
Funds or securities for implementation
Access to passive funds
Links to required wrappers
When and why changes in portfolio
Where on the cost wedge
Preferred degrees of delegation

Advisers' fee basis

The first screen for any IFA should be whether they are fee only or operate 'commission offset' with full rebate of any surplus. In other words, do they calculate a fee based on an agreed schedule instead of relying on commissions on the sale of products?

How an IFA charges is a valid proxy because it tells you whether the firm has thought hard about how to charge fairly, whether it is willing to be exposed to greater client sensitivity to value for money, and whether it wants to differentiate itself from the bad IFAs who use commissions to maximize their income at the expense of the customer's investment goals. Because the typical consumer cannot tell whether commission-taking IFAs are playing fair or bending the agenda, you need a general rule, with no exceptions. It really is that simple.

HOW AN IFA CHARGES IS A VALID PROXY BECAUSE IT TELLS YOU WHETHER THE FIRM HAS THOUGHT HARD ABOUT HOW TO CHARGE FAIRLY, WHETHER IT IS WILLING TO BE EXPOSED TO GREATER CLIENT SENSITIVITY TO VALUE FOR MONEY, AND WHETHER IT WANTS TO DIFFERENTIATE ITSELF FROM THE BAD IFAS

It matters less whether the basis of the fee is time, like a solicitor or accountant (with or without a retainer element), or assets under advice or management. The difference is likely to be most sensitive to the size of the investment portfolio. You are likely to pay more in asset-based fees in the long run but you may feel that is both fair and worthwhile if the adviser is offering a genuinely dynamic portfolio service. You may also agree more readily to an asset-based fee if the adviser is keeping the implementation costs as low as possible, such as by use of index-tracking funds. You are then paying more to your planner but at the expense of the rest of the industry.

If there is no genuine dynamism in the adviser's stewardship, it is as mad to pay an asset-based fee as it is to let an adviser pocket trail commissions for doing nothing more than producing a valuation statement every so often.

It also matters less whether that service is advisory or discretionary (which is a general point we explore later). The investment resources required and your investment outcome may be the same.

Beyond the principle of fees, issues of how they are combined with commissions are essentially practical. 'Commission offset' means that the adviser receives commissions from product providers but credits what it receives against what you owe, based on its fee schedule. Alternatively, most product providers dealing with fee-only advisers will, if asked, credit the customer with additional units out of the adviser's commission foregone. Though the mechanics are a bit confusing, the effect is you first pay the full sales commission but then get back, in the value of your investment rather than in your pocket, the proportion (usually 3 per cent) that would otherwise have been used to pay your adviser.

Commission offset makes sense where customers want to hold funds that charge a front-end load or where a trail can be negotiated, provided they produce a revenue flow back from the product provider that the customer could not themselves negotiate. It is a continuing bone of contention among streetwise consumers that if they buy direct, cutting out an adviser or 'discount broker', they still pay the full commission and get no credit in additional units. If low-cost funds, including trackers, are being used, capturing this opportunity does not apply.

There is another advantage of commission offset over pure fees: by some quirk of the tax code, commissions do not attract VAT but fees do. This inconsistency provides a handy excuse for advisers who want to see commissions persist but it is also validates combining fees with commission offset.

If you are offered a commission offset arrangement, make sure it includes a rebate of any surplus of commissions above the fees due. There should be a reasonable statement period, most likely to be quarterly, within which charges and receipts can be netted off before they are actually settled. This saves on actual money flows and will also prevent agents hanging on indefinitely to surplus commissions that are contractually due to you. (Where commissions are retained under an imprecise offset agreement, it may even constitute a breach of the FSA's 'holding client money' rules.)

Advisers' investment expertise

You want to see whether advisers see themselves as having investment expertise, not just to plan but also to implement goal-based strategies using packaged products. If they effectively delegate the construction of portfolios by recommending managed funds or with-profits funds, they are effectively telling you that they do not have the asset-allocation expertise you prize. If they want to limit their role to the strategy and leave you to do your own implementation, there is a good chance that they actually lack the investment expertise you need.

The amount of investment-related business an adviser does is not a substitute for a test of quality but it is still useful to check. Ask about the proportion of their business, the number of consultants with investment expertise and the number of investment clients. Ask particularly about pension planning and their qualifications to advise on pension transfers. Pensions are the area that most requires planning expertise and pension transfers require a higher level of examination qualifications, so they are good initial proxies.

Culture of selling

It is highly likely that any firm that gets past the earlier screens has moved on from the bad old IFA business model. IFAs hooked on the drug of commissions do not lightly give it up. It can take several years before time or asset-based revenues make up for the drop in revenues when coming off commissions and that is a business sacrifice only made very deliberately. However, you still want to be alert in conversation to signs of excessive selling pressure. It should be apparent from the way they market their services to you. Think about what it will be like dealing with them if they have a pushy or oily manner.

Probe particularly the culture within firms owned by (or part of a network owned by) public companies with shareholders. For instance, some 25 per cent of IFAs are now part of the Misys IT group following its purchase of another public company called DBS Management. It seems unlikely Misys is maximizing its industrial power to instil a culture of advice rather than to maximize product margins.

Several institutions have also stopped selling their own products and switched sides of the polarization barrier by buying IFAs. Both Chase de Vere and John Charcol have new parents who are probably gambling that polarization will be scrapped (a topical issue which will be followed on the website). They will then be able to pump out their own products through these supposedly independent brokerage channels. It underlines the importance of not relying on labels and always checking on the facts of the relationships and the culture.

Managers' customized and goal-based portfolios

The criteria specific to managers are widely exclusive because of the poor economics of offering genuinely customized service and the lack of planning expertise. The more their service looks and sounds like that of an investment-orientated IFA the better. In fact, you could ask them how they compare with the service you could get from an IFA.

High-level control could mean no more than carefully planning the initial parameters for the portfolio – which we have already seen is something they should do anyway, under the regulations. However, even at an early stage of the conversation you can look for proof of customization indirectly by asking about the range of investment results. Remember that there is an inherent conflict between the manager's desire to market a track record that speaks (supposedly) of their own skill and your desire for risk and return payoffs that are personal to you and 'owned' by you. The more results are the same, the less genuine customization is going on. A conversation about benchmarks can get you to the same place, as genuine customization means a theoretically infinite range of benchmarks!

Ask what they treat as risk-free assets and what use they make of them. As we have seen, the answer should be specific to the nature of the task and should differentiate between targets based on purchasing power and those with a monetary value.

Investment technology

At this stage you are merely trying to sort the amateurs from the professionals, knowing that the decision processes are too complex and too vulnerable to emotional inconsistency to be performed by eye and knowing a bit about what kind of decision technology institutional investors depend on. The direct way to find out about the engineering they have under the bonnet is to ask:

■ How do you arrive at your long-term assumptions for investment returns (such as if planning resources for a specific task)?

■ Do you use return 'models' to make assumptions about different markets?

■ Do you use your own or bought in 'optimization' models for portfolio construction?

The indirect way is to ask hypothetical questions, such as, 'If I tell you what I want to achieve and how much money I want to contribute, can you tell me what the odds are of achieving it?' Check that they can calculate probable outcomes in real terms rather than just money terms: money illusion is still widespread in the industry.

Language and mindset

Any firm, adviser or manager that has made it this far through your elimination screens is already exceptional. However, it is still possible that its culture is macho and knowing, and probably therefore boastful of past performance, rather than intellectually agnostic and respectful of the inherent uncertainty of markets. Be alert to language that advertises the wrong mindset.

The decision hierarchy

Ask them how they construct portfolios: is it from the bottom up, based on the most attractive individual investment opportunities or is it from the top down, via a deliberate and controlled asset mix?

Asset-allocation expertise

If they apparently believe in the hierarchy, you may still need to ask them how they deal with asset allocation, but it really should be redundant by this stage. If you have got this far without the firm mentioning asset allocation themselves, there is likely to be something wrong as believers typically build their entire process around it. It may have already come up if they are using computer-based techniques for asset allocation (some form of 'optimization' process). However they respond, beware of 'individual flare and judgement' and also of 'committees' who do not make good asset allocators and can hardly customize!

Required building blocks

For exposure to market systems, they should cover the major building blocks we identified: the UK, the USA, Europe and Japan. Don't forget to ask what they do about risk-free assets.

Funds or securities

If you only want exposure to systematic returns, you can get by with funds but ideally safe-harbour assets should be individual horizon-matched securities rather than funds and there are other securities you might want access to. You may also want to hold an entrepreneurial portfolio or you may have some money trapped by CGT liabilities. In either case, you will need some kind of access to holding and transacting in individual securities although it does not have to dictate the entire choice of relationship.

Active or passive

If you accept the premise – and evidence – of this book, you are likely to want to rely heavily if not entirely on tracker funds for your equity exposure. You could tell them this at the outset or, by keeping it under your hat initially, wait to see how they advertise their own thinking and preferences. Any adviser who normally invests in active funds for clients should accept your preference for trackers, but it must be better to work with like-minded tracker enthusiasts. It is more likely to focus them on asset allocation and the hierarchy, for instance.

Links to required wrappers

Your agent should be able to provide access to third-party wrappers (coming up in Chapter 17) to hold your investments in and maximize tax savings. The wrappers should be ones that can hold all the portfolio building blocks you need, as far as possible. They should show they are alert to the cost/benefit trade-off when using wrappers that involve additional cost.

Dynamic stewardship

Though there are advisers who will sell you a product and then lose all interest in you, they should not have made it past your screens. You want your agent to make changes in the portfolio mix from time to time, but you also want to minimize transaction costs, such as sales commissions, spreads and brokerage. You will have to feel for how they calculate the marginal benefits of rebalancing a portfolio and how sensitive they are to the nature of the trade-off. However, you can also be direct: ask for an idea of turnover, not just as an annual average but the typical range and frequency.

You need to know whether this is to alter an asset mix or to alter active fund choices. Remember that the more you use active managers the more likely you are to come under pressure to switch whenever performance (even randomly) hits a rough patch or the behaviour of a fund starts to look uncharacteristic. Advisers who use active funds may not be honest with themselves, let alone with you, about the likely turnover of active funds because it implies either a general fallacy or specific errors.

Where on the cost wedge?

This is a function of your agent's own fees, the typical all-in expenses within the products they use (allowing for your bias to index tracking funds) and (if they use active funds) an allowance for transaction costs within those funds. If you ask directly, I would be amazed if they can answer – though obviously they should! You are likely to need to push and prompt, perhaps using the cost wedge exhibit, Figure 11.1 (page 176).

Preferred degrees of delegation

This last criterion will dictate the formal or contractual nature of your relationship. I leave it to last because, as we are about to see, it is not necessarily a precondition and may be influenced by the particular firm you select.

Making your final selection

At some stage you need to move from elimination mode to selection mode, although the small number of firms offering what you want means that in the near future you are more likely to be narrowing it down by who gets closest. In selection mode, you might want to use additional criteria, such as ease of access (including the internet) and personal chemistry, or return to earlier criteria that lend themselves to sorting or ranking, such as fee levels.

You do not have to limit yourself to a single relationship. The general principle is that it is not worth sacrificing investment expertise to breadth of coverage. Any good agent should be perfectly willing to work with other agents and may help you with recommendations. If you do this, do not be overly influenced by the recommendation of your agent and always check the nature of the financial relationship between them and anyone they recommend.

What does make sense is having one agent for your overall goal planning, acting as 'ringmaster'. Other complementary and supporting relationships could be for securities trading and custody, venture capital advice, trusts, wills and other specialist tax advice. These requirements tend to increase with the level of personal or family wealth.

The contractual form of the relationship

Bear in mind that the approach of customized and customer-controlled portfolios cuts across the investment industry's traditional binary world, where arrangements are either advisory or discretionary. Though the analogy of the chauffeur works, it is as though that role does not actually exist in the marketplace: you either own and drive your own car or you select whatever public transport option best approximates your need. Try asking the bus driver to take you to your door!

Where arrangements are discretionary, the only chance you normally get to control the manner in which you are driven, or to say what markets or types of investment you will accept in your portfolio, is at the outset. Indeed, as we have seen, the regulations require the manager to agree and record in the customer contract the objective of the portfolio and the eligible investments.

As we have also seen, without quantifying the effect of such differences on the probable outcomes, any conversation about them is likely to be wishy-washy, open to unnecessary prejudice and vulnerable to the manager's agenda. How it then ends up worded in the contract is usually of little help to the customer later and any doubt will tend to benefit the manager.

Your willingness to accept a discretionary arrangement should be based partly on this initial setting up of the agreement being genuinely participatory, explicit and ongoing and including the following:

■ The defining features of your goal, in the form of the Three Ts or something equivalent, should be specified and quantified.

■ References to risk tolerance or descriptions of your own 'utility' should be related to these goal parameters rather than to general or firm-specific properties.

■ The eligible market building blocks should be explicit, including identifying a suitable risk-free asset and the eligible use of cash or conventional bonds (if not themselves the risk-free asset).

■ Exposure limits applied to any of the building blocks should be quantified and listed.

■ The basis for selecting the implementation vehicles (such as the balance between active and passive, or levels of diversification when active funds are used) should be specified.

■ The agreement should deal with how the portfolio mix will be adapted to shortening of the time horizon (usually referred to as 'lifestyle' investing).

■ Though it should go without saying, you may also want to see a specific reference in the agreement to your right to modify the parameters from time to time and the manager's willingness to adapt to them.

Even if your desire to control the portfolio is only at a high level, it is possible that this will be inconsistent with a manager or adviser's regulatory status or methods of operation. This is most likely to arise when you want to delegate the hassle of all the implementation or rebalancing decisions but the adviser's 'advisory' status means all these decisions have to come back to you for approval.

Though inconvenient, it is perfectly practicable for both parties to agree to act out the pretence of the agent proposing and the customer disposing. Provided the recommendation is consistent with the policy, you just say 'yes'. If implementation is via funds instead of stocks, such exchanges should not be very frequent. This is most likely to arise where the stewardship role is being performed by an IFA. In such cases, you still want the goal parameters to be specified and quantified in the agreement.

How to manage the relationship

Managing expectations

The goal parameters and the high-level control that they bring through the explanatory power of market exposure are the only means of ensuring that you are both responsible and in charge. Yet you also have a continuous means of influence over the way your agent treats you and the style of the relationship through the manner in which you advertise your expectations. The more you keep faith with sensible scepticism and respect for market uncertainty, and the more you signal your understanding of the role of time in the realization of your plans, the easier you make it for your agent to resist emotional pressures and irrational temptations.

DO NOT CONFUSE THE NEED FOR ACCOUNTABILITY WITH HIGH INFORMATION VALUE. IT IS THE ABSENCE OF ACCOUNTABILITY THAT SHOULD CAUSE YOU CONCERN

This does not mean you risk being forgiving of any outcome or appearing careless of the progress of the portfolio along the way. You can keep up pressure on your agent to justify their course of action but based on the technical expertise and mindset you hired them for, and their use of engineering under the bonnet. You want to see reminders from time to time, and particularly when the going gets tough, that these are still there and are still being applied to your own targets, time horizon and risk tolerance.

Performance reporting

Everything your agent has to do to account to you for what they are doing with your money is generally helpful but do not confuse the need for accountability with high information value. It is the absence of accountability that should cause you concern, not how you interpret the performance reports. Stay sceptical and agnostic.

Benchmarks

This applies particularly to portfolio performance benchmarks. Many customers see these as a means of controlling their agents, particularly in the case of discretionary managers. Be aware, though, that managers are likely to see benchmarks as the complete opposite: as a means of pushing customers into common pools, controlling how they view the progress of the portfolio and flattering the added value of their active management. When you come to discuss benchmarks, remember the hierarchy and the difference between the policy level and the strategy level and think about whether you want a benchmark to capture the first or the second.

If it is all about policy, then the logical benchmark is some optimized mix of risky assets. If it is a plan based mainly on regular contributions it is right to optimize on an assumption of normal market conditions but a single-premium investment requires a benchmark that reflects current conditions, even though their assessment is part of the agent's job.

The policy benchmark reflects your willingness to bear market risk but will also reflect any preferences for diversification. It picks up any bias to domestic equities and your agreed use of international equities, possibly including exposure limits. You might, for example, expect to see a benchmark mix of 50 per cent in UK equities, 20 per cent in Europe and 15 per cent in each of the USA and Japan. Only if your risk tolerance is very low or your horizon is very short should your policy mix include a proportion in your safe-harbour asset.

Is this policy benchmark helpful? As part of specifying the portfolio parameters and both parties understanding each other, yes. As a means of measuring and monitoring the performance of managers, not very. Any difference between the portfolio return and the benchmark return will be a mix of, first, the effect of assuming market conditions are not normal (hence the strategy will vary dynamically from the policy) and, second, all of the other performance contributions, including costs and implementation choices (of which active manager effects will rank large).

It is possible to try to isolate these two sets of performance effects by treating the strategic mix as a dynamic benchmark, rebalancing it whenever the asset allocation is altered. This allows the asset-allocation return to be compared with the policy benchmark and the actual portfolio return with the asset-allocation return. The first measures the effect of the strategy bets and the second the effect of the implementation bets.

This level of reporting is not common practice in the retail market and you may find managers unwilling to do it, unless your business is worth a lot to them. If they do, it will moderately increase the information content of progress reports, but remember that the inherent uncertainty associated with both asset-allocation and implementation decisions casts huge doubt on any conclusions drawn from the evidence as it unfolds.

The typically large differences between the short-run returns of different markets and the small number held means that the asset-allocation returns relative to the static policy-benchmark returns are not a meaningful measure of the manager's skill in identifying market conditions.

Remember also the random and unpredictable path of active-manager returns. This means that the portfolio return relative to the asset-allocation return, even over a string of several years (let alone in a single reporting period), is not a measure of a manager's skill in selecting how to implement the strategy.

Whatever the benchmarks you agree to, the golden rule is to avoid either party basing decisions upon them that implicitly attribute more significance to them than can be justified. Above all, watch closely to see that managers do not start managing the portfolio as if 'benchmark' risk is their real agenda. A useful way to ensure that both parties are constantly reminded of the underlying variance in the constituents of benchmarks is to ask your agent to include in reports the returns of each of the constituents. If, as recommended, you only have a few asset-allocation building blocks, this is not an unreasonable request. It can be presented as a more complete description of the investment environment in the reporting period.

Cost audits

Part of your agent's role is to balance the costs of market access against the particular benefits of the chosen means of access. You want to keep up continuous pressure on them to justify where they are on the cost wedge. They should therefore account to you from time to time for the total costs, reflecting both their own fees, any product charges and an estimate of transaction costs (including within any funds held in the portfolio). This is an unusual request but it is perfectly valid.

Keep looking forward

The ideal way to control the relationship, which deals with many of the potential problems of interpreting progress in the portfolio and third-party agenda distractions, is to ensure both parties keep looking *forward* to your targets at their own planning horizons. This forward look should complement and take precedence over, but not replace, the accounting reports *backwards* at some past interval or *sideways* at some benchmark (or even at what other people in different arrangements may be achieving).

This can only be done if your agent has the technology to quantify return probabilities specific to current market conditions and to time horizons, either in real or money terms. The value of this facility at every stage in your relationship cannot be overstated.

Meetings

How often you meet and whether in your agent's office or at home are not material to the management of your money when you have a consistent and disciplined framework in place. Though you may set an additional value on meetings, so will professionals: expect to pay! Remember that the main reason why financial advisers and company representatives have been willing to visit people in their own homes is to be better able to sell them something.

16
Selecting the right products

Products simply put

Whether your relationships are discretionary, advisory or self-directed on the net or the telephone, you are likely to have to think about whether you need 'packaged products'. Products are the cause of much of the confusion about personal investing. It was so much simpler in the days when all wealthy families needed was a stockbroker, what they owned were shares and bonds and what they held them in was a portfolio.

To deal with the modern complication of packaged products you need a simplifying set of principles. There are in fact four ways to think about them which should cover all contexts:

1 Products are *alternatives to individual securities* – for example, a unit trust is a packaged portfolio of individual securities, professionally managed.

2 Products may be a *substitute for a portfolio strategy* – for example, a with-profits policy or a 'managed (or balanced) fund' provides you with an off-the-shelf, one-size-fits-all asset-allocation strategy.

3 Products may be the *building blocks for individual asset class or market exposure* – for example, trackers or actively managed single-country

equity funds and bond funds can be used to build a portfolio with a deliberate and personalized asset-allocation strategy.

4 Products are *not the same as wrappers*; many of the functional attributes people give to products actually belong to wrappers – for example, a 'personal pension' is a wrapper inside which you could hold any number of either securities or products in any or all of the three capacities above.

The simplifying device of the decision hierarchy also helps with products. It reminds us that it is not products that explain portfolio outcomes, it is the asset exposure they in turn give you. Exposure can either be constructed *deliberately*, from a policy down to the contents of a portfolio that implement it, or *accidentally*, from whatever results from selecting contents individually. The first is what you are trying to achieve. The second, being more typical, is what you may already have but should be seeking to change.

This distinction provides a clear and simple framework for classifying packaged products, as set out in Table 16.1: *What is it? Where does it fit into a portfolio approach?* What are the issues? Because the portfolio approach and the issues have all been met before, in Part I or II, we rely on the index to guide you to earlier references rather than repeat them here.

Products as alternatives to securities

Two types of product act as alternatives to individually selected securities: 'open-ended' funds and 'closed-ended' funds. The confusing titles refer to how they are affected by people buying and selling them.

Unit trusts and OEICs

Unit trusts and their European equivalent, OEICs, are open ended, which means that the fund size shrinks or grows as people sell or buy units (like shares) in them.[33] They shrink or grow because the manager either cancels units or issues new ones in response to net selling or net buying at each trading frequency (usually once daily). This means the unit price at the time of dealing always reflects the underlying market value of the portfolio.

---

[33] OEICs and unit trusts are effectively interchangeable for the purposes of this chapter.

Table 16.1 ▨ **The main packaged products and where they fit into a portfolio approach**

	Controlled portfolios	Uncontrolled portfolios	
Approach:	*Using the hierarchy and playing the system*	*Delegating control over the asset mix*	*Investing like an entrepreneur*
Portfolio contents:	Safe harbour: deposits, gilts or gilt funds	With-profits insurance contracts	Undiversified securities
	Single country/region unit trusts	Balance or 'managed' unit trusts	Hedge funds
	Single country/region investment trusts	International (multi-market) bond funds	Venture capital funds
	'Exchange traded funds'	International (multi-currency) bond funds	Sector or industry funds
		Protected and guaranteed funds	Theme funds
			Emerging market funds
Issues:	Active or passive	Mismatch of policy	Unpredictable outcomes
	How to control active manager risk	Interference with system payoffs	Diversification
		Opaque strategy	

Returning to our normal approach of identifying sources of uncertainty and hence risk, an open-ended fund combines market risk and active-manager risk (the relative performance of the manager relative to the index – unless it is a tracker). These two types of risk are the same as for a portfolio of individually selected securities (although the levels of risk are not necessarily the same).

With otherwise identical risk factors, the key difference is that the packaged portfolio comes fully diversified and with a professional manager in charge. However, tax (as usual) also makes a difference. Unless a portfolio of individual securities is held inside a tax-sheltered wrapper, every time you sell a stock you are liable to crystallize a capital gain, which clearly interferes with efficient management. If you hold a fund, you only risk incurring a taxable gain when you sell the fund. The manager of the fund can get on with managing the portfolio without capital gains tax consequences. The different tax treatment may not in fact be relevant if the individual's likely annual gains are below the small gains exemption.

Investment trusts

An investment trust (actually a company) is closed ended because when people buy and sell shares they do so in the market and it is only the existing stock of issued shares that is being traded, like any listed company. This means there are two factors that are reflected in the price: the underlying asset value and the effect of net selling or buying. The difference between the two shows up as a premium or (more normally) a discount for the market price of a share relative to the asset value per share.

An investment trust shares the exposure to market risk and active-manager risk of a unit trust, plus it adds a third: the volatility of the discount. When you come to sell, the discount may be either higher or lower than when you bought. Discounts have proved very hard to model or understand and therefore to predict, but as a general rule when a fund is unpopular and is performing poorly the discount tends to widen, and when it is popular it narrows. A premium almost always happens only when an investment trust offers exposure to a very hot area.

AS A GENERAL RULE WHEN A FUND IS UNPOPULAR AND IS PERFORMING POORLY THE DISCOUNT TENDS TO WIDEN, AND WHEN IT IS POPULAR IT NARROWS

Investment trusts may also add a fourth risk factor: gearing. As a company it is allowed to borrow money to buy more assets and this tends to increase the asset value's sensitivity to market movements (in the language we encountered earlier, it increases beta).

Most people who prefer investment trusts are taking a view that these differentiating features relative to unit trusts will tend to increase their mean expected return. They are sufficiently confident about their view of the underlying asset returns to expect any discount to narrow and any gearing to raise returns yet further. It is also possible to be neutral about the discount but to want the long-term benefit of a 'geared-up' risk premium, or to want to avoid gearing but look for discounts large enough to make narrowing a better than random probability.

The tax treatment of investment trusts is the same as for unit trusts. The investment trust also represents a ready-diversified portfolio. Both are likely to be specialized or general and to have some market or spread of markets that they normally invest in, so the need to understand the exposure they bring is equally important.

You also need to make the same cost comparisons as with unit trusts. Investment trusts often appear to have lower expenses (particularly large funds) and have no selling commissions (which is why many IFAs ignore them). Note, however, that inside a wrapper investment trusts can be more expensive than a unit trust.

Products as a substitute for asset allocation

A packaged product can give exposure to either several asset types or to several markets within one asset type, in either case as selected by the manager. They can also alter the dynamics of market returns, as do 'protected products'.

One product, several asset classes

Both with-profits and balanced 'managed funds' come packaged with exposure to bonds, equities, possibly property and sometimes even some cash. Regardless of your own circumstances, this is what you get. What you see at the outset, though, is not necessarily what you get later, as the manager may alter the asset allocation a lot or a little over time.

A one-size-fits-all asset allocation actually fits hardly anyone except by chance, and will only continue to fit if their time horizon is constant or 'rolling'. As we have seen, the mismatch of exposure to personal needs is *inefficient* in terms of rational investing:

- For most long-term tasks, it increases vulnerability to unrewarded inflation risk by holding cash and bonds.

- It dilutes the risk premium for holding equities that investors given a well-articulated choice would probably accept.

- It increases the chance that fees will consume a high proportion of that risk premium.

- At the later stages of a task, the asset mix is likely to be too risky, with excessive equity exposure.

- Few of the assets held actually represent risk-free assets for most personal goals and that too only by chance.

If you hold with-profits contracts and think you want to replace them, remember the warnings given earlier about taking specific advice. This is something an IFA should be willing to do for a fee, on a one-off basis or as part of a new and continuous planning relationship.

One product, several markets

International funds offer a pre-packaged spread of different foreign equity markets. They are actively managed, so the spread changes. They are a popular short-cut to diversification but, as we have seen, the merits of diversifying long-term equity exposure without regard to expected returns and their predictability are usually overstated by planners and managers alike.

Advisers who do not have the capacity to perform international or global allocation, even to the few building blocks we recommend, are likely to want to include one or more international equity funds in a portfolio, where the mix of market exposure is delegated to the manager. This is a poor relation to treating the major international opportunities in exactly the same way as the UK, in other words so that exposure is a function of explicit expectations for probable outcomes. With explicit expectations, customers can then participate genuinely in the decisions about how exposure to foreign equities should alter their risks and payoffs, at least at the outset and preferably along the way.

Managed international equity funds also introduce agenda risk. This typically takes the form of crowd-following and so may tend towards either excessive caution or excessive enthusiasm. Delegating market choices can also weaken control over exposure to entrepreneurial investment exposure, such as a heavy emphasis on a single sector (like technology or energy in the past) or big bets in emerging markets. These bets are often not clear at the time and so can be the cause of regret.

Protected or guaranteed products

In recent years there has been growing interest in funds structured to provide some participation in equity-type returns but with downside risk closer to cash. The general principle that makes these saleable is that capital values are protected (if not actually guaranteed) and income is used to 'buy' insurance or participation in equity returns via some form of 'derivative' contract. The structure could be an equity portfolio plus derivatives to protect downside or a cash or bond portfolio plus derivatives to give some equity participation.

Mass market variations of these products have been popular with IFA customers and wealthy clients of private banks have been under pressure to buy the bank's own or third-party products. The common denominator that makes them easy to sell is the not very streetwise hope of a free lunch.

But customers also tend to be unaware of the importance of income to expected total return and the importance of looking at real returns, both of which were emphasized in Part I. The killer for the sales pitch for protected funds, though, should be the distribution of probable returns, or the odds on different outcomes. These are rarely quoted, for the same reason that premium levels for endowment mortgages were never based on expected outcomes at different levels of required certainty.

The point about using option strategies to control downside risk (as opposed to using a combination of safe-harbour and risky assets) is that in most eventualities you lose your option premium and to win you need an exceptional outcome: avoiding a loss so large as to make up for all the lost option premia. This would be more obvious if the distribution of likely payoffs was specified, or illustrated graphically. Taking costs into account, which any illustration should, will further shrink the area of the outcome distribution that the customer regards as satisfactory. Indeed, it may no longer be visible with the naked eye.

Some critics come at it another way, using the same logic and language of a systematic risk premium that we encountered in Part I. If the cost of the premium is normally equivalent to the equity-risk premium relative to your safe-harbour asset (which is logical), you are unlikely to benefit relative to a preference for staying cheaply and comfortably in your safe harbour – or at least leaving some of your wealth there.

Like with-profits policies that are sold on the basis of taking the sting out of market volatility, protected products sell because investors are not being encouraged to confront the choice between outcomes and what happens along the way. The premise of this book is that if you work with professionals who can articulate and quantify this key risk choice, and provide you with a clear route map once you make your choice, you are likely to choose to focus on outcomes. You will then dramatically lower the price you are prepared to pay for smoothing the path of returns along the way.

The story of the industry has always been about selling more complicated and expensive options than are actually needed to get a job done. Streetwise consumers know that and will always ask what cheaper or simpler ways are available.

Products as building blocks for playing the system

In Part I we defined two categories of asset: risky and safe harbour. Playing the system means controlling risk via the combination of risky assets and a safe-harbour asset specific to the task your money has to perform.

Safe harbour

The most reliable and cheapest way to obtain exposure to safe-harbour assets is via a security bought through a broker. This allows the maturity of the security to be approximately or perfectly matched to the time horizon of the task or, in the case of a series of time horizons (such as where an income is drawn down or capital is being consumed by, say, school fees), to a 'time slice' such as one year's needs. Where cash is the natural safe-harbour asset, deposits need to be arranged.

Using securities and buying them and holding them through your ring-master or another agent was described in the previous chapter as good practice and easy to arrange. But there is no denying it is more complex than buying another packaged product. Depending on the amount of money involved and the required certainty of outcome, you may prefer to keep it simple.

Unfortunately, the closeness of match between funds holding either conventional or index-linked gilts is not good. This may change as there is a mass market need for gilt funds that are differentiated by their maturity band, just as the gilt market itself is.

It is still possible to differentiate to some extent within conventional gilt funds and there is at least one short-dated fund. Most have a portfolio average maturity of around 10 to 15 years but even past average is not a good guide to the future as product managers tend to see themselves as expected to take interest-rate bets, moving their maturity longer or shorter depending on whether they see rates falling or rising. Why a manager should think he or she can outwit the market on interest rates is truly bizarre.

We have seen that conventional gilts are not in fact a true safe harbour for most long term tasks, as inflation risk is likely to call for index-linked gilts. Here the choice is severely restricted, except inside insurance wrappers.

Whether you use products, securities or cash, use a single agent or use a complementary broking service, your ringmaster's job is to allocate the individual safe-harbour assets to your goal-based portfolio structure in all planning and reporting procedures, so their function and impact on expected outcomes is always clear.

Corporate bond funds

Though these are becoming popular, they do not in fact fit easily into a systematic approach to investing, as they fall between the merit of equities (as uncertain but premium-carrying risky assets) and government-guaranteed gilts (when held as safe-harbour assets). Corporate bond funds have all the downside of poor protection against inflation risk and the added risk that any additional yield during the period you hold the fund or bonds may be wiped out by a single instance of company failures or widening of the yield premium to take account of greater perceived risk of failures. The irony is that such periods are most likely to occur at the very time that investors are most fearful of equities!

The rules for PEPs, on the other hand, make it impossible to hold any other asset class than corporate bonds as an alternative to equities. Government bonds are not eligible and scheme managers are tightening up on persistent holdings of cash. In such circumstances, a corporate bond fund is the obvious alternative and better than trying to select individual issues (unless you are desperate to stay near the five-year-minimum maturity that PEPS require, as the closest proxy for cash).

The selection criteria are simple: steer clear of above-average fund yields (associated with greater credit risk) or below-average yields (associated with equity-type risks) and look for performance paths over time (graphs are good for this) that look like the path of the gilt index. They will not frequently feature amongst the leaders in performance screens. There are several very large and low-cost bond funds managed by household names that in the past have met these criteria.

Equity markets

In Part I we saw that just four major stock markets (or blocks of markets) cover 90 per cent of the total world market capitalization: the UK, the rest of Europe, the USA and Japan. All four show the characteristics of market systems: a long-term trend of real total returns that act as a magnet preventing limitless deviations from the trend over time. These features provide a basis for estimating return probabilities, specific to today and to the time horizon of your goal, that are directly comparable with a known safe-harbour return that is also personally specific.

With technical professional help, this is all you need to plan the resources and strategies for customized and risk-controlled portfolios for each of your personal goals. Exposure to all four systems can be obtained (by your agent or by you direct) simply and cheaply using products. Your next choice is whether these should be actively or passively managed.

Tracker funds

If you are using the index at the back of the book and dipping into this section, out of context, because you think trackers are key to successful individual investing, you have already reached the conclusion a more linear reader of the book is likely to have reached.

In Part I we introduced the core principle of exposure to the market as a system. It is dynamic in the sense of its changing make-up, which was compared with a Darwinian model. A properly constructed market index is itself a dynamic replication of that system. An index-tracking fund simply ensures that a portfolio is exposed efficiently to those dynamics, with the least leakage and lowest cost.

In Part II the linear reader was shown overwhelming evidence that the alternative form of equity market exposure, an actively managed fund or portfolio, is a lottery with the odds stacked against the private investor by the high cost of playing. Viewed as the product of investor psychology, it is the triumph of hope over experience. Viewed as the product of a deliberate industry agenda, it is the triumph of marketing hype over common sense.

At the typical cost relative to an index tracking alternative, the chances of winning the active fund lottery are just one in four. If you move higher up the cost wedge they drop to about one in nine. If you assume that winning actually means outperforming by enough to pay you a risk premium for the gamble, the chances of achieving it with a higher-cost product are effectively negligible, yet these same funds are often the most popular and widely recommended.

It is no surprise that more and more investors (and some professionals) are opting out of the lottery and turning to index-tracking funds at a fraction of the all-in costs of active funds. They are available for all four of the systematic building blocks from top UK houses and competition is growing all the time.

In time, what are known as exchange-traded funds (ETFs) are likely to challenge tracker unit trusts and investment trusts. They are portfolios that are 'securitized', that is turned by an investment bank into a security traded on an exchange. To prevent the problem of discounts occurring that beset investment trusts, there has to be arbitrage between the securities and physical portfolios or index futures. This requires a wide following and deep liquidity, not just normally but specifically in periods of extreme market volatility. Liquidity is also needed to ensure dealing spreads are minimized. You can well afford to wait for these features to be demonstrated.

For unit trusts and investment trusts that track markets there is still a range of costs, from a management fee of about 0.35 per cent per annum up to 1 per cent or more, so it is worth checking. A good adviser will also check total expense ratios, reflecting the size of the fund. A valid short-cut if you are making your own selection is to go for the biggest of any two funds having the same management charge.

The choice of index matters. In the UK, the FTSE All Share Index is the true 'system' benchmark, thoroughly representative and reasonably frequently 'refreshed' in line with the dynamism of the economy. The FTSE 100 Index was not designed for the same purpose, being the basis of constantly traded derivatives. Though it alone may represent as much as 80 per cent of the All Share, it is not the system benchmark and may show different risks and payoffs.

Most managers tracking continental Europe, our closest system in terms of risk characteristics, choose the FTSE All World Index for Europe ex-UK. This is indeed the best benchmark of what has to be at the moment a combination of individual country systems that is only just beginning to take on the characteristics of a unified stock exchange for a partially unified economic system. It is weighted by the total market capitalization of each country rather than the accident of where the largest European companies happen to have their listing. (This also applies to the MSCI Europe ex-UK Index that is most commonly used by institutional funds around the world.) Avoid funds that track the company-driven FTSE Euro ex-UK 300 Index or the DJ Euro Stoxx Index.

Virtually all US trackers track the S&P 500 Index which is the true system benchmark, so no problem there. In Japan, on the other hand, it is very important to avoid the Nikkei 225, as indeed most index fund managers do. The 225 Index is the accepted benchmark of daily movements but not for long-holding-period returns. It is notoriously mistrusted for being unweighted and rarely refreshed.[34] Most UK-based Japanese trackers take the FTSE All World Index for Japan as their benchmark and this is fine.

---

[34] For a long time there were hardly any alterations to the constituents of the Nikkei 225 and when in 2000 its publishers finally woke up to the fact that it needed to be dynamic they loaded up with then fashionable technology shares, just before the global technology bubble burst!

Active funds

You know the odds but it is your money and your call. You can still follow the hierarchy and implement an asset-allocation strategy using actively managed funds, or by combining them with trackers. You simply need to select those that invest solely in one of the four building-block markets and which take the same benchmark. But there is no winning formula.

As a streetwise investor you will want to know what sort of impact your own active implementation strategy is likely to make on your range of expected goal outcomes. A good adviser or money manager should anyway quantify the impact. They ought to take into account the size of the active bets typically made by the fund managers, the level of diversification of active-manager risk within your own portfolio and the costs of the funds.

In Part II we looked at the persistency of manager's riskiness relative to the system risk and decided that there was clear evidence that you cannot rely on past characteristics. It is a waste of your time or a professional's time to pore over the historical standard deviations of all the potential contenders and the correlations between them if they are not likely to be reasonably constant from one period to another. Instead go for simple rules of thumb! Think about the logic here: two funds will be much less risky than one, because they are unlikely to do really well or really badly over the same holding period. Ten funds would really reduce the active-manager risk but at the expense of being condemned to earning pretty close to the system return but with all the extra costs of active funds.

So you might compromise on a combination of about two or three per building block, with allowance perhaps made for the proportion that actively managed building-block money represents of the total goal-based portfolio. This is common sense. If you have more money in the UK and all of it is active, you will tend to need more manager diversification than if you only have, say, 15 per cent in Japan half of which you anyway want to be passive.

If you are doing the fund selection yourself, you need some information about the suitability of equity funds for market exposure: What makes them a contender as an implementation option? If you are hiring an adviser or manager who will select the funds, you should ask them how they manage the active-manager risk. What funds do they regard as suitable and how diversified? Do they use style differences to manage the diversification? This is also a good common sense approach, though again it is spurious to read too much into the analysis of style differences using historical return data. You may nod wisely but should not appear overly impressed by their clever style-based fund selection technique!

If you are using a third party, you will be concerned to see that they have a sensible and not overconfident approach but it makes no sense to constrain them so much that they end up adopting an approach for you that is completely different from the one they are used to. This particularly applies if you are hiring a manager to pick stocks, not funds. Of course you should be comfortable with the suitability of their approach to management based on all the criteria covered in the previous chapter but, if you are, it makes sense to give them room to operate within the individual markets as they normally do.

IF YOU ARE USING A THIRD PARTY, YOU WILL BE CONCERNED TO SEE THAT THEY HAVE A SENSIBLE AND NOT OVERCONFIDENT APPROACH

Products for an entrepreneurial approach

Table 16.1 lists the main products that in Part I we described as suitable for an entrepreneurial approach rather than playing the system. Hedge funds, venture capital funds, undiversified securities portfolios, sector (or industry funds) and emerging markets funds were all scrutinized earlier.

Most of the entrepreneurial alternatives are attractive only on the basis of poor information, emotional or illogical responses and marketing hype. Those can be pretty strong attractors, though! Many that appeal most seductively are also excessively expensive, a problem which in the case of hedge funds is exacerbated by the fact that the only realistic route for even very affluent private clients is a fund of funds that loads an extra layer of costs.

The systematic approach is all that most well-informed and cost-conscious private investors should ever need. However, we must remain consistent and it is always the customer's right to select less rational alternatives to the purely rational.

The special pleading of the book is that these choices should at least be made in the context of a rationally planned framework for your investments. The entrepreneur in you is then unlikely to be the cause of regret, in the sense of bets made without realizing they were bets or opportunities scorned through lack of awareness of their presence or their merit.

The choice between products and securities for these entrepreneurial investment types is actually quite straightforward. Obviously, undiversified stock portfolios are better managed as portfolios of stocks, where the concentration and CGT angles are all specifically addressed. You hire or do it yourself with both in mind. Otherwise, diversification and cost angles point you towards funds. In the case of venture capital, there is no alternative as there is also a tax wrapper angle.

Any preferences for entrepreneurial investing likely to survive the process of rational planning will tend to influence your selection of an agent but, as suggested in the previous chapter, it is better to hire complementary managers or advisers for part of your wealth. It is not worth suborning the choice of ringmaster to whether someone happens to make a specialty of VCTs.

With a clear grasp of how products fit into the picture, the next logical step is to see how either products or securities can efficiently be placed in wrappers.

17

Understanding wrappers

How they fit, if they fit

Wrappers are responsible for many of the labels and acronyms that confuse individual investors. They confuse by blurring the distinction between a focus on market exposure and a focus on products and contents. They also confuse by their sheer number, particularly where pension contracts are concerned. Confusion also contributes to boredom with the complicated detail of all these different legal contracts.

There is a simplifying device for cutting through the confusion and boredom, in the form of the decision hierarchy, because wrappers are only relevant at the implementation stage:

- Investment is all about market exposure.

- Market exposure can be obtained through a product or securities.

- Products and securities may be held inside a tax-favoured wrapper.

Ignoring the industry's marketing agenda, readers know not to confuse wrappers with products or products with markets. Markets explain the return behaviour but products introduce other factors that affect returns, notably active-manager risk and the cost wedge. These factors continue to explain returns even when the product is held in the legal structure of a wrapper. What the wrapper adds is the tax benefits, the contractual obligations associated with them and a possible additional cost.

Dismissing them to the lowest level of the hierarchy does not mean it is not worth while understanding wrappers and how to make the most of them. Some familiarity is very helpful, both for DIY investors and for individuals who want to delegate. Because of the industry's accomplished art in using the allure of tax breaks to sell things you do not really need or are too expensive, it is also well worth knowing how to assess them or how to assess your agent's use of them. Much as I sympathize with complete boredom with contractual detail, it may carry a cost and is not very streetwise.

As a good start to understanding wrappers, we can divide them into those that are 'necessary' and those that are potentially 'beneficial':

- It is necessary to hold pension investments in one or other of the different types of pension wrapper if we want to benefit from the special tax breaks applicable to pensions.

- It is potentially beneficial but not necessary to use other tax-favoured wrappers in which to hold investments for other tasks: PEPs, ISAs and 'investment bonds'.

Any wrapper should be cost-effective: in other words, the benefits of favourable tax treatment need to be weighed against the additional cost of using the wrapper (although in some cases the cost may be the same or even less than the same product outside a wrapper). The use of the term 'potentially beneficial' recognizes the fact that the tax savings may not be worthwhile (such as if there would not anyway be a charge to income or capital gains tax) or that the costs may be too high. You cannot assume that a wrapper is always better than no wrapper or even that a pension wrapper is always better than a non-pension wrapper.

The distinction between pension wrappers and the rest is used to give this chapter a structure. Because the cost-benefit trade-offs are specific both to individual circumstances and to the costs of a particular wrapper, we will see what we need to find out but not necessarily what the specific answer is. I look at how different wrappers can be used to hold the assets recommended in this book. Lastly, we show you how a good planner will use wrappers in conjunction with goal-based planning as a series of different 'pockets'. The logic of what goes in each pocket derives partly from the nature of the task and partly from whichever asset most benefits from being inside each type of wrapper. Though this is what a good professional planner should do, it is also within the grasp of dedicated DIY investors.

Pension wrappers

As a quid pro quo for enjoying tax breaks, we have to hold our pension investments in a wrapper administered and marketed by authorized financial institutions under a set of rules. In the minds of governments and tax authorities, these rules provided a 'trust' framework to protect the investor and a 'mistrust' framework: to prevent cheating, such as by contributing more than the earnings level allows or dipping into the pension fund for other purposes before we retire.

Until now the only firms allowed to run pension plans have been banks and insurance companies. Behind whoever else nominally appears to run a pension lurks a bank or insurance company, and probably the latter. Some money managers and actuaries, for instance, have in the past formed life companies specifically to conduct business as a pension provider. Only now is this opening up to allow other investment product providers, such as unit trust managers, to get in on the pensions act without having to form a life company.

The rules governing both pension contributions and how you take your pension benefits are, like most things governed by the UK's tax code, complicated by the cumulative weight of decades of tinkering and partial reform. For once, the fact that there may be some choice as to which form of contract to go for is an inconvenience, because it means you have to go into the detail in order to make a decision. For all its advantages, stakeholder unfortunately poses this same problem. In a really simple world, the arrangements for pensions would be standard and transparent and would be different from other investments only as the different tax treatment required. Some hope!

The details of the rules are beyond the scope of this book because of their scale and because they are so specific to individual circumstances. Though the website is also a reference source, that too is far from the last word. However, it can at least point to publications and other websites, including those of the Inland Revenue and the FSA, where objective factual information is available.

In any event, as a general rule, most issues relating to your retirement plans are valuable enough to warrant either intensive DIY effort or taking professional advice. If you follow the guidance provided in Chapter 15, you will be able to identify pension experts who are willing to give you one-off setting-up (or reorganization) advice for your pension planning, for a fee. In many cases where individual resources are limited and planning needs are simple, this is all that is needed. In some cases where resources are limited, there may not even be a need for customized advice.

What this section of the chapter aims to do is provide an overview that informs both any need for specialist and individual advice and ties in with the need to ensure the right investment approach can flourish within the actual contract.

For an overview, we can start by looking at the tax benefits of pensions as these tend to be common to all rather than dependent on the wrapper. The general principle in the UK has been that we let money grow tax free in a fund and only tax it when it is taken as a pension. Some countries do it the other way round. Either way, there is a concession. However, the big incentive for pensions is the fact that contributions benefit from tax credits.

The value of the relative benefits of accumulating money tax free has anyway been eroded over the years. The introduction of the indexation of capital gains to inflation means that only the real growth of capital outside a tax-favoured wrapper is taxed and then only if it exceeds an annual exemption for small gains. However, since indexation was replaced for the years after 1997/98 by 'taper relief', which is based on the number of years an asset has been held, the link with inflation is now weaker. After its election in 1997, the Labour government was also quick to withdraw most of the relief from tax on dividend income that pension funds used to enjoy; being a form of tax rise most members of the public would be affected by but few would notice.

The income and capital gains advantages of a pension wrapper are small compared with the benefit of tax credits. All contributions are deductible against income tax and even if you are not actually liable to pay tax at the rate of 22 per cent the government still injects that amount into your plan against every contribution you make. A liability to tax at 40 per cent instead of 22 per cent entitles you to set the difference against your income when you prepare your tax return, so the total tax credit is always at your own marginal tax rate.

The costs that you need to offset against this tax benefit are traditionally much higher than for investments outside a pension. As we saw in Part II, estimates of a traditional personal pension policy's total costs, even without any penalties for failing to keep the policy going, amount to about 40 per cent of the final plan value! This is why the government has introduced the new concept of stakeholder pensions.

Some of this extra cost is undoubtedly accounted for by the inherent inefficiencies of collecting small monthly contributions but the willingness of investment firms to offer stakeholder pensions shows that it is possible to get these administrative costs down. Without it, it was entirely possible for savers with modest means and paying tax at or below 22 per cent to find after the event that all of their tax benefits had been consumed by charges!

The stakeholder pension's job as a fifth column for the Treasury is to infiltrate the market and drag down costs on older pension contracts. Though it is clearly working, for some time there will be a difference between old- and new-generation wrappers. Some typical cost differences between wrappers will emerge as we go through them and we also look at how their costs may change.

With pensions, as with all tasks, you are always primarily concerned about the market exposure, as the return driver, and the next level of decisions, about products and wrappers, will tend to be helped by seeing 'packaging' as a commodity business, practical and unglamorous. Keep this in mind as we look at the individual types of contract.

We start with the various forms of personal contracts where you make all the contributions and you have to choose the wrapper provider, the product providers and the contents, as well as the degree of delegation if you want to go through an agent. Then we look at schemes organized by your employer but whose investment outcome and eventual benefits depend on investment choices you are able to make. These give you both an opportunity and a responsibility for high-level control of outcomes. Both types of pension arrangement make you an individual investor, whereas with a 'defined benefit' scheme organized by employers, they bear all of the investment risk and you are a beneficiary, not an investor.

Retirement annuity plans

Also known as Section 620 or Section 226 schemes, RAPs are the oldest form of personal-pension contract or wrapper for the self-employed. They were replaced in the Conservative reform of 1988 with the new flexible personal pensions. Since no new RAP contracts have been sold since then, the only choice is whether to keep a RAP going. Their advantage is higher contribution levels, and among high earners this is nearly always the reason for keeping them going. Though the benefit rules are tighter, they can be switched when contributions end to different wrappers to increase flexibility in taking the pension, so you get the best of both worlds.

Almost by definition, their value is greatest for people best able to afford high-quality pension planning advice. Take it! Even if you have some time to go to retirement, take it now. This is because the investment strategy is likely to be affected by knowing in advance of retirement how you plan to take the pension, including whether you intend to switch into a personal plan and do a drawdown, extending the investment time horizon dramatically.

Personal pension plans

The 1988 reform brought some genuine benefits but it sowed the seeds of the binge of marketing abuses we encountered in Part II. It also encouraged the popular view that pension planning was all about product performance and choosing the best provider, when it was really about making an investment plan and choosing an implementation wrapper for your investments that met your need for contents and had sensible contract terms, including cost.

Personal pension plans typically invest in products managed by the provider though the trend to give access to other managers' products is growing. The funds have to be managed separately and are specific to pension contracts (because of the different tax treatment) although they often replicate the strategy of tax-paying products and may even share the same name. Over time the list of accessible funds has grown and for most large providers covers all areas of their own expertise, as well as the managed fund and with-profits options this book rejects. Since you are not limited to one wrapper or one pension provider, there is effectively all the choice you could possibly need.

As we saw in Part II, early contracts included punitive penalties if people could not keep up regular contributions, replicating the same penal practices that the Conservative government at the time had rightly seen as a despicable feature of occupational schemes. It is now much easier to find contract terms that allow full contribution flexibility and these are worth having.

General to all personal pension plans are the rules on contributions, by reference to earnings levels, and the rules relating to benefits. These include what used to be the only option for the early contracts: using the fund to buy an annuity when you retire that provides the pension itself, with the option to take 25 per cent of the fund as a lump sum tax free. There were no restrictions on what you did with the lump sum.

Changes to the rules allow you to defer the purchase of an annuity until aged 75 and there is a lot of lobbying going on to have this extended or removed. You do not have to buy it from the wrapper provider and you should always get quotations from other annuity providers – this is called the 'open market option'.

Likewise, if you want to defer the annuity and start a pension drawdown you can change provider, including setting up a SIPP (coming up) for the purpose. As we saw in Part I, drawdown should be thought of as a task in itself and not as a product. All investment tasks involving drawing down capital require careful investment planning, with particular importance to return assumptions and costs. Many of the providers who first signed up personal pension clients will disappoint on both counts. This is a key area for IFAs to advise on but you have to be sure their allegiance is not to the product providers and that they have the right skills. [35]

Even entering into the pension contract can benefit from professional advice about how to set it up so as to maximize your flexibility about how to take the benefits. As an alternative or complement to drawdown you can 'phase retirement' by 'vesting' parts of your fund (ie starting to take the benefits) at different times, but only if it was set up in the first place in 'segments' (technically each segment is a separate policy). This may not seem like a high priority if you are a long way from retirement but it is important. It may also have a cost.

---

[35] Many advisers will not even consider advising phased drawdown unless you have or expect to have assets at retirement in excess of, say, £250,000. Though not an FSA rule, the FSA is concerned about people with smaller assets being sold drawdown plans. They are concerned about the consequences of poor performance and high charges if investors have no other financial reserves to fall back on. With the professional and highly technical approach this book commends, I would argue that it is more important at low levels of nominal wealth to have proper advice about financial risks associated with retirement. In particular, the purchase of a level annuity, with no inflation protection, is potentially a greater risk than a well-organized and low-cost drawdown. The £250,000 'rule' is not a substitute for understanding what can happen in both cases and thinking about the possible consequences of both.

Rebate-only personal pension plans

Also known as 'protected rights' or an 'appropriate personal pension', these relate to a planning decision that is itself highly technical: whether or not to contract out of SERPS. If you do, the government pays you an 'incentive' (in the form of a National Insurance rebate, plus basic-rate tax relief). This must be paid directly (on an annual basis) by the DSS into a separate wrapper (although if you already have a personal pension plan you might as well use the same provider).

Protected rights refer to the fund at retirement. Slightly different rules apply to how you take the benefits. You or your employer can also contribute (within the normal contribution rules) to a plan formed to hold protected rights in which case the fund value is split between protected and 'ordinary' rights and the different benefit rules will be applied to each.

Self-invested personal pension plans

SIPPs are the ideal wrapper for personal pensions where an individual, their adviser or discretionary manager wants a customized, controlled and dynamically managed portfolio, particularly if it is to contain individual securities or to combine funds and securities. Members can individually select most permitted investments and there is an additional list of more esoteric investments that professional managers can select.

SIPPs are used by individuals who want to manage their own investments, including 'entrepreneurial' investors, by stockbrokers who can manage a portfolio of stocks within the wrapper and by IFAs who can use it to hold either products or securities under a continuing stewardship contract.

They are tailor-made for the approach this book recommends and will accommodate the different degrees of delegation to professionals that the individual might prefer. They are particularly useful as the wrapper for the management of pension or other drawdown tasks, because the careful matching of time-sliced horizons benefits from control of the individual investments and from combining horizon-matched gilts with low-cost tracker funds.

The SIPP wrapper market is dominated by a small number of specialist providers but the access to them is normally through a professional firm, be it a stockbroker or an IFA. Some advisers or managers have 'own label' SIPPs but they are usually provided by one of the big three and then 'badged' with their own name. There are a number of online SIPPs, mostly through web-based stockbrokers.

The cost of the wrapper (as distinct from any product or adviser charges) is usually in the form of a setting-up charge, a fixed annual charge and a schedule of transaction-related charges. The setting-up charge is usually around £400 but own-label providers may waive this. The annual charge is usually upwards of £300. These extra costs are onerous for small amounts of money. Costs are tending to erode fastest for stockbrokers as they may feel they can subsidize administrative costs out of their expected commission flow. You may not want to prove them right, though. If you plan to hold a simple range of assets such as trackers plus perhaps a few active funds, all from a single provider, a wrapper provider may set a lower cost on the basis that their administrative costs will be lower.

Stakeholder pension plans

The new low-cost and genuinely fully flexible pension was not created to alter the essential structure (or complexity) of contribution or benefit rules for personal pensions generally. These are essentially the same for stakeholder and conventional personal pension contracts though the government did take the opportunity when introducing stakeholder plans to alter the contribution rules for both types. The good news was they allowed contributions for five years to remain pegged at the level of your highest annual earnings even if they subsequently fall. The bad news was they removed the ability to carry forward unused contribution capacity, reducing funding flexibility.

The main difference in stakeholder contribution rules is that you can make contributions of £3,600 per annum (initially) even if you have no earnings, which means policies can be taken out for non-working spouses and for children. The benefits of stakeholder pensions are taken in the same way as conventional personal pensions, including the distinction between protected and ordinary rights and including the option of deferring annuity purchase, phasing retirement or doing a drawdown. The inherent benefit inflexibility of all pension contracts means that less affluent families may want to use non-pension wrapper capacity first, in spite of the remaining tax differences, unless they (or their parents) value the fact that the capital is out of reach.

A catch permanently low-income earners need to be aware of is that they could end up using their own money to pay for an income they could have had for free in the form of the State Pension 'minimum income guarantee'. If in doubt, any IFA should be able to check your situation and advise for a fee, perhaps for less than an hour's work.

The cost and flexibility drivers behind the stakeholder concept are revealed in a limit of 1 per cent per annum expenses, no sales commissions and in the exclusion of penalties for stopping contributions, altering the contribution rate or transferring. The arrival of stakeholder has already (as intended) led some providers to meet the flexibility requirements even for products that are too expensive to be registered as stakeholder.

With-profits are not totally excluded as suitable products for the stakeholder wrapper but offerings are likely to be rare and should be avoided. The fund has to be separate from the existing life fund and so will have to start with the injection of fresh reserves. Given the 1 per cent charge limit, this will bear on profitability as well as fund performance.

Stakeholder pensions can be used in conjunction with other personal pension arrangements: they are not mutually exclusive. In practice, this means that advice is more likely to be needed in respect of what to do about contracts you already have than about the merits of starting a stakeholder.

There is a good chance that the low-cost and high-flexibility features of stakeholder pensions will inject a dose of Darwinian economics in an industry that, as we saw in Part II, has so far resisted them. The fittest to survive in this new environment will have mastered IT challenges, both for internal administration and customer liaison, have good brand names and customer-centred values and learnt how to come to terms with operating in a commodity market. Though large organizations will emerge as winners, size alone does not guarantee that the technology and branding challenges will be met. It is not easy for individual investors, or even advisers, to spot the winners but the whole point about flexible terms (and about avoiding with-profits) is that it is then no longer vital to spot them.

Individual pension accounts

Introduced with stakeholder pensions at the start of the 2001/02 tax year, this is actually a wrapper within a wrapper because you still need to choose between a stakeholder and a conventional personal pension as the legal framework that applies the appropriate contractual rules. The purpose of IPAs is in tune with the suggestion above as to what a simple pensions regime would look like, with the underlying investments being identical whatever the tax treatment and the tax and contract differences all residing in the wrapper. A similar idea already operates in the USA, in the form of the Individual Retirement Account or IRA.

The greater flexibility of the stakeholder, particularly for using the £3,600 allowance for several members of the family, suggests this is the way to use IPAs. Yet that may waste their intended advantage, which is extending the choice of funds or institutions to those who do not currently offer funds (or versions of particular) funds that are eligible for pension accounts. Examples are unit trust groups which do not yet compete in the pensions market or actively managed specialist funds that are not accessible by a firm's pension account customers.

From the user's point of view, the presumption must be that they attach a high value to a particular unit trust group or to an individual unit trust (or investment trust). This runs counter to the more realistic idea that products are only commodities, easily replaced. To the extent that more flexibility is needed, such as for mixing trackers and safe-harbour securities, for including particular active funds or even holding individual equities, using multiple managers and different transaction agents, the SIPP is already available.

Perhaps these are reasons enough for providers to think they are neither a mass market opportunity nor a tool for the more affluent and why so few have so far decided to offer them. However, it is likely that we will see large management groups using IPAs to promote their entry into the pensions market, including foreign-owned groups and UK-based international groups who see products as global (or at least European) and wrappers as the means of localizing them as required.

These are essentially all the options for individuals not employed or self-employed. Next up are the options for employees, including the options for personal pension arrangements that can coexist with membership of a defined benefit or occupational scheme.

Employers' defined contribution schemes

To clear up any confusion with labels, these are also known as 'money purchase schemes' or 'group personal pensions'. Treat them as interchangeable. I prefer 'defined contribution' only because it underlines the key distinction as to whether the employer or member bears the investment outcome uncertainty. If only your contribution is defined, you definitely bear the investment risk.

Though you have some choice, it is prescribed by the employer: they typically choose the provider to whom they pay their share of the contributions on your behalf. This has two downsides to it. First, you may not have access to the kind of portfolio building blocks you want, notably trackers. Second, you may end up paying high charges, both in relation to the underlying product costs and because the provider (or the intermediary) stitched up your employer with ridiculous commission levels.

Fortunately, the fifth column is at work here too. In most circumstances companies with defined contribution schemes will have to offer a stakeholder alternative (or switch their existing arrangements to a stakeholder format). The new rules also let you take out your own stakeholder contract, which is a valuable option if the company contract does not give you the investment choices you want.

It is a safe bet that the industry will try to justify selling products that do not meet the stakeholder criteria, using all the discredited arguments exposed in Part II. The IFA trade press is full of articles and letters debunking the commodity nature and tracker bias inherent in many stakeholder offerings and promoting the old performance myth, so that is obviously what is emerging in client advice too. You must make your own mind up who is right and how important it is for you to work your way down the cost wedge.

Top-up arrangements for members of employers' schemes

Topping up an employer's defined benefit scheme is known as 'additional voluntary contributions' and as we discovered in the context of mis-selling it come in two forms of contract: AVCs and FSAVCs where FS stands for 'free-standing'.

As the mis-selling scandal demonstrates, the choice between a company arrangement and your own arrangement is likely to be significantly affected by employer benefits and tax rules. The benefit differences may be so obvious that you need no advice but if there is any doubt you should definitely take specialist advice, using the criteria set out in Chapter 15. The contribution and benefit rules are also quite complicated and although there are websites and publications which can add to the help you get from your employer it is not every investor who will want to do their own analysis and hope to get it right. Controlling directors need to be particularly aware of rules that affect them.

Executive pension plans

EPPs were a popular form of occupational pension scheme for small companies, limited to directors and small groups of executives. The structure is essentially the same as group personal pension schemes but they had their own rules for contributions that were and are no longer so advantageous.

Small self-administered schemes

SSASs are a popular form of scheme for owners and directors of small companies (they can only have up to 12 members and many have far fewer). The contribution regime is similar but a SSAS has more flexibility as to what it can hold. This includes shares in the sponsoring company and commercial property (or loans to purchase property) used by the company.

SSASs have independent trustees, like all occupational schemes, and these are normally professional firms, including a number of actuarial practices. Because this is a small market segment and the trustees are also not large firms, the economics of running a SSAS do not make it a low-cost wrapper.

In the context of this book's recommendation, the pooling of members' money which is implicit in an occupational scheme can make it tricky to match assets to the needs of different members. Also implicit, though, in any SSAS arrangement is that the members are willing to co-operate on how the fund should be invested. It does at least allow the full range of building blocks recommended in this book, including a mix of products and securities, to be held in the wrapper. A good investment-orientated IFA should be able to make the most of the SSAS wrapper.

Personal equity plans and individual savings accounts

Because PEPs and their replacement, ISAs, are not tied to a particular type of investment task in the way that pension contracts are, it should be harder to confuse these two wrappers either with products or with the return source: market exposure. However, the heavy promotion of individual products and the way the marketing season ties in with the end of the tax year sows the seeds of confusion and drives customer choice towards the fashionable, the emotional and the expensive. This is a pity, not just because it is likely to lead to disappointment but because it wastes the true potential of tax-efficient wrappers as an integral part of an investment-led planning approach.

Old PEPs and new ISAs, which can now be flexibly transferred between providers, offer a great deal of freedom about how to maximize the tax benefits by deciding where assets chosen for goal-based investment reasons can best be held. This is a combination of knowing the rules about eligible investments specific to each wrapper and valuing the tax breaks.

At the time of writing it is not clear whether providers will be required to allow partial transfers of PEPs, a doubt arising because their software may not let them allocate current values to different plan years. If you are putting in place new arrangements consistent with the principles outlined in this book, the chances are you will anyway want to transfer all old PEPs.

Organizing (or, more likely, reorganizing) PEPs and ISAs is a sophisticated planning exercise but is not beyond the DIY investor and is certainly a key part of a good adviser's job. However, for those with fewer resources and less choice, who are perhaps unable to take full advantage of their annual wrapper capacity (currently £7,000), it is a simple decision. Though boundaries based on income or wealth levels have typically been avoided in this book, I plan to risk dividing this section this way, starting with small resources or simple needs.

> ORGANIZING PEPS AND ISAS IS A SOPHISTICATED PLANNING EXERCISE BUT IS NOT BEYOND THE DIY INVESTOR AND IS CERTAINLY A KEY PART OF A GOOD ADVISER'S JOB

Small investments

If your income level puts you below the taxable threshold the freedom from income tax in a wrapper has no value compared with direct investment in a unit trust or investment trust, because of the principle in the UK tax code that these should only be taxed once. (This does not apply to investments that are inseparable from an insurance policy, such as with-profits or investment bonds, because the life company suffers tax.) You can also achieve the same tax relief by transferring assets from a spouse who pays tax to one who does not, to use up their personal allowance.

If the freedom from income tax in the wrapper has no value, you would not be prepared to pay an extra cost for an ISA wrapper or to maintain old PEP wrappers. However, many wrappers do not involve an extra cost and the use of the wrapper may actually increase the ease with which you can follow your investments.

If you are liable to income tax but your expected capital gains are likely to be below the small gains allowance (£7,500 for 2001/02) there is no value to the freedom from gains tax in the wrapper. You may anticipate that, when you take the gains, the combination of a low or zero rate of income tax and the benefit of the small gains allowance will leave you very lightly taxed, even outside a wrapper. Bear in mind, though, that realizing gains should not be forced to fit into your annual tax position and that the freedom in a wrapper to take them when it is right for investment reasons has a value.

So in most cases it will be sensible to keep any old PEPs running and to use as much as you can of your ISA allowance. However, it is not worth using a cash-only ISA to hold cash in if you are not a taxpayer.

The other decision criteria are ones covered already, that is to say, your investment needs should have been identified in relation to tasks you give your money, your strategy should flow from that and the implementation should be efficient and low cost.

A recurring theme throughout the book is that for investors constrained by their resources, once they have decided they want to accept the uncertainty that goes with equity investing, they might as well keep it simple and stick to a UK index fund. This will guarantee the diversification of specific company risks and remove active manager risks as well as keeping costs down. The value of international diversification is not so important but even that can be achieved simply and cheaply with a small investment in each of the other three building blocks, also through trackers.

All of these options are available today through index tracking funds in an ISA from leading household institutions, in some cases (such as Legal & General) online. Because you have avoided active-manager risk, you can concentrate all your products on a single provider and follow them by accessing a single account. There are some virtues in only having small amounts to invest!

Large investments

Many individuals have accumulated large amounts through regular contributions to PEPs and more recently to ISAs, perhaps for both husband and wife. However, the chances are that they are with lots of different providers and have no coherent strategy. This must be the first place to start. How you use wrappers should then be part of the implementation strategy.

The knowledge you need in order to do your own implementation is not extensive or off-putting. Remember that old PEPs can now hold equities anywhere: the old restriction to UK and Europe has been lifted. However, the restriction on gilts remains, hence in the previous chapter we decided that corporate bonds might have to act as a poor alternative to a true safe-harbour investment in a PEP.

None of these restrictions need be a problem if you organize your wrappers so that they act as depositories for different tasks, depending on what you can hold where. In other words, not being able to hold cash or index-linked gilts in a wrapper is not a problem if you can hold the safe-harbour asset outside a wrapper and allocate some of the assets that are using up the wrapper capacity to a different task. Getting your head around this is easier if you think of each goal as having identified investments but you then allocate all or part of each goal's investments to different pockets. Each wrapper is a different pocket but so is a stock-broker's account or investments you hold directly.[36]

The idea of wrappers as pockets is also helpful when you use non-pension wrapper assets as part of your retirement income goal if, for example, the resources you need to meet your income target are in excess of the contributions the rules allow you to make. You can then allocate part of your PEP and ISA capital to the pension task.

Though most product providers offer ISAs, the flexibility you seek to operate wrappers efficiently in a hierarchical approach as well as to maximize tax efficiency may call for a stockbroker-sponsored PEP and ISA, usually prefaced by the title 'select'. Their normal purpose is to hold individual securities, often on an execution-only basis, but in most cases you can also hold funds. There are also likely to be an increasing number of online PEPs and ISAs that allow you to hold funds, particularly in conjunction with a 'fund supermarket' transaction platform. We explore these in the next chapter.

These arrangements have the advantage of linking all your different products and providers in one place. However, if you are using an agent, such as an IFA, this is their problem not yours and they should easily be able to cope with it.

There is considerable debate about whether it is more tax efficient to maximize the income tax or the gains tax freedom in a PEP and an ISA. This can make a difference to what assets you first allocate to your wrappers. The argument presumes, though, that individuals will wish to hold high yielding investments for long periods. That means fixed-

---

[36] In fact, most packaged investments do not now have certificates as proof of ownership so even a DIY investor does not have to worry about where, physically, to hold them. Even if they are 'certificated', the pocket does not need to be a bank, for instance.

income bonds. But we have seen that these are not suitable matching assets for most investment tasks because of the uncertainty about inflation for long horizons.

Investment bonds

Viewed strictly as a wrapper for implementing part of a hierarchy-driven investment strategy, these insurance company contracts become an exception to my rule about not mixing insurance and investment, but they are essentially an investment vehicle and any life cover is largely irrelevant. Viewed as a product, without any advantages specific to tax treatment, investment bonds have absolutely no intrinsic merit. They also carry a cost, so the tax benefits have to be measured against that cost.

Viewed as a wrapper for products that the insurance provider manages and that are inconsistent with a systematic and hierarchical approach, such as managed funds and guaranteed products, even the tax advantages should not outweigh the lack of intrinsic merit in the underlying investments. These underlying products account for a large part of the investment bond market, though.

The first thing to do is to clarify any confusion arising from the insurance industry's hijacking of the term 'bond' which in general usage means a fixed income security. As a wrapper, the insurance company investment bond takes its return characteristics from whatever it is invested in, which could be a number of different funds, and there is nothing otherwise in its behaviour to link it with bond investing.

Investment bonds are either single-premium (lump sum contributions) or regular- premium (for example, monthly contributions) but most common is the former, particularly among the constituency who most value the wrapper, which is high tax payers, notably CGT payers. They are also either offshore or onshore.

The main feature of an investment-bond wrapper is that CGT is deferred until the bond matures, at which stage a tax payer may be on a lower rate. Making changes to the actual holdings in the wrapper, for instance, as part of a dynamic management approach, does not give rise to a chargeable disposal whereas switching the same investments outside a wrapper would.

A feature many bond users value is the right to withdraw up to 5 per cent of the original amount each year tax free. In fact, there is a contingent liability at maturity and there is also an implication for older persons' age allowance, so the situation is quite complicated. This withdrawal feature appeals to investors wanting a steady income but this book makes the point that drawdown, whether for retirement income or any other purpose, should affect the investment strategy, as part of a planned matching of time horizons. No such planning is usually going on in the arbitrary withdrawal of capital or income in an investment bond. However, it is possible to construct the contents of the bond so it is approximately matched. This is what a good adviser will recommend.

The advantage of offshore versions of the wrapper is that income rolls up tax free, whereas onshore bonds suffer tax at the rate paid by insurance companies. Because equity yields are quite low and because many income sources offshore will be subject to unrecoverable withholding taxes (including UK equity dividend income) this particular tax saving is likely to be small and the difference between savings on- and offshore is possibly marginal. This may make the products they give access to a more important criterion.

A few providers offer both on-and offshore bonds with links to third-party funds, including some trackers. This includes Skandia Life which originated the concept of investment bonds as a wrapper for third-party products, but there are others, such as Clerical Medical, which offers both versions with a wide range of its own funds including trackers. These options make investment bonds a useful addition to a shrewd planner's wrapper strategy but they may be beyond the justifiable effort of a DIY investor.

18

Using the internet

Flake.com

Flake.com was, believe it or not, an American portal for breakfast cereal enthusiasts but it could just as well describe most of the functional focus and content of the first 60-odd UK investment websites. In its earliest form,

IN ITS EARLIEST FORM, INVESTMENT ON THE INTERNET HAS BEEN DISAPPOINTING, TOO CROWDED WITH SITES THAT OFFER NOTHING OF NOTE

investment on the internet has been disappointing, too crowded with sites that offer nothing of note and replicate the lowest common denominator of offline investing. The internet is amazingly powerful for searching but this only increases frustration when the object of the search so often turns out to be trivial. At the time of writing, the cull has started and sites are fast joining flake.com in the internet graveyard.

From the particular point of view of this book the early stages of online investing have fallen short in three key respects:

1 In terms of the hierarchy, websites have focused on trivia.

2 They have encouraged entrepreneurial investing by pretending 'we can all be professionals now'.

3 In terms of the enemy within, they have played on our worst instincts and vulnerabilities.

Falling so conspicuously short has not stopped web-based businesses wrapping it all up in hype about 'power to the consumer'. The early marketing messages wanted us to believe that access to information and a transaction platform is empowerment worth having. But DIY on or off the net is dangerous without a general understanding of investment principles and, as we have seen, dealing direct with the industry is always dangerous without streetwise awareness. There is some good educational content out there but you have to spend a lot of time trawling through the trivia before you run into it.

It is not really surprising that the early business model has been trans-action-based. It is an obvious way to use the ability of the internet to cut costs, short-cut middlemen and save time. However, this was ideally suited to financial choices that do not require more than basic infor-mation, of which price alone may be the main item, such as insurance cover and mortgage terms. The advantages of direct access to low-cost transaction platforms and to market information are less obvious in making investment choices where knowledge is more important than information and strategic planning more important than transactions at the margin.

Out of 60 investment-related sites I managed to identify at the end of 2000, some of which have now gone, more than half do not even execute. They feed off advertising revenues from brokers or product providers or sponsorship by a particular agent on the basis of sharing commissions on the traffic generated. Their customers expect to pay nothing for passing through their gateway so they have to be able to generate traffic to survive. These include so-called portals like eXcite, financial services gateways like Interactive Investor, and virtual magazines set up by publishers of offline journals like FT Your Money, This is Money and Times Money. Collectively they tend to be known as 'infomediaries'.

There is as yet no sign that people are willing to pay subscriptions for these services, though the best sites in the USA are demonstrating that the right quality of information and education, coupled with a strong enough commitment to independence, will command a subscription.

The number that do execute investment-related transactions, though the smaller part of the total, are nonetheless too many to fight over the DIY business. They are dominated by online securities brokers. I only identified 14 but I read of a number as high as 25. Though it is clear that there will always be a genuine call for online share dealing, whether or not supported by research or news, it is not yet clear how many firms it will support.

Another early category was discount brokers dealing in packaged products, particularly unit trust and funds in PEP and ISA wrappers. These are online versions of an offline model. They are usually regulated as IFAs and they allow individuals to buy funds with full rebate of the selling commission. They live off the trail commissions that the customers may not realize they are generating. These discounters exploit the product providers' reluctance to rock the traditional IFA boat. If a provider was to waive or rebate commissions to customers who buy direct, circumventing the IFA industry, IFAs might strike back by not recommending the offending provider's products to their clients. As long as this industry practice continues, there will be a call for online fund discounters.

The last core category that actually execute transactions are fund supermarkets, which started to appear in 2000. They have had to choose between challenging the IFA distribution network or working through it. Cofunds, which groups several unit trust groups as backers, chose to work exclusively through IFAs. Egg and Virgin Money chose to go direct to private investors. Fidelity (whose supermarket also goes by the name of Funds Network) decided it was strong enough to do both. In the USA Fidelity and Schwab also do both and effectively operate as a duopoly.

Whether transacting in securities or products, these sites have relied on the appetite of the investor for news and facts to support individual decisions. Hence security stories tend to focus on the daily noise of markets in exactly the same way they do in newspapers and fund ideas tend to flow either from news stories or from search facilities based on past performance, following equally silly behaviour offline.

While it could be argued that this does indeed put the individual investor in the same position as professionals, all this hype should do is remind us how futile and marginal is the typical professional approach to both security selection and fund selection. The internet can do much better than this.

Lagging a long way behind the stand-alone net businesses are the individual providers themselves who we can assume will eventually all have web-enabled platforms for customers to buy and sell products and monitor their holdings. Those best able to take advantage of the net as a generator of incremental business with different kinds of relationships appealing to different types of investor are the firms who have been able to accept the commodity nature of their products. A good example is Legal & General which has been a leader in cutting fund charges and promoting trackers and has a perfectly efficient website for transacting and monitoring.

In time it is likely that advisers and portfolio managers will also widely provide internet access to customer accounts as a standard feature of their service, probably supported by third-party businesses.

For both individual providers and the firms that try to act as multi-product intermediaries, moving forward requires them to address the kind of relationship they want with the customer.

Intimate relationships: the next generation

As the initial frenzy about the internet dies away and the flake is gradually discarded, we can already anticipate how online investment services will evolve. Because America is several years ahead of us in the use of the internet, I have looked closely for features that are likely to cross the Atlantic, either by imitation or by export to the UK subsidiaries of groups like Fidelity and Schwab. I have also looked at what 'business to business' services are in development and what their long-run vision is. From talking to firms like Misys, Interactive Investor, Fidelity, Egg and Virgin, I am beginning to feel more confident about who will shape the future and how.

I believe that the key to next-generation thinking is the customer relationship that web-based investment firms want. Looking at the early consumer-facing services, how they initially saw their customer relation-ships is a mystery. Whether they are sites sponsored by off-line parents or backed by venture capitalists, the people with the money do not seem to have been asking the right questions about the sort of relationship they want the customer to have with them.

The mistakes that have been made are common to many web-based businesses, including underestimating the promotional cost of acquiring customers. The implication for investment sites is that the early emphasis on transaction platforms with marginal cost savings or time savings has misunderstood the low value most investors attach to a remote relationship based on price. By promoting a role of disintermediation, or replacement of offline intermediaries, they have devalued the importance of customer relationships and left themselves nothing to differentiate their offering or business culture.

At the heart of web-based investment business is the dichotomy that the internet lets the light in on the commodity nature of investment products that businesses have spent decades disguising from the customer. Like grocery shelves, transaction platforms emphasize the sheer volume of customer choice, with literally hundreds of items to choose from, most doing only a small number of different jobs.

To operate successfully as merchants of commodities (or what in this book we call building blocks), institutions have to personalize other aspects of their service. To do this online, which is by definition remote, is at first sight a major challenge. But in fact, the reticence that people have about discussing their financial affairs with outsiders and their mistrust of financial intermediaries is a strong suit for web-based firms to play. It should be possible to develop more intimate relationships online than person to person.

Intimacy in investment relationships can take the form of the personal information a system holds, the knowledge it has of what you want to achieve, how you think about risk, how you take decisions, how much you want to do yourself and how much you want done for you. A service can be intimate in terms of the dialogue and interaction that typically occurs when you log on. It can be intimate too in the way you come to trust advice, even if you exercise a degree of freedom as to how, when and if you implement it.

The style of the 'conversation' is very different in this kind of relationship. You are more likely to listen because it is adult to adult, personal and relevant. There should be no trace of selling pressure or even decision pressure. It should come across as helpful, with options to ask more questions, seek more information, go deeper.

The notion that a remote relationship can actually be intimate is not the only irony implicit in the potential of the net. This book has challenged the folly of blind trust and the corruption of systematic dependency created by keeping customers confused or locked in by penalties. Yet the fact is that you could end up willingly dependent on an online 'navigator' for goal-based journeys that might last for the rest of your life, without in any way being contractually bound or inflexibly tied in by practical arrangements. Free to leave, you choose to stay.

The keys to these new mutual dependencies are being on the side of the customer, giving up control to the customer and letting the customer design the way the service is to be used. The internet lends itself to all three. It does so with an unusual combination: spirit and technology. The web has and will hopefully retain for some time a healthily anarchical and subversive spirit. It can cut costs and we now know that in investment this can be presented not as a short-term gratification but as a huge contribution to long-term satisfaction. It can use technology to transfer control in a way that offline relationships may find difficult.

Web-based customer relationships will also tend to break down many of the artificial and accidental historical distinctions about who does what in investment. A life-time navigator or ringmaster could in fact be a product provider, a stockbroker, a pure portfolio management house or an IFA. Online businesses may even end up carving out an entirely new form of agency relationship. It is also clear that the contractual nature of online relationships could be either advisory or discretionary and here too on line firms could end up redefining a hybrid combination of the two that might never be commercially feasible for offline firms.

The net has already cut the costs of commodity functions like share dealing and insurance but I believe the most dramatic change it will make is to the cost of customized portfolio management or advice. To indicate the potential, in the USA an online investment adviser called Financial Engines offers style-based fund selection for members of defined contribution schemes, using a model built by that Nobel prize-winning economist Bill Sharpe, for just $15 per quarter! This is institutional quality investment process, fully customized and customer-controlled, delivered at a genuinely mass-market price.

Decision support

The key element of intimate customer relationships that is missing so far is decision support. Customization, participation, control, individual responsibility all call for the user to make choices and there is no point working with a firm online, or for that matter offline, unless they want to and can help you make your own choices. Decision support is therefore central to what they are offering and how they see their relationship with you. It should not look like an optional extra, with standard toolkits bolted on after designing the functions, look and feel of the site.

Whatever the exact functions performed by an online investment business, the main categories of decision support are likely to be these five:

1 resource calculators

2 risk profiling

3 asset allocation

4 fund selection

5 security selection.

Most are available to a limited extent today but they just do not convey an impression that management understand their importance to the customer, let alone their business building potential. Talking to business managers, however, I find some are definitely switched on and have development plans but are proceeding cautiously. In terms of the approach this book recommends, the issues for decision support are quite clear:

■ To get away from the detachment and remoteness of transaction sites, help in taking decisions has to be highly personalized and relevant to individuals and families and not just to people working in the markets.

■ To be aligned with the customer's agenda, firms must shake off the culture of disclaimer that typifies the early-generation sites.

■ To give a firm character and personality and to establish credibility in its approach, it must tell us what it believes is important in investing, what sort of process it believes in and how its decision support ties in with that mindset.

■ To operate remotely and interactively, decision support has to make more use of investment technology.

■ To be robust, the engineering must be more sophisticated than the superficial toolkits available today.

■ The screens that the customer uses to interact with sophisticated engineering must be clear, intuitive and easy to use.

■ Support must allow for a wide range of experience and knowledge, from beginners to experts.

■ It must never require or presume expertise or rely on self-diagnosis.

A set of beliefs

My impression is that most firms have not thought it necessary to differentiate a transaction platform by an underlying attitude or way of thinking. One of the most successful sites (it does not provide execution but nonetheless ultimately depends on the transaction business model) is the Motley Fool, because it strikes an attitude. A voice does not need to be challenging or mocking to be heard. As examples of a more serious approach, in the USA (where the Motley Fool has generated a strong following) InvestorHome and the American Association of Individual Investors manage to combine the independence of the Motley Fool with a more conventional dedication to professional integrity. It shows in a commitment to educational content, attachment to institutional ideas and techniques and reluctance to trivialize or talk down.

Firms may resist differentiating their voice and their ideals for fear of alienating sections of the market but all the evidence is that there are too many firms fighting over the available business to warrant a universal approach. An individual voice is critical, even for big business.

The role of advice

Decision support has to mean a willingness to give direct advice where it is sought, even if the function of the site is to provide an execution service. Education, underlying principles and general rules, such as this book and its website offers, can only go so far in informing individuals. They will expect some degree of customized advice and guidance, relevant to their particular situation. Though they will also accept that for some decisions the best advice is to take advice in the old-fashioned way, they will not accept that with modern technology decision support has to be stripped down to the most basic and exclusively generic. Indeed, they are likely to suspect that purely generic support may be worse than no advice at all.

Neither will the customer understand or sympathize with the difference in regulatory risk between execution and advice. Disclaimers and recommendations about the need for personal third-party advice may remain necessary but there is something fundamentally wrong with the relationship when legal disclaimers run to several pages of A4, which is not uncommon.

In all five areas, it is perfectly possible to lead users through a decision logic whose exact course is dependent on the individual information the user inputs. In this key respect, the answer is always qualified and responsibility resides with the user. Where the decision logic leads could be a specific recommendation that is not covered by the Financial Services Act, such as recommended asset-allocation percentages or amounts of money, or to a shortlist of qualifying investments that are covered by the Act, such as individual securities or funds.

This support can in fact be offered even in an execution-only environment, let alone where the individual signs up to an advisory relationship of some form. After talking to the FSA about this, I believe execution-only sites are being excessively risk averse. Perhaps it is largely a cover for not having the decision support customers should have.

The techniques

A recurring theme of this book is that individual participation and control, even if only at a high level, depend on technical resources more than individual professional skills. Because technology is as much at home on the internet as sitting in office networks or a professional's laptop, the internet has a big advantage relative to many other professional services, like law or medicine, that depend on personal interaction and cannot easily be reduced to systems or routines.

Since the book is so critical of the technology used by most retail investment firms offline it is hardly surprising that the early use of decision technology on the net comes up short. The state of the art on the net, with examples, is described on our own website where in a rapidly changing world it can be updated.

The main flaws at the time of writing (which are unlikely to vanish over night) can be summarized as follows, under five headings:

1 failure to integrate resource planning, risk tolerance and asset allocation

2 reliance on questionnaires

3 self-diagnosis and a presumption of investment knowledge

4 assumptions that do not allow for uncertainty

5 reliance on categories as proxies for customization.

1. Failure to integrate resource planning, risk and asset allocation. Several sites offer asset-allocation advice but not all include some form of risk profiling as a step towards a recommended asset allocation, either for market exposure or for a combination of funds. Asset allocation is expressed using percentages and is therefore independent of any amount of resources. There are also a number that offer resource calculators, with more or less allowance for risk preferences, but not connected to any asset allocation process.

Clearly, then, there is very little scope to foster understanding of the underlying principle that there are trade-offs to be made between investment targets, the resources applied and the risks taken.

This structural and communication flaw runs through the entire sector. The origin is partly the limited ambition of the host websites and partly the necessary complexity of technical platforms for combining the three planning components rationally and explicitly, without short-cuts, proxies or dependence on questionnaire responses. A contributory factor may also be an assumption that explicitly customizable solutions require more complexity than the customer can handle. The insight missing is that the explicit inputs sought from the customer should be ones that relate to parameters for their personal goals and these are not complex and do not require any investment knowledge.

2. *Reliance on questionnaires.* Questionnaires are mainly used on the net in asset allocation and risk profiling. They typically require the user to think in terms of the purpose of the plan and to quantify some planning parameters. Asking investors to say what the money's purpose is and to give it a time horizon is not necessarily difficult for the user or error-prone and is within the area where self-diagnosis is reasonable. After that, questionnaires cope poorly.

THE WEAKNESS OF QUESTIONNAIRE-BASED METHODS OF CUSTOMIZING ASSET-ALLOCATION STRATEGIES IS WELL UNDERSTOOD

The weakness of questionnaire-based methods of customizing asset-allocation strategies is well understood. They require an inflexible logic to interpret answers and they do not usually contain any process for countering illogical inconsistencies between responses. You are asked to respond to hypothetical situations and seemingly unimportant word choices, phrasing, and question sequencing will influence your answers and therefore the suggested allocation. You can find out for yourself how small differences in your answers affect the resulting recommendation if you have the time and the patience.

A general construction problem arises with questionnaires because they seek to make explicit inferences from general questions or general inferences from specific hypothetical suggestions. Typical examples are:

- Answers about time horizons are interpreted by assuming an arbitrary matching asset but the significance of a particular horizon is not specified.

- Answers about investment experience are used without specification to deduce risk tolerance.

- You are asked to anticipate responses to hypothetical volatility changes, such as 'a 25 per cent fall', assuming perfect anticipation of reactions.

- You may be asked how you actually responded to past actual events, assuming consistency each time whereas you may modify your response in the light of past experience.

- Answers to the effect that you already hold equities may be assumed to mean you can tolerate equity risk whereas the current exposure (let alone incremental exposure) may not be appropriate and your risk preferences are likely to vary from task to task.

- There is no specified solution for dealing with differences in sources of risk, such as outcome risk, volatility risk, capital to income conversion risk and inflation risk, several of which have conflicting implications for the 'right answer' in logic.

When Charcolonline added the first fully regulated personal advice area to its website, limited to advice as to what fund to put in an ISA (and specifically not to whether an ISA is itself suitable), it claimed it had conquered the weaknesses of questionnaire approaches. So many of the weaknesses listed above are present in the decision logic as to call into question what the FSA saw that made it any different, let alone any better. I single it out only because it is the first to be regulated to give customized advice.

As an approach to defining risk, it is flawed by the inadequate selection of descriptive choices offered, and the woolly flannel each is couched in. For instance: 'I am prepared that the value of an investment might fluctuate quickly but I accept the risk in the expectation of greater potential returns.' Exactly what logical inference could be made from this: 'If an investment in your ISA fell in value you would hold it but would keep a close eye on it and might consider selling it if the bad performance continues?'

Some clues to the interpretative logic are given in its Appendix headed 'How we reached our recommendation'. The links to personal circumstances are not obviously logical in investment theory ('As you are investing to generate growth, you can take slightly more risk than someone investing for income'). They are not even common sense ('as your proposed ISA investment is relatively small in relation to your income, you can afford to take a bit more risk with it' and 'as your income is likely to rise you can take a little more risk with this investment than your current circumstances suggest').

3. Self diagnosis and a presumption of investment knowledge. The online world replicates one of the commonest failings of traditional advice which is expecting you to be able to diagnose yourself and hence presuming you have investment knowledge. This recurs in questionnaires and fact finds and takes its worst form in 'box ticking'.

Typically, investors are asked to define whether their risk tolerance is 'high', 'medium' or 'low', without any guidance as to what the measure of risk is, what defines the differences between each or what the adviser will infer from the response. Another example is on the Egg site. One of the 'Investor Profiler' screens asks the customer to define their 'ideal portfolio' by 'specialized', 'well diversified' or with 'minimal stock market exposure'. This puts the answer before the question!

The worst example of putting the answer before the question defies belief, yet is amazingly common. It is to ask the customer to define their expected investment return or inflation assumption. These assumptions make up the real total return that frames the outcome in spending power terms of any investment programme and so they are a key part of the answer in resource planning. Yet time and again they are put as one of the questions.

4. Assumptions that do not allow for uncertainty. By definition, self-selection of investment assumptions will prevent the use of a 'probabilistic' framework for forming assumptions, that is, one that comes to a sensible accommodation with the uncertainty inherent in investment plans. However, even when the assumptions come from an adviser, they are not usually based on uncertainty ranges. Not surprisingly, resource calculators on websites are likewise not probabilistic.

This has been a widespread shortcoming of private client advice on both sides of the Atlantic and the words of Bill Sharpe in an interview with the magazine *Dow Jones Asset Manager* in 1998 are just as valid in the UK:

The software versions and some of the human versions of the advice that people are getting often seem to ignore risk. They're bookkeeping schemes in which you earn 9 per cent every year like clockwork. You die right on schedule. There's no uncertainty at all. Making a decision as to stocks versus bonds versus cash and about how much to save, without even acknowledging uncertainty – let alone trying to estimate it – seems to me the height of folly.

In Part II we saw that a realistic framework for quantifying all the sources of uncertainty and for modelling the relationships between them is beyond the scope of the individual, whether amateur or expert, and beyond the functions of a calculator. This technical complexity no doubt excuses the short-cuts that have typically been made but it is no longer justifiable to ignore probabilistic and explicit planning tools. The technology is available in the institutional market, already computer-based and can readily be web-enabled so that individual investors can interact with it.

5. Reliance on categories as proxies for customisation. A typical short-cut on the net is to use categories as a form of semi-customization. These typically replicate categories used offline, such as product categories differentiated traditionally, for example, 'income' and 'growth' equity funds, or needs expressed similarly as 'capital growth' or 'income with growth'. A typical trap is to oversimplify the asset-allocation process by suggesting approximate matches for individual situations, particularly based arbitrarily on age. This is becoming popular as 'lifestyle' investing catches on but it works specifically not generally. Several sites, for example, suggest moving into gilts as you approach retirement but, as we have seen, this is only a match for your needs if you plan to buy a level annuity.

Fund selection tools

If we accept the evidence that we should normally prefer using funds to individual securities, then for DIY investors using the internet fund selection tools are likely to be a major part of the decision support. However, if we also accept the evidence that active management is a lottery, random and not predictable, then automatically all decision support that claims some information advantage in selecting active funds is based on a false premise. This is indeed widespread amongst offline intermediaries but on the internet fund selection tools tend to be more agnostic and leave the user to set the criteria.

However, there are exceptions, though all these are 'at the time of writing' so not as up to date as our website coverage. This Is Money is an example of a journalistic site feeding the interest of DIY investors who then have to go elsewhere to transact funds or securities. The style of the site suggests it is aimed at investors with a limited knowledge of financial products and investment. Their 'Unit Trust Search Engine' starts out 'If you are new to trusts or are looking for general pointers, one of the top-performing trusts may be the place to start'. The default ranking is one-year performance. Oh dear! So much for setting novices out on the right path!

Egg also has a 'Fund Search Facility', including a search engine for screening funds by user-determined criteria. But the required fields include two which assume a knowledge of the return environment and which might easily be incompatible: the growth over a chosen period and the required quartile ranking over the same period. The quartile ranking is limited to top quartile or top half! The fund selection engine on BT's broadband site, Openworld, which is powered by Interactive Investor, is also limited to performance criteria using only the top half.

UK-iNvest's site is mainly geared to stockmarket investing but on the product side it has a link to discounted ISAs from Chase de Vere. In its section titled 'Best Buys' are listed the top performing unit trusts over the past five years in several fund categories. Best buys indeed?

Many of the online investment businesses will not be able to shake off the cynicism or ignorance of the industry: their entire business model depends on people's vulnerability to hype and emotional appeals. In fairness to them, web-based businesses that depend on fund transactions may also reasonably assume that the people wanting to use their service are those likely to believe in the myth, in which case there is no point trying to disabuse them.

The clear message is that the criteria for identifying the motivation and beliefs of the people in between are really no different whether online or on the high street. The streetwise investor will avoid the agenda benders and the myth peddlers like the plague.

Future postscript

'Seen this about Japan?' said Sally, jabbing with one hand at a headline as she pushed the newspaper towards her husband with the other.

'I know', said John. 'The market's just hit another of those airpockets – no pun intended, Sal.'

'As long as you're online, why don't I check what's happening.' She pulled the laptop towards her and for a brief instant newspaper, laptop, mobile phone and drinks all seemed to be in perilous motion together.

Sally clicked on the RingMaster®[37] icon on the laptop's desktop, went through the security checks and straight to the Task Summary screen. This grouped summary information for a number of investment tasks that they had set up together when they first signed up to the RingMaster® service. Though they had originally worked with a fee-based financial planner, Mary, who was licensed to use the RingMaster® software, they were now comfortable operating the accounts themselves, usually

---

[37] The service described here does not exist – but it brings together all of the best elements of on- and offline relationships recommended in this book and relies on investment modelling and software applications that are already perfectly possible. Invidual aspects of the service, including some of the underlying modelling, are certainly available from some professional firms. They should be uncovered by the search process described in Chapter 15. As services that measure up are developed, they may also be accessed via the website for the book.

entirely online. They had used the programme to set up three different investment tasks for their money that they had named, prioritized and set targets for: a Rainy Day Reserve Fund, their joint Retirement Fund (which they both contributed to) and what was left of the need to fund school and university fees for their two sons. It was the Retirement Fund that had exposure to several equity markets, including Japan, all in index tracking funds.

John and Sally were not fanatical about checking the progress of their investment plans. They understood that the short-term ups and downs of stock markets did not necessarily have a bearing on the outcome of any of their three investment plans, each of which was organized to take account of the likely fluctuations up to the chosen time horizons for each. Though certainly not complacent or uninterested, they felt calm and emotionally detached and that was the way they liked it.

Today, they had a particular interest because they knew that any weakness in equity markets would eat into the sizeable planning gain that strong markets, notably in Japan, had already delivered. At first, the term 'planning gain' had been a bit of a novelty but they had quickly got the hang of it. In RingMaster® parlance, a planning gain arises when the resources applied to a task, be they existing capital or planned contributions, are sufficient to achieve the planning targets at a higher than required level of certainty. They result from markets' past actual returns exceeding the expected returns the plan was based on. It does not mean the return forecasts were wrong, just that they had turned out better, or better *quicker*, than had been a sensible planning assumption.

Planning gains offer the client the opportunity to do several things that could be to their advantage, such as reducing contributions, re-allocating capital to a task lower down the client's priorities, raising the floor target or switching to safe-harbour assets. The effect, for instance, of cutting exposure to risky assets is to reduce the probability of falling short of the primary target but it holds the floor target unaltered. Because these choices are entirely personal, RingMaster® leaves it to the client to decide but spells out the options, with probabilities.

John and Sally had originally been alerted to the planning gain on their retirement task by an e-mail about six months before. Tempted to lock in the gain and lower their downside risk, they had nonetheless decided to accept the possibility of giving up some of the ground gained and to stick to their original goals. It was not so much that they were being lazy, just willing to accept the risk – for a while. Since then the planning gain had increased slightly, largely because of Japan, so what was happening to the market now made them think it might be time to lock in the gain.

In fact, from the Task Summary screen Sally could see that there had been little change since they had last checked. Going to the Goal Control screen for that particular task she clicked on the performance icon. From the numbers for each holding she could see that the reason was that while Japan had indeed been weak recently the Yen had strengthened sharply and so in Euro terms returns were holding up. However, the recent returns for the other markets, including the UK, were all looking quite weak but here too Euro weakness had come to the rescue. These were all index funds, so the only influences on short-term performance were market movements and, for Japan and the USA and (to a much smaller extent) Europe, currency movements against the Euro. The Active-Manager Return columns for each period were all blank, but had they held active funds this factor would also have contributed to the short-term progress of the portfolio.

It would have been easy, had they in fact wanted some active fund exposure, to opt for it either at the outset or indeed later. They could screen for no load funds, for instance. (Virtually all the top fund-management groups had dropped front-end loads, stung into action by the Sandler Report and the arrival of low-charging investment groups like Vanguard from the USA, as well as by technology-driven independent services like RingMaster®). With the Fund Suitability Tool it was a simple matter to see which no-load funds appeared to behave closely with the relevant market building block. (Most fund supermarkets also had programmes that ranked funds by tracking error as asset-allocation building blocks. It seemed that fund managers were themselves responding to the new look to fund selection and clearly positioning their funds for different matching purposes and tightening up on their own internal risk controls. Stupid labels like 'income with growth' were happily a thing of the past.)

John and Sally had found the active versus tracker choice an easy call to make. When discussing the option of active funds with the planner, they had input cost criteria and played around with various 'Tracking Error Ratings' in the Goal Control Panel. With each new setting, RingMaster® recalculated in a nanosecond the probabilities of hitting their targets. Sure, they could reach a higher outcome by taking on some active-manager risk but it also lowered the chance of hitting their primary target for retirement income and unless they were willing to increase their contributions even a modest amount of extra risk was pushing them through their floor target at 98 per cent certainty. This all came up on screen in slick graphics. They spent less than a minute deciding trackers were for them, at least for their retirement task.

'Don't you think this is a bit silly, John? I think I may start to regret it if we miss the opportunity to lock in the gain.'

'You're right, Sal. Let's go for it. You know what to do.'

Clicking on the link to the transaction details that would rebalance the portfolio as earlier prompted by RingMaster®, Sally saw that the model was now proposing to switch 15 per cent of their combined retirement goal portfolio from a combination of Japan and the USA into index-linked gilts. A little image, like two overlapping funnels, showed the old and new range of expected outcomes (shown as usual as monthly after-tax pension income in real terms). By locking in the planning gain by switching some money from risky to safe-harbour assets, the funnel for expected returns narrowed slightly at the top end but all of the expected outcomes were above the red line representing their floor target. Also on the screen were the exact proportions of each fundholding to sell and the actual gilt issues and amounts to buy, broken down in each of their own names.

Sally clicked to action it.

Sure?

Sure.

The confirmation flashed up. They had standing instructions set up with RingMaster® that would deal with the sales of the HSBC trackers, the purchase of the ILGs through Barclays Stockbrokers and the instructions to PPM which managed their own SIPP wrappers and looked after the settlements. RingMaster® would make sure the actual trades would be timed so that funds from the sale were physically available to settle the purchase. John and Sally had nothing more to worry about.

Had they chosen a discretionary contract with RingMaster®, instead of an advisory one, the same deal would have been done six months ago but the mechanics would have been identical and the third parties involved would have been the same. In neither case would they have to be involved in the transaction processes. Both required the same goal-planning process and even with a discretionary contract they were free to change the goal parameters at any time, such as raising the floor target or altering the required certainty of hitting their primary target for retirement income. The main difference is that they would have had an e-mail advising them of a transaction done instead of one that was being proposed.

'Before you exit, Sal, I want to check my bank balance.'

More risky manoeuvres. John and Sally had also signed up to the RingMaster® aggregator facility. This took a regular peek at their balances at IF which they had moved to so as to take advantage of the netting off of mortgage interest paid and deposit interest received, saving them both the banking spread and tax on deposit interest. (Such savings had come at a high price initially, though, in terms of teething problems worse than any of the frustrations they had experienced at HSBC. 'Frying pan' and 'fire' were words that had frequently come to mind as they grappled with the ever so gentle Scots in the IF call centre. Such were the rewards of early supporters of banking on the net.)

John used the back button to return to the Task Summary screen. This showed their Rainy Day Reserve. The numbers came from IF. Only a fixed amount of John and Sally's own cash balance were grouped as an integral part of their investment goal planning. When they set up their plans, they were prompted by their planner to treat part of their cash reserves as available, in exceptional circumstances, for investment in risky assets. Mary could see that John and Sally were normally keen to keep a very generous cash 'cushion' even if it meant running a higher mortgage balance than was really necessary. It was a characteristic many of her clients showed. She demonstrated how it might be worth setting up a task for their cash cushion so that when future real returns were exceptionally high they would be prompted by the system to invest part of it in, say, UK equities.

If they chose a rolling five-year horizon, the inherent uncertainty in equity returns over such a short period would mean that in most market circumstances they would not be venturing out of their safe harbour. The projected downside risk when holding some equities, on the cautious assumption they were forced to sell at any earlier stage, had come up on the screen and did indeed look tolerably low relative both to the size of the normal cash cushion and to the potential gain. The graphics also showed this trade-off looked much better if the tracker option was used. Another easy call.

With mean expected real returns from the UK projected by the system still well below average, even after the falls in UK equities, John knew not to expect any such prompting yet but he still wanted to look anyway.

It seemed like he had a little time left so he also took a look at their School Fees Task. This was almost complete and there were only a couple of zero-dividend preference shares left in the portfolio. When they had set this task up they had opted for a discretionary relationship because the plan was more complicated and the transactions were anyway all driven by the need to tie in with the cash-flow needs of each year. Even so, they had had to answer a lot of questions, including about whether they were willing to use horizon-matched zeros, which were a good way of turning income into capital gains to use up each of their small gains allowance, and if so what criteria they would accept. It had explained, for example, that the underlying investment trust portfolios, and hence the projected yields on the zeros, were subject not just to market risk but also to active-manager risk and possibly gearing risk. Though this was all coming from the system, it was their planner who at that stage was walking them through the process as they sat round the big screen in her office. With Mary's help, they had opted for no gearing risk and 'blue chip' UK equity exposure. Each holding matched these criteria and also matched, to the nearest year, the timing of the fees due. It was a slightly complex structure but the logic and the principles were all so obvious.

By opting for a discretionary relationship with RingMaster® they had given up control over the implementation for this task yet they still felt they were in control of the overall plan and had not given up their responsibility for the outcome. That was one of the things they really liked about RingMaster®.

The co-pilot came on the intercom: '… tail winds … arriving a little ahead of schedule … close down laptops and end your calls'.

About two more hours and I'll feel the sand between my toes, thought John as he snapped the laptop shut.

'Thank God we didn't buy that house in Castellina, Sal', he mused out loud. 'I prefer to feel free.'

Notes

i   Sources are several: Barclays Capital Equity-Gilt Study for gilt yields since 1919 and previously Mitchell & Deane (1962) plotted in David Wilkie 'More on a Stochastic Asset Model for Actuarial Use', Institute & Faculty of Actuaries 1995; retail prices from Global Financial Data.

ii   Gary P. Brinson, Brian D. Singer, and Gilbert L. Beebower, 'Determinants of Portfolio Performance II: An Update', *Financial Analysts Journal*, May / June 1991.

iii   http://www.ibbotson.com (go to Research and look for Asset Allocation).

iv   Hensel, Ezra & Ilkiew, 'The Importance of the Asset Allocation Decision', *Financial Analysts Journal*, July / August 1991.

v   Emerging and developed market indices (for longest common period) from Lipper.

vi   *Anatomy of Britain Today*, Anthony Sampson (1965) Chapter 25.

vii From 'Through the Chairman's Eyes', an extract of company meeting reports published in *The Times* during 1955.

viii Sampson, Chapter 25.

ix   Bogle's speech can be downloaded from the section devoted to his writing on the Vanguard web site at http://www.vanguard.com under the title 'What the past half century can tell us about the future'.

x   'Through the Chairman's Eyes'.

xi   As at the end of 1954.

xii New Policy Institute research paper, 'Quality Assurance or Benchmarking? Presenting Information about Pensions', June 1998, Guy Palmer (ed) (subscriptions from www.npi.org.uk).

xiii *The FSA Information Guide*, August 1998, page 20.

xiv   *Money Management*, September 1998.

xv   Peter Ward, *The Great British Pensions Scandal*, second edition, 1996 page 36.

xvi   Ward, page 35.

xvii   The Consumers' Association, *Which? On line*, 'Who has had to pay compensation?'

xviii   FSA News Release, 1 December 2000.

xix   These estimates are all taken from the FSA News Release of 1 December 2000. Though subject to review as more cases are completed the pattern of claims is now clear enough to make for accurate projections.

xx   FSA News Release 28 February 2000: 'The FSA and PIA issue a policy statement for the review of specific categories of FSAVC business'.

xxi   FSA News Release 24 May 2000: 'Mortgage Endowments: the Facts'.

xxii   Financial Services Consumer Panel Mortgage Endowment Reprojection Research Report, Autumn 2000 (in full on the FSA website).

xxiii   FSA Consultation Paper No 75, November 2000 'Endowment mortgage complaints' page 43.

xxiv   FSA 'Better Informed Consumers' April 2000.

xxv   http://www.actuaries.org.uk.

xxvi   The Myners Report page 34 and the Consumers' Association Report February 2001, 'Profits at the Consumer's Expense'.

xxvii   The Consumers' Association.

xxviii   Money Marketing Conference, May 2001.

xxix   Volume III Research undertaken by the OFT for the Pensions Enquiry, 'Passive Fund Management' by Paul Klumpes, Department of Accounting and Finance, Lancaster University Management School.

xxx   My recollections of this are exactly as set out here, without embellishment and any inaccuracies should not detract from the generality of the example I have selected from my own experience.

xxxi   Eugene F. Fama, 'Random Walks in Stock Market Prices,' *Financial Analysts Journal*, September/October 1965 (reprinted January/February 1995).

xxxii   Quoted in an interview with Eugene Fama on Dimensional Fund Management's website (http://www.dfafunds.com).

xxxiii   A subsidiary of Deutsche Bank, originally part of brokers Wood Mackenzie whose initials were echoed in its first name as a separate entity, World Markets.

xxxiv   http://www.index-tracking.co.uk.

xxxv   Association of Unit Trusts and Investment Funds.

xxxvi   Occasional Paper 9 'Past Imperfect: the performance of UK equity managed funds'; available at http://www.fsa.gov.uk/pubs/occpapers.

xxxvii   Agarwal and Naik, London Business School: 'On taking the "alternative" route: risk, rewards, style and persistence of hedge funds', February 1999; and 'Multi-period performance persistence analysis of hedge funds', February 2000. Both can be downloaded from Social Science Research Network: http://www.ssrn.com.

xxxviii   Examples are the Information Ratio (absolute or relative return divided by standard deviation of same series) and the Sharpe Ratio (some measure of excess return divided by standard deviation – for purposes of comparing equity funds the excess measure may use the index return as the 'risk free' rate). Calculations of relative return series in different research services variously divide by or subtract the benchmark return, leading to different ratios for the same funds and periods.

xxxix   Based on Lipper data for 496 non-pension UK unit trusts filtered to 301 (by excluding index funds, institutional funds and accumulation units) with the following distribution features: only 15 funds below 1.00%, 70 at 1.00%, 90 at 1.25% and 121 at 1.50%).

xl   From *Financial Times*, 24/25 August 1996.

xli   Occasional Paper 6; available at http://www.fsa.gov.uk/pubs/occpapers.

xlii   Murthi, Orszag & Orszag, Department of Economics, Birkbeck College, University of London: 'Administrative Costs under a Decentralised Approach to Individual Accounts', a paper presented to the 'New Ideas about Old Age Security' conference sponsored by the World Bank on September 1999. May be downloaded from http://www.econ.bbk.ac.uk/ukcosts. Cost impact is measured by estimating actual costs, assuming a target value for pension income and applying the Minimum Funding Requirement assumptions for inflation and market returns (equivalent to a real return of 5 per cent per annum).

xliii   Attributed to DTI reports.

xliv   Quoted on the website of Vanguard, http://www.vanguard.com.

xlv   My estimate of £58.8 million is based on reported net new business of £2.8 billion, a reported 70% share being through IFAs and an assumed average 3% commission.

xlvi   Brad M. Barber and Terrance Odean: 'Boys will be boys: gender, over-confidence and common stock investment', University of California, Davis, draft, September 1999.

xlvii   *The Times*, 2 December 2000.

xlviii   Benjamin Graham, *The Intelligent Investor* HarperCollins.

xlix   Brad M. Barber and Terrance Odean: 'Trading is hazardous to your wealth: the common stock performance of individual investors', *Journal of Finance*, April 2000.

l   Compeer Survey 1999 for APCIMS.

li   Compeer.

Useful addresses

Association of Independent Financial Advisers (AIFA)
Austin Friars House
2–6 Austin Friars
London EC2N 2HD
tel: 020 7628 1287
fax: 020 7628 1678
website: www.aifa.net

Association of Investment Trust Companies (AITC)
Durrant House
8–13 Chiswell Street
London EC1Y 4YY
tel: 020 7282 5555
fax: 020 7282 5556
website: www.itsonline.co.uk

Association of Private Client Investment Managers and Stockbrokers (APCIMS)
112 Middlesex Street
London E1 7HY
tel: 020 7247 7080
fax: 020 7377 0939
website: www.apcims.co.uk

Association of Solicitors for Investment Management (ASIM)
Baldocks Barn
Chiddingstone Causeway
Tonbridge
Kent TN11 8JX
tel: 01892 870065
fax: 01892 870160
website: www.asim.org.uk

Association of Unit Trust and Investment Funds (AUTIF)
65 Kingsway
London WC2B 6TD
tel: 020 7831 0898
fax: 020 7831 9975
website: www.investmentfunds.org.uk

Financial Ombudsman Services
South Quay Plaza
183 Marsh Wall
London E14 9SR
tel: 020 7964 1000
fax: 020 7964 1001

Financial Services Authority (FSA)
25 The North Colonade
London E14 5HS
tel: 020 7676 1000
Consumer helpline: 0845 606 1234
Leaflets line: 0800 917 3311
fax: 020 7676 1099
website: www.fsa.gov.uk

IFA Promotions Ltd
117 Farringdon Road
London EC1R 3BX
tel: 0117 971 1177
fax: 0117 972 4509
website: www.unbiased.org.uk

Institute of Financial Planning (IFP)
Whitefriars Centre
Lewins Mead
Bristol BS1 2NT
tel: 0117 945 2470
fax: 0117 929 2214
website: www.financialplanning.org.uk

Personal Investment Authority (PIA)

Contact FSA

Society of Financial Advisers (SOFA)
20 Aldermanbury
London EC2V 7HY
tel: 020 7417 4419
website: www.sofa.org.uk

Solicitors for Independent Financial Advice (SIFA)
10 East Street
Epsom
Surrey KT17 1HH
tel: 01372 721172
fax: 01372 745377
website:www.solicitor-ifa.co.uk.

Index